D1202001

# Destined to Lead

# DESTINED TO LEAD

## Executive Coaching and Lessons for Leadership Development

*Karol M. Wasylyshyn*

palgrave
macmillan

DESTINED TO LEAD

First published in 2014 by
PALGRAVE MACMILLAN®
in the United States—a division of St. Martin's Press LLC,
175 Fifth Avenue, New York, NY 10010.

Where this book is distributed in the UK, Europe and the rest of the world,
this is by Palgrave Macmillan, a division of Macmillan Publishers Limited,
registered in England, company number 785998, of Houndmills,
Basingstoke, Hampshire RG21 6XS.

Palgrave Macmillan is the global academic imprint of the above companies
and has companies and representatives throughout the world.

Palgrave® and Macmillan® are registered trademarks in the United States,
the United Kingdom, Europe and other countries.

ISBN: 978–1–137–35776–2

Library of Congress Cataloging-in-Publication Data

Wasylyshyn, Karol M.
    Destined to lead : executive coaching and lessons for leadership
development / Karol M. Wasylyshyn.
        pages cm
    Includes bibliographical references and index.
    ISBN 978–1–137–35776–2 (hardback : alk. paper)
        1. Executive coaching—Case studies. 2. Leadership—Case studies.
    3. Executives—Case studies. I. Title.

HD30.4.W374 2014
658.407′124—dc23                                        2014006016

A catalogue record of the book is available from the British Library.

Design by Newgen Knowledge Works (P) Ltd., Chennai, India.

First edition: August 2014

10 9 8 7 6 5 4 3 2 1

Printed in the United States of America.

*To the eight courageous business leaders
who permitted me to publish
their executive coaching experiences.*

*My thoughts are joined by your words—and together, we've ignited a
fuller understanding of what really matters in this work.*

# Contents

# Figures

# Foreword

It is the very nature of a story to transform. The stories in *Destined to Lead*, told by a master storyteller, will transform the practice of executive coaching. Authored by Karol M. Wasylyshyn, a pioneer in her field, this book teaches, inspires, and provokes.

I've known Dr. Wasylyshyn for more than 20 years. We met when I was on track to finish my doctorate. I recall after expressing my desire to marry my love of psychology to the business world, my colleagues telling me repeatedly, "Talk to Karol Wasylyshyn; she's the expert."

They were right: gracious and generous with her time, Karol gave me invaluable insights that helped guide me into a diverse and very rewarding career in leadership development. I have served as an executive coach, an action learning partner, a professor, and most recently as a vice dean for executive education at The Wharton School.

Throughout my career, I am often asked if one can really "learn" how to lead. My answer? Yes. Absolutely. Leadership is not a mysterious formula; it's a set of skills. It's the ability to apply these skills to a meaningful goal. Mastering the role of leader requires two things: first, a clear sense of the context in which one is leading; and second, a willingness to understand the nuances and complexities required in the role. I believe that if you have the right formula—intelligence, drive, ambition, and a compelling reason to lead—you can be a successful leader.

Today, many leaders also need the guiding hand of a confidential partner—someone courageous enough to cut through the noise, speak the truth, and provide a safe space for reflection, experimentation, and exploration. Karol embodies this type of leadership mentor. She's served as a trusted advisor to some of the top business and nonprofit leaders in the country. Her clinical orientation, combined with her experience as a businesswoman, creates the right fit for the evolving practice of executive coaching.

Throughout her career, Karol has been known for quality and focus. She never accepts an assignment without a complete immersion into her client's business, a focused plan of action, and a strategic view of their competitive landscape.

- She knows the culture.
- She challenges her clients to deepen their commitment to leader development.
- She's vigilant about holding a critical but compassionate mirror before her clients.

She herself may not have "invented" coaching, but she surely is one of its pioneers, visionaries, and architects.

And, in *Destined to Lead*, she invites us to share her knowledge and wisdom, giving us a unique view "from the balcony." Through Karol's example, we all can gain innovative practices and views into ways a trusted advisor can challenge and channel executives. She knows how to help an executive find his or her leadership voice and stay true to it.

In the years since our first meeting, Karol and I have often lamented the commoditization of coaching. We've seen the debate about the role of executive coaches intensify as more people entered the field. Is it, as some suggest, a perk for the high-potential leader, a "fix-it" prescription to ensure success at the top? Or is an executive coach simply a cheerleader to replace your favorite aunt who came to every ballgame? Or is the coach the external voice that keeps one from saying the wrong thing or making too many political blunders? It's possible that executive coaching is a little of all of these things. But, in the hands and heart of an expert like Karol Wasylyshyn, the practice becomes a personal and intimate partnership that honors the executive client, provides a trusted source of advice, and enables these individuals to grow and achieve their ambitions and goals as transformative leaders.

There are no qualifying criteria or universally recognized certifications for becoming an executive coach. The question of whether our discipline is a profession has been heated for the last ten years. Even today, anyone can join the ranks of coach. And regardless of whether you call yourself a life skills, or presentation coach, if you are side by side with an executive, you must bring more than your business background to bear. Inexperienced but well-intentioned professionals who enter this field can give advice that might bring damage to reputations, business results, and perceptions of leadership readiness.

If you want to learn the power of a deep, trusting coaching relationship, open *Destined to Lead*. Reflect on Karol's lessons as one of our industry's true innovative thinkers, and apply them to your own methodology and practice.

As coaches, we walk with our executive clients through the ups and downs of their leadership journeys. To add value, we must go beyond the fundamentals. The craftsmanship inherent in this book is hard to teach. I have tried. But through Karol's compelling cases, we begin to discern the art of coaching. We discover that being a trusted adviser means many things: rigorous self-awareness, disciplined understanding of organizational systems, an immersion in the scholarly underpinnings of personal development, and a belief in the power of dialogue. Balancing the tensions of a complex relationship, keeping focused on the goals of your client, and having the courage to confront and critique someone you care about and respect—these attributes are the gold standard of the practice.

It's rare to have someone with Karol's background, experience, and gifts share knowledge so openly and with such clarity. I urge you to immerse yourself in this treasure of leadership coaching. *Destined to Lead* is a gift to the profession. Karol puts her hand out and asks you to walk with her and her clients. I firmly believe that if you take her hand, your thinking about experience coaching will be transformed.

MONICA McGRATH
Vice Dean of Administration
Aresty Institute of Executive Education
The Wharton School of the University of Pennsylvania, USA

# ACKNOWLEDGMENTS

My mother, Stella Winczo Wasylyshyn, was a Polish immigrant with a very fast eye and a tongue that could pierce right into the heart of you. When I graduated college, I remember her urging, "Don't just do something; make sure you do something *different*." So in some primitive and catalytic way, she influenced my career choices—choices through which I sought span of impact—and ultimately, placed me among the pioneers of executive coaching in the United States.

The actual catalyst for this book was a comment made by my colleague and friend, Lois Juliber, retired Vice Chairman and COO of the Colgate-Palmolive Company. She gave me the memorable prod, "So when are you going to write your *definitive* book?" With that word "definitive," and in that unexpected "Stella moment," I realized other books I'd written had been a dress rehearsal for this one. It was time.

My marvelous and ever-encouraging agent, John Willig, not only found a home for this project quickly at Palgrave Macmillan, he also reconnected me with Charlotte Maiorana, an editor with whom I had worked on another leadership book. Later, I would be rewarded by the guidance of Leila Campoli, Sarah Lawrence, and Kristy Lilas who all contributed to this becoming the instructive legacy work I intended it to be. I am grateful too for Elisabeth Tone's wise marketing instincts. Surely this manuscript would never have been completed without the stellar efforts of my Office Manager, Carol Testa. For over 20 years, her anticipation, resourcefulness, steady competence, superb accountability, and infectious sense of humor have propelled my best efforts. I am beyond indebted to her for the work done here—including every table and reference.

A special mention goes to the talented artist Joseph Williams, who drew all the Visual Leadership Metaphors® (VLMs)—a key coaching tool in most of these cases. Further, his patience through many iterations of the illustration for my conceptualization of the *trusted advisor* (see figure 10.1) is especially praiseworthy.

An inner circle of provocative thought partners was always "there" to read chapter drafts, to guide me to the right references, and/or to keep reminding me of the timely contribution this work would be to the field of executive development. Notably this group included Marisa Guerin, Tom Kaney, Rick Ketterer, Frank Masterpasqua, Frank Smith, and David Washington. I am especially indebted to Paul Koprowski who with great discernment, kindness, and insight gave me critical input for many segments of this manuscript.

My deepest gratitude goes to Monica McGrath for the brilliance and stunning generosity of her foreword for *Destined to Lead*. Her faithful encouragement throughout this book's three-year gestation, as well as her fierce and loyal presence in my life—surely have made her as much sister as colleague and friend.

I am grateful too for my professional home, Division 13 (Consulting Psychology) of the American Psychological Association. My colleagues here include Jim Quick with whom I had a pivotal conversation as I planned this project, and who later wrote a review of the proposal that helped "sell" it to the publisher. Important conversations with Dick Kilburg and Vicki Vandaveer have always stretched my thinking. And I have also been rewarded by the collegiality of other Division 13 members including Bill Haas, Bob Mintz, Jeremy Robinson, and Randy White.

The executive coaching outcomes captured in this book would not have been possible without the human resources professionals or other company insiders with whom I forged such strong, transparent, and trusting partnerships. Further, without their endorsement and confidence in my capabilities, I would never have received these senior coaching engagements. While they are not all living still, I honor them here: Benito Cachinero, Gene Carroll, Mark X. Feck, Joe Forish, Valerie Gervais, Gayle Gibson, Don Johnson, Tom Kaney, Jim Tabb, and Deb Weinstein.

In the category of people who "kept me going," I include Bill and Anne George who welcomed me on and off the tennis courts in Cape May, New Jersey. Props too to my fitness trainer, Alma Qualli, who motivated my workouts even when I was away from Philadelphia.

Believing deeply in the interaction among creativity, productivity, and *place*, most of this book was written with the sea (Villas, NJ) as my constant companion. Up on a dune, in the lolling rhythm of that stillness within the home of my friends Bob Kaeser and Don Stremme, it all seemed possible—even on the days when the words refused to flow. One bittersweet morning there, Bob and I mourned the passing of their beloved dog, Miko, prompting my thoughts about how death and birth (of this book) had merged with the primal power of the sea.

While I have dedicated *Destined to Lead* to the eight business leaders at the center of these case studies, I acknowledge them again here for their ready willingness to participate. I feel especially indebted to each of them for the time he or she took to write an "executive's reflection" to accompany his or her case study. Such explicit client input is rare in the executive coaching literature, and in providing it these leaders have made a distinctive contribution to the field.

Finally, for my husband, Ken Butera, there is the most fervent love and appreciation for all his supportive patience, vigilant checking in as I was writing, timely good humor, and fine grammatical scrutiny/editing of this entire manuscript. While we often joked about who was going to cook his "spaghettis" whenever I left home to write, there was always a hefty bag of tasty food that he had cooked and packed for my sojourns "al mare." A little of Ken in the fridge . . . and fully warm in my heart. Sempre.

*KAROL M. WASYLYSHYN, PSY.D.*
*Philadelphia, PA*

# Introduction

What exactly happens during executive coaching? This question is as pressing now as it was when Kilburg wrote, "For all of the work that has been done to illuminate the subject of coaching in the past 15 or 20 years...I have been concerned about the lack of detailed case studies that describe what practitioners actually do with their clients."[1] Equally pressing is a question about what coached leaders themselves value most from coaching, and the implications of such information for research and sound practice in the realm of executive coaching.[2] *Destined to Lead* sheds light on these questions by including inputs *both* from business leaders who have been coached and from the author, a clinical and consulting psychologist, who coached them. Specifically, each case study presents a comprehensive account of the coaching work, and each is concluded with a candid "executive reflection" written by the leader on his or her coaching experience.

This collection of case studies is focused on senior business leaders[3] who chose executive coaching as a resource for their becoming even more effective, and/or to help them realize their career aspirations. I concur with Ennis et al. regarding a general definition of "coaching" as a developmental resource.[4] Further, based on nearly three decades of coaching senior business leaders, I believe this resource is optimized on valued performers who are intentional about their own continuous learning. While I have had heated discussions on this point with numerous colleagues, once a senior executive is perceived as failing or truly derailing,[5] engaging an executive coach is usually more of a rescue fantasy than anything else.

The subjects of these case studies were, for the most part, focused on the behavior "how" dimension of leadership.[6] While this is a core area of my coaching expertise, it was the *combination* of my business background and training in clinical psychology that established my initial credibility with these executives. In other words, I was seen as someone who had worked in and understood their world, as well as a professional who could help them make behavior changes and/or amplify the positive leadership behaviors they already possessed. I have often been asked that familiar question about whether leaders are born or made. I step away from either of those formulations with the belief that the best leaders are *destined* to lead, and hence the title of this book. I suggest that three primary destiny factors are: (1) education, (2) experience, and (3) behavior. In my experience, most senior business leaders are highly evolved in terms of their education and business experiences; where they need the most help is with the behavioral aspect of *how* they lead.

The reader may be intrigued by how a clinical psychologist maintained the necessary *coaching* intention of these engagements, that is, did not tilt toward a more psychotherapeutic stance.[7] Surely my clinical training was a powerful resource in the conceptualization of these cases, and in how I thought *with* my clients about the work. However, it was this training, in combination with a grasp of clients' business challenges, their company contexts, their leadership preferences, and the nature of our *presence* in this work together that most informed the actual coaching process. Further, in the coaching meetings, I avoided what executives might hear as psycho-babble, and remained vigilant about the right timing and tone of relevant psychological interpretations. These interpretations often fostered clients' deeper reflections and insights that, in turn, fueled lasting behavior change and convictions about how they needed and wanted to lead differently.[8]

While these engagements represent an insight-oriented coaching model in which a process of self-discovery, deeper self-awareness, and the exploration of relevant psychodynamic factors[9] lead to more effective leadership, each client's experience was customized. In practice this meant that I focused on meeting them where they needed to be met, and drew from humanistic, existential, Gestalt, behavioral, and psychodynamic psychology. It is hoped that the flexibility of my coaching within this model is both evident and instructive. However, I hasten to add that this approach is not for everyone; nor do I contend that it is more effective than other coaching models used by seasoned executive coaches—especially those who integrate their knowledge of human behavior with a solid grounding in business.[10]

While the identities of these talented leaders have been masked, each executive has reviewed his or her case study and provided permission for publication. It was difficult to choose from the hundreds of cases in my files; but in the end, I was influenced most by three criteria. First that the cases represented gender, racial, and ethnic diversity. Second that they involved a variety of behavioral coaching indications. And third that they fulfilled the overarching intention of this book: to leverage the power of story-telling, that is, to tell compelling stories about real business leaders for whom coaching catalyzed and supported their strongest aspirational pursuits. I wanted these stories—and the comments of the protagonists in them—to be memorable, to be more than an intellectual exercise, and to arouse both the reader's emotions and energy thus serving as a potent *learning resource* for anyone practicing or otherwise involved in the burgeoning field of executive coaching.

On some level, I am embarrassed by the decidedly positive tone of these engagements and their outcomes. Given the commitment of these executives to their coaching and superb coach/client chemistry, perhaps this was inevitable. However, this is not to suggest that all coaching engagements unfold well. Even in the wake of diligent precoaching scrutiny, unexpected individual and/or organizational culture issues can sabotage a successful coaching outcome. I have had these experiences, too—some fairly noxious ones with leaders who had no interest in coaching but felt it was politically correct for them to fake it; and with others who actually considered the mere suggestion of working with a coach a narcissistic injury. While I would have preferred to include such coaching experiences in this book, getting permission from any of these executives was a daunting, if not impossible, prospect. (Such permission is an ethical necessity for any licensed psychologist.)

These combined case study and executive reflection pieces are presented in chapters 1–9 and are distinguished by the fact that they were assembled "blind." None of the executives read his or her case before the reflection was written, nor did I read any of the reflections before I had written each case. Further, since my relationship with most of these leaders continued over many years with my role eventually shifting from executive coach to *trusted advisor*, chapter 10 details the dynamics, versatility, and utility of such longitudinal relationships with business executives—including CEOs of global entities and/or CEO succession candidates.

A discussion of my perspective on factors related to the outcomes of these cases versus those of my clients is provided in chapter 11. While these business leaders confirmed my major beliefs about key coaching factors (traction, trust, and truth-telling),[11] their executive reflections brought some surprises as well in terms of what they found most helpful. I offer them as a catalyst for research and practice guidance. As Quick and Nelson state, "The exchange between theory and practice should be such that each informs and feeds back to the other so that we are advancing both sound research and useful practice."[12]

Finally, in partnering with the executives in these cases, I have had a fierce reminder. I have been reminded that successful executive coaching outcomes often have less to do with coaches' tools of the trade, or the elegance of our interpretations, or even with the courage of our observations. Yes, all of these are essential, but they are not, in my view, what distinguish our ability to aid business leaders in their dealing with the stark and relentless pressures of twenty-first-century business dynamics. As capable and resilient as these executives typically are, they can be besieged by the weight of their duties, the ongoing threats of an unstable financial and geopolitical world, the constancy of criticism, the absence of a relevant peer group, and surely by the loneliness of it all.

It is in this sense that what happens during the coaching of top business executives—and what is meaningful to them—is simultaneously and equally focused on (1) leveraging their leadership competencies,[13] and (2) marshaling their behavioral resources.[14,15] Such coaching is significantly more subjective, visceral, and enduring—as the coach influences the realization of executives' destinies as leaders. It encompasses the steadfast *presence*, compassion, and empathic *intimacy* executive coaches/trusted advisors maintain and protect in their uncommon relationships with these business leaders. This is the red thread running through each of these cases studies, and I offer this truth as a springboard—or perhaps a provocation—as this still nascent field of executive coaching continues to evolve.

# CHAPTER 1

# The Relentless Champion

Most executive coaching cases begin in a fairly predictable manner. An experienced coach is contacted by the boss or human resources (HR) partner of a talented senior leader, and they discuss the prospective coaching engagement. The coach and executive then meet and in the presence of good chemistry and a clear contract, the work commences—work that is focused on helping a gifted individual become even more effective. Depending on the coach's model, there can be other steps in between but basically this reflects how the use of executive coaching has shifted from a remedial intervention to that of a powerful development resource. In the words of management consultant guru Ram Charan, "As coaching has become more common, any stigma attached to receiving it at the individual level has disappeared. Now, it is often considered a badge of honor."[1]

Nothing about the work with Ted was predictable. This executive coaching case began differently. It unfolded differently. It ended differently. In its totality, three coaching practice points are emphasized: (1) the importance of precoaching scrutiny (*Is coaching really the right resource?*); (2) the partnership with an HR professional; and (3) the value of life stage development theory[2] in the conceptualization and management of a case with a lasting coaching outcome.

## THE COACHING REFERRAL

This referral started at a meeting I was having in London with a senior HR professional who said, "I need you to coach one of our most brilliant scientists." However, the more I heard about Ted, the less inclined I was to work with him. The HR Vice President in this global pharmaceutical company described Ted as "highly forceful, out-of-control, rude, and too much of a hassle for most people." When I asked him how he thought Ted perceived himself, his response was both intriguing and revealing—"an idiosyncratic genius." While he also told me that another consultant had tried to coach Ted, he believed the "hook" for coaching at this juncture was that he was about to be promoted and would be reporting to a new boss who found Ted's behavior "unacceptable."

Since I had been consulting to this company for over a decade, I checked out Ted with another HR contact there. She described him as explosive and with a tendency to "ream people out" in both live meetings and teleconferences. On one occasion, when he was championing support for a particular drug, he told members of the company's top executive team that their resistance to developing it indicated that they had "shit for brains" (I'm thinking to myself, *Oh boy, this is not sounding encouraging*); then she started to emphasize his "warm and mushy side." Given this observation, I decided to dig further before I made a final decision about whether or not coaching could be the right "medicine" for Ted at this point in his career.

Serendipitously, the external consultant who had previously coached Ted had once reported to me, so it was easy to get his candid input. He described Ted as "egotistical, abrasive, and combative (with anyone who disagreed with him)." In my follow-up phone call with the HR manager in London, I expressed doubt about Ted's making the behavior changes that he reportedly needed to make; but I also suggested I have an introductory "no commitment" meeting with him to assess this directly.

## THE FIRST MEETING

Ted was punctual and appealing, wearing one of the softest leather jackets I'd ever seen. While the business world was in "dress down casual" mode by then (1998), Ted's version was decidedly high quality. He was also quite engaging—smiling, listening, and remarking on his surroundings. After our polite settling in, I asked how coaching might be helpful to him now. In his words, "The focus needs to be on my temper because I just don't tolerate fools too well." When I probed about the manifestations of his temper, he said, "I'm perceived as heavy-handed and that I can pummel people, especially if they're getting in the way of delivering on our objectives."

Ted went on to say, "I'll do anything to get a drug to market— and I can continue to fight even after I've won!" Sensing his volatility and perhaps retaliatory nature, I explored this further. Ted commented almost gleefully, "Oh yeah, I can be retaliatory all right! There was once a physician who was blocking my progress, and I actually wanted to destroy her!" As our conversation continued, his seemingly softer—or at least more reasonable—side emerged when he described how he'd never had a secretary or a direct report quit, and the loving nature of the relationships with his wife and three children.

When I probed his volatility, Ted said, "It's a reflex, I just go into auto-pilot. I have a real mean streak, and I don't know when to pull back. I want to punish after I've won. I expect people to yield to my opinions because generally they're better, but I realize now that this behavior has really cost me." When I questioned how his behaviors had "cost" him, he said he had missed an earlier promotion because he was "too immature." In his words, "There are no shades of grey for me, but I'm at a different stage in my career now that I'm dealing with senior people who have their own well-formed views, so I need to better deal with them."

While Ted's comments were encouraging in terms of him as a viable coaching client, I still had a lingering doubt. Using paradoxical intention, I asked,

> So tell me, why would I want to work with you? You made minimal progress with your first coach, and I'm not sure that I'm the right medicine for you. I suggest you go away and think about two things. First, would you make coaching the priority it needs to be for behavior change to happen? And second, are you ready to work with someone who's going to push hard for you to take a deeper look at your volatility and its implications for more effective leadership?

Within a few days, Ted debriefed our meeting with the two HR contacts (as had I) and then called to say he wanted to begin the coaching as soon as possible.

## DATA-GATHERING PHASE
### The Coaching Agenda-Setting Meeting

In addition to Ted and me, the coaching agenda-setting meeting was attended by his boss and his HR partner in the United States (who reported to the HR person in London). I crafted an agenda that covered: (1) the coaching process (data-gathering, feedback, coaching, and consolidation phases conducted over 12–14 months); (2) our respective roles (boss and HR in collaborative partnership with Ted and me throughout the coaching); (3) the boundaries of confidentiality (Ted owned all data gathered, however, the specific coaching foci, as well as the quality of his participation in the coaching process would be shared with his boss and HR partner); (4) coaching areas (boss and HR to provide explicit input); and (5) the identification of a sample of respondents for 360 data-gathering. (There were 17 people in this sample, that is, a representative mix of senior executives, peers, direct reports, and Ted's wife as well.)

As expected, Ted's new boss highlighted two interrelated areas for coaching: (1) explosive behavior that needed to be modified, and (2) executive presence in terms of Ted's behavior not sabotaging the collaborative organization his boss was trying to create. Ted's boss wanted him to censor his overtly negative comments about other senior executives whenever they disagreed with Ted. He also thought Ted needed to "let go" and thus empower his direct reports more fully.

### The Life History

Of all the data-gathering, none was as revealing—and helpful in understanding the underlying basis of Ted's explosive and retaliatory behaviors—than his life history. At the outset of this four-hour meeting Ted said, "I have no contact with my family. I don't think about them and I don't like them. They make my skin crawl." The oldest of three boys, his tilt toward the pharmaceutical industry was not surprising in light of the fact that both his father and paternal grandfather had been pharmacists. He described his mother as "nuts, and emotionally and physically absent" as she had been institutionalized for mental illness when he was a child.

His father was an alcoholic who expressed no affection, provided no affirmation, and yelled at and beat Ted. While he never attended any of his son's sports events, his athletic ability was an early source of pride and accomplishment for Ted. By junior high school, for example, he was the leading swimmer in his state and became an All-American.

Well-cared for by his swimming coach, a former member of an Olympic swimming team, he moved in with this family when he was 14 years old. In his words, "I was so glad to get away from my family—and I never went back. I lived in their basement, maintained a strict discipline, worked two jobs, and I mostly ate Kraft's macaroni and cheese." Ted received a swimming scholarship from Ohio State, majored in pharmacy, and graduated with top honors. He also completed his PhD there and had great mentors including a Nobel Prize winner.

Regarding his first job in the pharmaceutical industry Ted said, "I saw that I could do basic research in a pharma company and make a really good living, too." After several years there, he joined another big company where, in his words, "I could advance my career without giving up science."

He would spend nearly two decades in this company where his major career highlight was the development of a drug that saved millions of lives and proved to be one of the company's blockbuster products. On the personal side, he formed a few very close friendships with colleagues and also met a woman (the "absolute love of my life") whom he married. His habit of indulging her and his three children, making holidays—especially Christmas—an extravaganza of gifts was an expression of his generosity and also a reaction to the misery and deprivation of his own childhood experiences.

## Feedback Phase

### Organization-Based Data

As Ted and I began to discuss his 360 feedback,[3] I was reminded that beneath his outwardly aggressive and confident persona, there were strong elements of sensitivity and insecurity. Seeing his mix of anticipation and anxiety, I reminded him that this type of feedback was no more than a set of perceptions, that is, a point in time and not the absolute truth. But despite this, it was better to have them because, as the axiom went, "Perceptions were reality in corporate life." When he said the feedback was making him "feel flat," I reinforced my support and optimism that, in the presence of his intention to do so, he could accomplish the necessary behavior changes to be successful at this senior level in the company.

I also emphasized that his many distinctive strengths far outweighed problem behaviors. I even suggested that if others in R&D (an organization I knew well) had more of his bold and tenacious drive, the company might, in fact, accelerate its success.

### Core Strengths

The 360 data underscored a number of core strengths. These included his: (1) scientific knowledge (respected on a world stage); (2) reputation for selecting winning compounds; (3) knowledge of the pharmaceutical business; (4) innate intelligence (agile and creative mind); (5) work ethic, energy, and passion for what he believed in ("relentless champion"); and (6) kind, caring, and compassionate nature (with people who got to know him).

### Development Areas

The three development areas tracked with what Ted and I had already discussed as well as with what his boss and HR partner emphasized in the coaching agenda-setting meeting. The first focused on his lack of emotional control—how his passion was a significant double-edged sword that could lead to explosive outbursts, insults, the desire to *crush* adversaries, flaming emails, and intimidation. Our HR partner captured it well when she said, "We all know how brilliant Ted is, but what he needs to do now is channel this brilliance into collaborative relationships with others versus fueling combat."

The second area involved his executive presence—specifically, the level of maturity he projected as a senior leader. As his boss had underscored in the coaching agenda-setting meeting, Ted needed to be more circumspect in his comments about top company executives, and he needed to further empower his direct reports.

The third area was not identified in the coaching agenda-setting meeting, but it connected to what I had learned from his life history. The majority of people in the sample described Ted as an obsessive-compulsive workaholic whose sense of identity was completely dependent upon his work-related accomplishments. In tandem with this, he was seen as inexplicably insecure and in need of frequent recognition and affirmation.

### Distillation of Coaching Areas

After merging Ted's organization-based data with input from his boss and HR partner, we settled on two areas for the coaching phase. Further, I recognized that the life history data would likely jumpstart the coaching, and the construct of emotional intelligence would be a helpful learning vehicle. The two interrelated areas were: (1) self-regulation—minimizing his explosive/volatile behavior; and (2) executive presence—Ted behaving as a mature and enterprise-focused *statesman* who did not define himself solely on the basis of his work-related accomplishments.

Given the emotional intelligence he displayed with family members and certain others, I emphasized that developmentally it was easier for one to "generalize something that's already there" than it was to try to "build in" something that's not. This seemed to have a palliative effect on the doubt Ted was having about whether or not he could deliver on his behavior change agenda. In a conversation with his boss a few months later, he said that Ted was indeed "making real progress."[4]

### Conceptualization of Case

Clearly Ted illustrated what Kaplan and Kaiser[5] have described as a lop-sided leader. His massive innate left brain capabilities had fueled distinctive and stellar career accomplishments, but limitations in right brain-based interpersonal/relationship skills limited his full effectiveness as a leader. Further given his childhood history, there were psychological attachment issues[6] that influenced leadership behaviors that were not appropriate—especially at this level of responsibility. Specifically, Ted's limited perspective-taking skills influenced his reflexively negative behavior (*I have a real mean streak and I don't know when to pull back*) that could be dominant, harshly competitive, hostile, and even insulting.[7]

The coaching would have to address the combination of Ted's "lop-sidedness" (*I expect people to yield to my opinions because generally they're better*) and his underlying attachment issues that, in addition to the behaviors cited earlier, fueled mistrust and lack of collaboration. Ted's understanding of and insights about this powerful combination of underlying forces (the *deeper look at his volatility*) would have development implications for his increased emotional control and his executive presence (evolving statesmanship). Further with this conceptualization, I resisted a more clinical formulation as I did not want to blur the boundary of the engagement's remit, that is, it was not psychotherapy nor did I want to run the risk of overpathologizing my client's behavior. Was this guy talented? A resounding YES. Was he screwed up? Probably not any more so than countless other high-functioning and creative people. Was he narcissistic? Yes that too—but on a par, in my view, with many other distinctively gifted leaders.

In the coaching, I would focus on his previous successes, his potential, and how I might help release that potential as we explored and exploded any barriers to it. Given his intention to become a more effective leader, I believed that, to some extent, his greater self-control and growth toward statesmanship would evolve as a function of what Maccoby[8] has described as productive narcissism. While Ted would remain supremely confident in his capabilities, simultaneously he would also have to set direction, drive results, *and* step away from the more visible activities that had gratified him earlier in his career. This was why his greater empowerment of others would be so crucial. In other words, his ego would need to adjust, that is, be as well fed by his *influencing* events as it had been by his being the recognized force driving key objectives (*I'll do anything to get a drug to market*).

Ted would also learn that it was his unproductive narcissism that could trigger an overly aggressive defense against perceived attacks and/or resistance to his ideas, his objectives, or things being achieved his way. And on a deeper level, he would come to understand not only that he often used the force of his intelligence, his fierce need to achieve, and his retaliatory instincts to ensure that his ego needs (for affirmation and recognition) were met, but also that the vanquished "other" was eliminated as a threat.

We could examine how any one of these issues—and surely how any of them in combination—could trigger his most explosive "pummeling" or other politically troubling behaviors. However, rather than striving to eliminate them completely, the more realistic coaching goal would be—using a pharmaceutical phrase—helping Ted to "titrate the dose" of these behaviors. In addition to my helping Ted understand the underlying basis of his "problematic" behaviors, I would leverage the deepened trust of our coaching alliance in striking the right balance between honoring Ted's strengths and helping him blunt his sharper edges—the edges that caused unnecessary wounding and/or discouragement for others.

## COACHING PHASE

Ted began our first coaching meeting by putting his wounded narcissism right on the table. In his words, "I still feel embarrassed by that 360 feedback. It made me think that I really don't like myself. I don't like the image of me as that out-of-control, explosive person depicted in this data." I told him that his observation was actually good news—in terms of where we needed to be in the coaching process anyway. He then added, "I have made a major commitment to myself: Zero tolerance for emotional outbursts."

### Key Coaching Tools

Given Ted's limited capacity for introspection about his behavior as a leader, I applauded his "zero tolerance" objective. I also focused on giving him other concrete and imminently accessible tools to foster his change agenda. Two of the most helpful coaching tools were: (1) a "model" leader for him to emulate; and (2) an in-the-moment "prod" to ensure his best behavior—especially in meetings or other high stakes interactions with others.

Regarding the first, we identified another senior R&D person whom Ted especially admired as a leader. As he described this person, we recognized that he was as brilliant as Ted but probably the polar opposite behaviorally. Ted described him as "[a] really well-respected leader who is always controlled emotionally, has empathy for others, never crushes anyone, and who makes room for others' good ideas." Yes, he would be an ideal person for Ted to emulate and to keep front-of-mind through the coaching effort. The fact that they were already good friends was quite helpful.

As to the behavioral "prod," I suggested Ted envision me sitting next to him in meetings and during other key interactions as a way of bolstering his observing ego. I anticipated that this would work well given his need for my approval. Within a few months, Ted reported, "This has really helped me censor potential explosions. It's got me thinking about other ways to say things, and it's also helped me keep my mouth shut on things I shouldn't be sharing with a broader audience. Overall, it's also helping me make progress on being calm." Clearly, this Gestalt technique was having the dual effect of his censoring explosive outbursts, and his projecting a more mature executive presence, that is, his moving toward *statesmanship*.

Ted's other efforts at *statesmanship* included: (1) giving his direct reports more autonomy; (2) trusting in their having the "right stuff" to deliver objectives; and (3) practicing greater patience especially now that he recognized that they could succeed without the force of his "scary intensity." Regarding the development area of self-regulation, Ted's learning about the four dimensions of emotional intelligence and the interrelatedness among them proved helpful particularly in terms of his being less volatile (see figure 1.1).

**Figure 1.1** SO SMART®—Emotional Intelligence.

| Four Dimensions of EQ | |
|---|---|
| **Self-Observation (SO)**<br>• Awareness—of one's emotions<br>• Accurate assessment of own strengths and weaknesses<br>• Self-confidence<br><br>Core ability: Perceiving emotions | **Self-Management (SM)**<br>• Self-control—can channel emotions effectively<br>• Discipline<br>• Resilience<br>• Motivation—bias for action<br>Core ability: Managing emotions |
| **Attunement (A)**<br>• Focus on others<br>• Empathy<br>• Awareness of organization dynamics<br><br><br>Core ability: Using emotions | **Relationship Traction (RT)**<br>• Authenticity<br>• Influence and persuasion<br>• Consistency<br>• Connecting to others<br>• Collaborative teamwork<br>Core ability: Understanding emotions |

### Breakthrough Insight

As Ted learned about/increased his emotional intelligence, our focus on self-awareness and attunement—especially his having more empathy for others—produced a breakthrough insight. Ted saw how he had fostered a culture in his R&D area where it was alright for his direct reports to "take shots" at those in other departments, that is, those whom they perceived as less effective scientifically.

In Ted's words, "I've cultivated this in my department and now I see what a problem it is and how immature this is of me as a leader. So now I have to tear this down and I'll have to begin by being really clear that we're not going to do this anymore. I have to insist that this kind of behavior is not acceptable for me or for them. The behavior we want is collaboration—we need to be more collaborative with everyone and have some empathy too for the issues they're facing."

### Coaching Update Meeting: Heroes versus Leaders

Six months into the coaching, people in R&D were talking about the "new Ted." In a coaching update meeting, both his boss and HR partner highlighted his progress. His boss commented,

> Your change in behavior has been remarkable. I can see the increase in collaboration and the decrease in your volatility. Going forward—and in the spirit of your being more of a statesman—I need you to think and behave like you own the whole of this part of R&D and not just your patch in it. I want you to help me change the culture. I believe there are differences between heroes and leaders. The hero jumps in and saves the day. The leader creates an environment in which the problems can be fixed by others. I believe you will inherit my job and it's important to me that you do it in the right way—as a leader, not as a hero.

Our HR partner made the astute observation, "Your focus now is definitely about intensifying the behavior shift to statesman from father-of-the-family." Ted, struck by this comment, reacted, "I've really believed in the family thing, but I see the problem with it now because it feeds a bad us-and-them dynamic. At this point, I want to avoid creating any 'enemy camps' in the organization."

While debriefing this meeting with Ted, I emphasized that his father-of-the-family orientation was no accident. It was a reaction formation given what he had experienced with his own dreadful and punishing father. He was going to be a good and generous father—better than the rest. And wasn't his inclination to "crush" perceived adversaries, that is, this meanness, an overidentification with an aggressor (his father) and/or an unconscious attempt for Ted to stay safe by doing unto others what his father had done to him?

At the end of a year, Ted's boss gave him feedback from the recent R&D Talent Review meeting. In his words, "People have really noticed how your behavior has changed but there was also a lingering question: *Is your change real, will this behavioral transformation be sustained?*" His boss repeated his desire for Ted to succeed him and that over the next couple of years, he (Ted) needed to start framing his thoughts about what he would bring to this role. On the basis of this likelihood, Ted and I commenced a second year of coaching.

### Year Two: Shifting from Coach to Trusted Advisor

In this second year, the coaching focused on key actions that would help Ted *internalize* his version of statesmanship.[9] In addition to his first action of "zero tolerance for explosive behavior," the following actions proved helpful:

- Elimination of the us-and-them dynamic in his group; this meant no defensive sparring with other R&D groups, no silo mentality, and no petulant acting out when things didn't go their way. Collaboration would replace a pattern of combat and unproductive competition.
- Intentional efforts to convey his wisdom/experience/perspective—especially to high potential employees, thus grooming them for the future and ensuring talent bench strength in R&D.
- Stronger "political attunement"—his better reading of signals from senior management, carefully monitoring the tone of all his communications including email, and his censoring of overt negative comments about top company leaders.

By this time, Ted and I had formed an extremely close working alliance. Given all that we had discussed—including his serious health concern unknown to others—there was a strong reciprocal bond of trust and respect. I was now more trusted advisor than coach having guided him through crises and having celebrated with him too. On the eve of his leaving for Italy to receive one of the most prestigious awards in his field, I sent him an email that was intended to both congratulate him and reinforce core attributes of the *statesman* he was committed to being. It read in part:

> In a few days, you will receive a most prestigious award and be honored by colleagues from around the world. I join these other voices in praise and acknowledgement of all you've accomplished, and I also make a request: When you rise to accept your reward, think about the revered place at which you have arrived in your career and savor the hell out of it. You are well on your way to becoming the STATESMAN you want to be and my expectation is that you will remain mindful of all that's inherent in this: Knowledge. Station. Respect. Confidence. Wisdom. Patience.

Resilience. Grace. Generosity of spirit. Good will. Optimism. Forgiveness. Stewardship. Generativity.

At this point in our work, Ted had moved into frame 3 of his Visual Leadership Metaphor® (VLM), a technique I used to gauge coaching progress (see figure 1.2). This was another positive indicator of his continued success, but certain relationships and events would influence an unexpected course in his career.

### Ongoing Issues with Boss... and Other Senior Leaders

Given the combination of Ted's crucial role in the commercialization of one of the company's most successful drugs and his passion for teaching, he was often invited to give Grand Rounds lectures at medical institutions throughout the world. While his HR partner did a good job of trying to keep this activity in perspective, his boss was agitated about the time Ted spent doing this. While I thought this had more to do with his boss's frustration about his own career, nevertheless it was something Ted needed to manage.

In addition to Ted's tension with his boss, he did not respect and did not get along well with the new President of R&D. Ted

**Figure 1.2**  Ted's Visual Leadership Metaphor® (VLM)

Drawing by Joe Williams

| FRAME 1 | FRAME 2 | FRAME 3 |
|---------|---------|---------|
| An explosive, volatile Research Manager. | A calmer and more influential Research business executive. | A greatly respected, admired and inspirational leader within an R&D organization. |

found him to be "imperious and monolithic" in his view of what constituted effective leadership behavior. Given Ted's potential for negative transference with leaders he didn't respect, I knew this was a major problem. Further, based on what I had learned from others about the new R&D President, I knew Ted's view of him was justified, that is, no amount of coaching could neutralize the situation. So how was this going to play out?

### Sudden Business Development

With the announcement that Ted's company was merging with another global entity, the inevitable organization turbulence began. It was intensified by the fact that the CEO of Ted's company did not value the importance of culture, so no culture change initiative was even considered. This meant that for at least a decade post-merger, two of the primary US locations continued to duplicate activities, and little happened to leverage the potential in their functional areas to say nothing about harmonizing R&D and commercial activities. But I digress.

Back in R&D, the new President was exerting his power and vision through the creation of an organizational structure that would break apart the areas that Ted and some of his closest colleagues ran. Considerable turmoil, resentment, and anxiety reigned as people waited to see who would be appointed to the major roles in this reorganization. Ultimately, Ted received one of the big jobs, and my advice was that he stay focused on delivering stellar results, that is, not be distracted by the fray around him. His boss did not fare as well, which was not surprising as Ted and others had come to see him as a duplicitous leader who could not be trusted.

### Team-Based Leadership

Even in the wake of Ted's getting a top role, I sensed things would not unfold well when he said of the new R&D President, "Right now you just need to keep quiet and tell him what he wants to hear. He wants total order and obedience." It was hard to pierce Ted's cynicism; what I did instead was focus our work on the importance of team-based leadership. In addition to emphasizing this in our meetings, I gave him pertinent readings, and knowing how he enjoyed watching movies on his many trans-Atlantic flights, I assigned a film, "The Gladiator." I urged him to think about the protagonist, Maximus who, like Ted, had endured great adversity and containment in his life.

From the team-based leader perspective, we considered the power of Maximus's inspirational line, "What we do in life will echo in eternity." I believed it was important for Ted to stretch beyond the fruitless political speculations and gossip that preoccupied many, and concentrate instead on the ultimate recipient of their work: the patient. Increasingly, I was concerned about how toxic the R&D atmosphere was becoming as a result of the actions taken, and the decisions made by the new President of R&D. This concern was confirmed by a comment from my HR partner, "You can't believe how badly people are behaving—I've never seen this much bicker-ing and back-stabbing."

### Leadership Void: Catalyst for Retention Issues?

While Ted's aversion to the new President was intense, I had enough collateral data from others in the organization to know that Ted was right about him. This leader was described as inscru-table to the point of provoking others' fears, micromanaging, demoralizing, heartless, and ruthless. One instance that was espe-cially confirmatory was the phone call he made to Ted to con-gratulate him on his new role. His message was brief and chilling, "Congratulations, and don't mess up because if you do, I'll fire you." What I feared was that some of the more talented scientists would begin to leave—and unfortunately, this is precisely what happened.

While Ted had not responded to calls from executive recruiters in the past, he was ready to now. In his words, "I can't respect this leader, the morale has sunk to an all-time low, and it's just not fun working here now." I knew he was not overreacting, but at the same time, I wanted him to stay on the high ground continuing to keep his organization focused and productive. I reminded him that whenever people look for a new role elsewhere, the story about their most recent accomplishments needed to be as strong as their past achievements.

While I preserved confidentiality, I suggested to HR that Ted was becoming a retention risk, but no one leaned in to ameliorate that possibility. After 17 years with the company, Ted resigned to become President of R&D in another respected entity within the industry. Highlighting the importance of a dignified farewell, I collaborated with him on the message he sent to his organization. He received an outpouring of good wishes—and expressions of much sadness as well. True to form, when Ted met with the President of R&D to inform him that he was leaving the company, the President laughed at Ted's news, ridiculed his new employer, and said that Ted—who would now be in a comparable role to his—would fall flat on his face.

## DISCUSSION

There's a fragile dynamic that needs to be managed carefully whenever a longtime client company asks a consultant to do something the consultant is resistant to doing. In this case, a senior HR person near pleaded with me to take on a "mission" that involved one of the company's most brilliant scientists. Others in the company and another external consultant had "failed" to coach Ted, the brilliant scientist. The more he described Ted, the warier I became because I heard little regarding his intention to evolve as a leader. I didn't want to raise an expectation upon which I could not deliver. Nor did I want to waste the company's money or tarnish the reputation of executive coaching as a valuable development resource.

Not to damage my relationship with the HR professional, I agreed to have a "no commitment" introductory meeting with Ted. My precoaching scrutiny also included conversations with others in the organization, as well as with the previous coach who had worked with Ted several years before. However, in the end, it was Ted who convinced me of his readiness for coaching. He emphasized his need to change certain behaviors, and I emphasized the need for our deep trust and frequency of meetings if we were to have a fair shot at this change occurring.

Since Ted's leadership issues involved so much unconscious material, as someone trained clinically, I had to manage the boundary carefully between the contracted work and clinical considerations. As Kilburg wrote, "[U]nconscious material in the form of past experience, emotional responses, defensive reactions, underlying and unresolved conflicts, and dysfunctional patterns of thinking and behaving can contribute to poor leadership and consequently to decreased organizational effectiveness."[10] Fortunately, Ted and I were able to connect these considerations within the parameters of the coaching contract.

Further, in this coaching engagement, I was fortunate to have one of the best HR colleagues I've ever encountered. She did not filter or hold back anything, which was key given the often tense and acrimonious "political" dynamics that swirled about this case. We also maintained a frequent flow of collateral information— especially around the time of the merger and also when Ted contemplated leaving the company. Since I came to question the motives of Ted's boss, this rapport and truth-telling with my HR partner were invaluable.

Taking a cue from Gestalt psychology,[11] perhaps the most valuable coaching aid for Ted was my suggestion that he envision me beside him in all key meetings and other interactions with senior executives. Years later when we met for a year-end luncheon, he mentioned that this coaching tool was especially important to him because it helped him to both censor his explosive behavior and garner my approval. It also appeared that the coaching had helped Ted ease up, see himself in a steadier and positive light (minimal negative self-talk), and to have more self-compassion too.[12]

Using an insight-oriented coaching approach, I made linkages between the psychological residue, that is, issues related to Ted's childhood development, and how he behaved as a leader. Ted grew to understand the psychogenic basis of his less appealing behaviors; and while he made progress in beating back his inner demons, he realized, too, that certain struggles would continue. These struggles, he learned, could be attenuated if he stayed mindful of integrating the manner in which his left and right brain processed information. I referred to this as "total brain leadership."[13]

Inevitably, he would have difficulty trusting others—but when he did trust, it was a deeply held commitment to the other. He would always question how good he was, and he would need doses of affirmation and recognition to feel happy. However, given his undeniable accomplishments, awards, scientific articles, books, and ongoing magnificence as a lecturer, I anticipated that he'd achieve a strong sense of contentment and ego integration in his retirement years.

Finally, in all of my executive coaching experience, this was the first time I had to "hand off" my client to another consultant before a consolidation phase was completed. This was because my working agreement with Ted's longtime employer prevented me from consulting to an industry competitor. This meant that I was not able to assist Ted in his assimilation into the new role. Instead, I introduced him to another consulting psychologist whom I thought would be a good match with Ted. Their first meeting went well, and I believe the careful effort I made upfront to debrief the consultant fully and, with Ted's permission, to share the data I had gathered, helped support that success. Within a few years, Ted was voted Chief Scientific Officer of the Year by a jury of industry and academic peers. To be sure, Ted did not fall flat on his face.

## CONCLUSION

This is a case that almost never was. It taught me the importance of suspending my own alarm bells about the viability of an executive coaching engagement long enough to sit with a prospective client and just listen. Listen openly and hard. With significant reservation at the time of this referral, it was the sincerity of my client's expressed intention to change that pulled me into the work. All of the negative information I had heard about him faded in the presence of his painful recognition that he needed to modify behavior to be a better leader but had not a clue about how to make that happen. It would be my privilege to chart—and travel—this journey with him.

While we were rewarded by his diligence (making the coaching a priority) and immense progress (using insights gained), in the end, he left the company—taking his lessons learned to a competing organization. In between, it had been a roller coaster ride characterized by his self-discovery, taming of retaliatory urges, suppressing immature petulance, and navigating in a sea of massive egos. It had been a reminder of the power of one's early deprivation and struggle as forces for pursuing significant achievement. It had been a coaching challenge that, in the end, was mostly about harnessing the warrior instincts of this relentless champion. While it had been loud and unruly, I saw Ted's relentlessness as a gift to channel rather than a weakness to suppress. Rarely had I seen someone transcend such significant early psychological trauma and achieve at this remarkable level.

Executive coaches are often asked to blunt the sharper edges of a business leader's behavior. Surely Ted could explode and cut others deeply. While I focused on ways to help him minimize undue wounds created, I understood the inevitability of this behavior as part of his existential struggle *to be*. This fundamental understanding was the glue in our relationship and some of the fuel that helped propel his ongoing achievements. Ted would not self-destruct. Instead, his intense needs to be admired and to achieve on a grand scale would become well-channeled. They would take him to the heights of a career in which his single-minded pursuits were more than an antidote for the emotional and physical trauma of his youth. They made the difference between life and death for millions of patients throughout the world.

# Executive's Reflection

I was a senior leader in the Research and Development (R&D) organization of a global pharmaceutical company when the head of human resources (HR) for R&D, whom I trusted and respected immensely, urged me to work with Karol so that I could become an even more effective executive and leader. I had a coach several years previously, but that experience wasn't particularly satisfying. There were several reasons for this: (1) the coaching was forced on me and I didn't see a reason for it; (2) I was newly promoted and really didn't have sufficient time to devote to it; (3) I had no personal chemistry with the coach; (4) the lack of depth and discipline in the coaching approach; and (5) my limited trust in the coach.

The HR head emphasized Karol's reputation and experience with senior leaders in our company and also the fact that this was going to be a costly investment that the company wanted to make in my development. He also said Karol was discerning about the executives with whom she worked and would have to be convinced of my willingness to be coached. Based on information she had received about me from others in the company, I knew that her initial reaction was to not take me on as a client, but she agreed to have an initial meeting with me.

Much to my surprise, Karol shared all of her concerns, and that actually motivated me. In addition to the stated goal of my becoming a more effective executive, I wanted to prove her initial assessment of me wrong and impress her with the changes that I was capable of making in a successful coaching endeavor.

By this time, I had a very successful career and was considered to be a world-class scientist respected for my technical knowledge and for driving tough objectives to completion. However, I was also known as someone who was "tough as nails," "did not suffer fools easily," and who "went for the jugular" when I got into conflicts. Whenever I got into a conflict, I approached it from a win-lose standpoint, and I always had to win.

I remember distinctly the first days of working with Karol. She conducted what seemed like endless psychological tests—including an emotional intelligence (EQ) measure, which developmentally was my major issue. She also gathered 360 data from people at work and from my wife as well. Through her interviews at work, she got confirmation of what she already knew about my "temper" but from my wife, she learned that I was a sensitive, deeply caring, extremely generous person, kind, loving, and totally devoted to the family.

In other words, I was a very different person at work than at home, and Karol saw real potential in this. In her feedback, she emphasized that I had more EQ than most people thought—including the capacity for empathy. She went on to say that if I could bring this side of me into the work environment, it would help me become a more effective executive because I'd be softening the "hard edges" that had been causing problems in certain relationships there.

There were a number of factors that distinguished my work with Karol. They stand in contrast to the work with my first coach and included: (1) my readiness for coaching, that is, it was not forced upon me this time, and I could see its potential benefit; (2) I respected the person who suggested coaching and it was positioned as a major investment in me; (3) the intensity of Karol's commitment to the work; (4) great chemistry with her; (5) strong trust; (6) the use of effective tools; (7) coach gender—women have always intimidated me a bit and intimidation is a good motivator for me; (8) a disciplined and holistic coaching model; and (9) the notion of my realizing a "legacy."

Early in the coaching, Karol asked what I thought my career "legacy" would be and that proved to resonate with me greatly. I was in my mid-forties at the time, had been successful, and wanted to be more successful so this was the time to be thinking about legacy. I liked that. Coupled with this, she asked me how I wanted people to perceive me when the coaching was done. After a lengthy discussion, we focused on the term "statesman." I wanted to be a statesman, and I realized that people certainly did not see me as a statesman at that time. As one of the coaching tools, Karol asked me who I wanted to be like in my statesman mode and immediately I said I wanted to be like former President Ronald Reagan whom I considered to be the ultimate statesman. We then agreed to a key statesman rule, a rule I was to obey at all times when at work: I would never lose my temper again no matter the circumstances. I knew this would be a really tough rule to adhere to, but I agreed.

At this point, Karol introduced another key tool, something that worked quite well in terms of reinforcing the commitment to not losing my temper. She asked me to envision her sitting beside me in meetings and that whenever one of my hot buttons was pushed, I should think of her kicking me under the table as a reminder for me to react with good reasoning and EQ—not explosive anger. I think she knew how helpful this tool would be given how much I wanted to please her. The combination of acting on the job like Ronald Reagan and envisioning Karol next to me really proved powerful for me developmentally in achieving my objective of becoming a more effective leader. For the ensuing 15 years of my career in the pharmaceutical industry, I never again lost my temper at work. I became the "statesman" I wanted to be and realized my career legacy.

However, becoming the "statesman" did not occur overnight. While people noticed that I was behaving differently, not everyone believed the change was real. People at work had two names for me; the "old Ted" with the temper, and the "new Ted" who was the statesman. But after a few years of my staying with this behavior change effort, I was seen and accepted as the "new Ted," the statesman.

One real test of this came after my boss and another colleague had been injured seriously in a car accident. On a temporary basis (approximately one year), I was asked to assume the roles of both my boss and colleague, along with the role I had. My responsibility increased exponentially and I had to interact with many additional leaders throughout the organization versus just in my line. Inevitably, conflicts arose but given the coaching I already had, I was able to remain steady, calm, and effective in these leadership roles. I was given many kudos for holding my boss's and my colleague's organizations together and, after a year, I received a significant promotion. I also received a major role in the wake of a merger with another global entity.

Shortly thereafter, I was recruited to become President of R&D of another global pharmaceutical company. While this job was a real stretch with a much larger operating budget than the comparable role at my company, I felt coaching had helped prepare me for a job of this magnitude. Because Karol had an exclusive contract with my employer, we could not continue to work together. But the lessons I learned from working with her were cemented in my brain and she arranged for another executive coach whom she trusted to continue our work.

The work I did with Karol had become an ingrained part of my behavior. First and foremost, I maintained my commitment to never losing my temper at work. I received numerous awards and recognition including the prestigious Chief Scientific Officer of the Year Award presented to the best head of R&D in all of the pharmaceutical and biotechnology industries. I was also profiled and featured in many newspapers, and in business and trade publications, and I was universally credited with completely reengineering R&D in my new company, as well as for being a "visionary" (other people's words, not mine) for how pharmaceutical R&D should be done. To attest to the progress that Karol made with me, today—approximately five years after I retired—I am frequently invited to symposia, and hired as a consultant by many pharmaceutical companies to opine on executive leadership of large R&D groups, and to help these entities manage R&D effectively. Imagine, me being hired to present lectures on executive leadership!

Through this executive coaching, I became the effective executive, the *statesman,* I desired to be. While Karol gives me most of the credit for the successes I have had, I acknowledge her role—her vast experience, determination, and belief in my potential all of which contributed significantly to the crowning achievements of my career.

# CHAPTER 2

# Destined to Lead

Imagine the variations of an ocean...ebb and flow, undulating quiet and sudden waves crashing, possibility and imminent danger for person and property. Metaphorically, these are the variations in this case study—a case that involved the complicated dynamics of a CEO's succession. Blending their business and psychological wisdom, Saporito and Winum wrote of CEO succession, "Issues of power, control, legacy, competition and ego can operate throughout all phases of a CEO succession process and significantly compromise the best outcomes."[1] My effort to reveal and navigate these issues—as they played out for a CEO candidate—was at the core of this executive coaching engagement.

At the suggestion of one of his board members, the CEO of a global consumer brands company contacted me to discuss the potential of my coaching an internal succession candidate. While there was no formal succession process in place, and he was not amenable to one, he perceived coaching as an appropriate and sufficient development resource. He had had his own positive coaching experience, and the successor candidate, Kathryn, was receptive.

Prior to meeting with the CEO, I sought input from the referring board member whom I knew well given consulting I had done in his company, another global entity. I learned that my prospective coaching client was perceived by the board as an "emerging CEO" who had been a stellar performer since she joined the company a decade earlier. He described Kathryn's development need as "projecting a more CEO-like presence." Specifically, Kathryn needed to listen more, be less reactive to criticism, and interact with the board in a more impactful manner blending strong business acumen and interpersonal skill.

Based on my first meeting with the CEO, I knew he agreed with the board member regarding Kathryn's development need, had enormous confidence in her, and did not want to recruit from the outside. I also thought he would likely be an effective partner with me in this high stakes engagement.[2] While he was indefinite about the actual timing of his succession, he indicated a four- to five-year time frame.

## First Meeting with the Coaching Client

In my first meeting with Kathryn, I was struck by a number of factors beyond her obvious intelligence, business experience, passion for work, sense of humor, and stylish beauty. Most of all it was her candor evidenced clearly in the response to my question about her leadership. She exclaimed, "I'm terrible! I'm totally hard-nosed, I don't shirk from big risks, and I don't ask for permission." She also expressed a pointed question regarding the coaching, "Is he (the CEO) playing me to keep me here or, is he really serious about me as a potential successor?"

Her ready self-disclosure and confidence were apparent in her words,

> I've never viewed myself as different, and I think, "Hey let the gender thing go." I believe that if I'm comfortable everybody else is likely to be comfortable. Women have to overcome the myth that they aren't comfortable with risk or that they're not committed to being successful in business. I love what I do and I think I'm a much better parent because I work than if I didn't. If you love it, you'll find ways to make it work for you.

(I remember thinking, "Good, we're not going to lose any traction based on gender considerations, and she's figured out how to manage the work-family integration issue."[3])

## Setting the Coaching Agenda: Joint Meeting with the CEO

In our joint meeting with the CEO, I provided an overview of the four-phase coaching model (data-gathering, feedback, coaching, and consolidation) and reviewed our respective roles in it.[4] I was especially intent on Kathryn's hearing the CEO's support of her as a potential successor to him and that he would be an active partner in the coaching. I was also explicit about the boundaries of confidentiality and that the focus of the coaching was completely *developmental*. In other words, my sole objective was to foster her readiness to become CEO, and at no time would I be expected to "vote" on her CEO candidacy.

The CEO agreed with Kathryn's view of the coaching areas: (1) increasing executive presence in terms of staying even-keeled especially when things were not going well; and (2) being more discerning with her time, that is, less time spent on external activities. He also added a third area: the need for her to become more effective in using the corporate functions to accomplish results. Regarding executive presence, I added active listening and increased interpersonal effectiveness with key stakeholders including board members. We ended this meeting with the identification of a sample of people for my 360 data-gathering—a representative sample of respondents Kathryn knew well and who would provide thoughtful and candid input. I also advised her careful attention to the message she sent inviting their participation for this was not a culture where such data-gathering was common practice.[5]

## Phase I: Data-Gathering

My taking of a full life history preceded the 360 data-gathering and helped forge the connection I wanted to have with Kathryn before I gave her any feedback. From the perspective of Erikson's development stages,[6] it was clear that she had accomplished the psychosocial tasks of each of her life stages, which, in my view, further underscored her strength as a leader.[7]

Key aspects of her life history paralleled those of other successful senior business executives with whom I'd worked. These included: (1) caring parents who expected her disciplined achievement, (2) her playing competitive sports (*I loved the competition of sports*), (3) an early and fierce sense of independence (*I'm even more motivated whenever someone says I can't do something*), and (4) a strong desire to earn money.

Kathryn identified greatly with her mother who worked outside the home as a teacher. She described her as steadfast (*I was taught to never break down emotionally*), resilient, able to handle a lot simultaneously, more reactive than reflective, outgoing, and capable of being stern—but always fair. (I was already thinking, "The apple doesn't fall far from the tree"). While she identified less with her father, his entrepreneurism rubbed off, she admired his work-related intensity, and strove to please him with both her academic and athletic accomplishments.

A high school mentor noted Kathryn's achievements in math and science and encouraged her to pursue engineering in college, which she did. While she was an anomaly as a female engineering student, her description of this time carried no gender distinction. In her pragmatic view, "I was right at the transition from slide rule to computer."

Kathryn spent the first decade of her career in sales and marketing roles and she also received an MBA in this time frame. Having met her husband in grad school, they relocated a few times and eventually settled in the Northeast. They were adept at juggling the demands of their lives—including raising two children. Remarking on the more rapid trajectory of her career Kathryn commented with gratitude, "My husband was willing to give up a lot for me and my career."

By the mid-1990s, Kathryn was running a global business, and by the end of the decade she was reporting directly to the CEO. Given her strong preference for autonomy and maintaining pace, she had a mixed relationship with him. In her words, "I don't think he enjoyed working with me mostly because I didn't ask for permission; I just did things." However, she acknowledged his excellent mentoring in terms of picking one's battles carefully, bringing people along versus moving too quickly, and forcing others to think.

When I probed about what her inner "demons" might be, again Kathryn was forthcoming and direct. She laughed,

> There must be something in there about thinking I'm not as good as others, so I just keep pushing hard. I don't have a chip on my shoulder but sometimes I do question why I'm doing this. I think it's about the company and what I believe we can do in the world. The day the business is ever *about me*, that's when I'll fail.

Her perspective was consistent with Maccoby's concept of productive narcissism.[8]

Another key probe related to what she thought her career legacy might be. Her response was telling, "I've begun to think about that more. For the company, it's significant expansion into emerging markets. For me, it's influencing things so that this happens. The CEO and I are having some real conversation about this now."

## Phase II: Feedback

The results of the psychological testing data[9] confirmed Kathryn's many leadership strengths. Her strong critical thinking capabilities ensured analytical problem-solving, as well as her getting to core issues quickly, setting sound priorities, and arriving at logical conclusions. Energized by people and fresh ideas, she was reflexively focused on customers and thrived on pace and effective execution. Low on neuroticism, she could withstand stress well and rebound quickly from disappointments.

While Kathryn's emotional intelligence (EQ) was adequate for someone at her level, the need for greater empathy was indicated. In our discussion of this, she commented, "I'm so driven to get results or to fix things, I can get pretty impatient and not hear the other side as fully as I should. I just want to get it done and keep moving."

Cautions in this data indicated the potential dark side of her behavioral strengths versus any serious limitations as a leader. These cautions included the need for her to: (1) monitor her fierce independence

(*Yes, the CEO has counseled me to pick my battles carefully*); (2) channel her drive for results (*Yes, I do need to make sure people are aligned with the direction I've set*); and (3) titrate her forcefulness so she did not shut down collegial dialogue with peers or appear intractable (unwilling/unable to compromise when necessary), and didn't make her quests for information feel like interrogations.

Based on my interaction with the CEO, the joint meeting Kathryn and I had had with him, and my conversations with her, I wrote an interview protocol that would elicit the information we needed for the coaching phase.[10] These questions can be found in figure 2.1. There were 16 people in the interview sample plus a "self" interview with Kathryn so we could discuss the convergence and/or contrast between the Self and Other data.

For the most part, Kathryn's Self and the compilation of Other data were well-aligned underscoring her leadership capabilities and further potential. Of note, on the question that probed best possible next roles, half the sample said CEO. In response to the question regarding her development needs, the most frequent response (over 75 percent of the sample) was *executive presence*. On a more granular level, this focused on her (1) increasing EQ, particularly attunement to others' concerns, greater patience and awareness of her impact on others (especially when agitated), and forging relationships that were not just transactional; and (2) being less defensive when results lagged in her areas of responsibility.

After our discussion of all the data and Kathryn's private follow-up discussion with the CEO, we settled on three areas for the coaching phase. These were: (1) executive presence (more even keel/less reactive/defensive when frustrated, active listening, greater patience, and stronger EQ especially attunement to all stakeholders—including board members); (2) increased integrative approach in working with corporate functions; and (3) greater discernment regarding time (spending more time with people reporting to her and less on external speaking engagements).

### Case Formulation

My formulation of this case involved two parallel tracks. One track was clear and straightforward focused on the identified coaching

**Figure 2.1** Interview Protocol—360 Data-gathering Questionnaire.

1   Describe Kathryn's strengths.

2   What are Kathryn's limitations, if any?

3   When are they especially apparent?

4   Describe Kathryn's management style.

5   On a 1–10 scale, how effective is she in her management of people?

6   Analyzing people assets: From 1 to 10, how effective is Kathryn in analyzing capabilities of people reporting to her? In putting them in roles for which they are best suited?

7   Keeping the "keepers:" From 1 to 10, how effective is Kathryn at keeping the best people? What's the bench strength within her group?

8   On a 1–10 scale, how's her time management?

9   Executive presence: On a 1–10 scale, how well does she react when things are NOT going well? (Staying even-keeled and positive, walking that middle ground even when things are problematic/disappointing).

10  How would you rate her (1–10) in terms of understanding and using corporate functions to accomplish established objectives?

11  Focusing on results: From 1 to 10, to what extent does she focus on the "intangibles" like morale, trust, and loyalty?

12  Showing a sense of urgency: 1–10, to what extent does she display a sense of urgency and ignite the followership of others?

13  Providing psychological paychecks: How effective is she at acknowledging others' work well done (1–10)?

14  Communication: 1–10, how "current" do employees feel in terms of key business developments—knowing what they need to know to be effective? Having sufficient access to Kathryn? How open, direct, and honest is she perceived to be?

15  Vision. Fire. Goal passion: To what extent, 1–10, does Kathryn's group have a shared vision?

16  Team: How effective is Kathryn as a team player (1–10)?

17  Do you see another role in which she would be even more effective? If so, what?

18  What specifically does she need to do to be ready for further responsibility?

19  Advice: If you were to give Kathryn one piece of advice that would enable her to be even more effective than she already is, what would you tell her?

20  What did we miss?

areas and how Kathryn's progress in these areas would advance her candidacy as a CEO succession candidate. The other track was clear in its focus on helping Kathryn manage a set of interconnected relationships (with the CEO, other leaders in the company, and the board). However, this was a more circuitous path littered with psychological underbrush particularly that of the CEO. This was evident in my meetings with him when he vacillated between a high degree of contentment regarding his tenure as CEO, and discontent given tension he was having with the board on issues including the timing of his succession.

Given the boundaries of the coaching contract, I knew that I might—or might not—get a full handle on the psychodynamics of the succession for him. However, I would attempt to do so because as Kilburg states "[E]vents, feelings, thoughts, and patterns of behavior that are outside of the conscious awareness of executives can significantly influence what they decide and how they act."[11] I wanted to help ensure that his interactions with Kathryn contributed to her readiness to succeed him and eased any undue anxiety she may have harbored about the succession.

Finally, I thought Kathryn and I would be misguided by an overemphasis on the dark side of her fierce independence and bias for action. Instead, I believed the coaching would have more impact if it focused on her leveraging these fundamental strengths while minimizing the adverse effects of her impatience. The coaching would focus on her building empathic resonance with others (including the CEO), getting the right talent in place to accelerate her ambitious business objectives, and her staying focused on ways to increase the board's comfort level with her. Since she was more pragmatic than reflective, I would use a primarily cognitive-behavioral approach amplified with insights that would abet her relationships particularly with the CEO and board members.

## Phase III: Coaching, Year 1

Focusing on the three aforementioned areas, the coaching phase (monthly, face-to-face 90-minute meetings) lasted a full year. This contract was renewed for two more years after which I transitioned into a *trusted advisor* relationship (see chapter 10) with Kathryn that continues at this writing. In this capacity, I serve as an objective sounding board for issues related to her leadership effectiveness and key people issues/decisions.

### Coaching Tools and Actions

The Visual Leadership Metaphor® (VLM), an effective tool for anchoring the course of a coaching engagement, reflected

Kathryn's strong action orientation and emphasis on execution (see figure 2.2). In my mind, this tool indicated that Kathryn's coaching breakthroughs would involve her channeling her need for pace effectively, and her making the transition from *doing* to *influencing* the strategic course of the company. This was confirmed in my ongoing conversations with the CEO and had obvious implications for her executive presence development area.

Further, her learning about EQ and its significance for fully effective leadership would prove to be an important learning/ behavior change tool in the coaching. This information was conveyed through both our discussions and carefully chosen literature that I believed would resonate with Kathryn quickly.[12,13]

Through the first year of coaching, numerous other tools were introduced. These included: (1) mindfulness as a technique for keeping her focused in-the-moment,[14] (2) an emphasis on her using a *collaborative/seeking clarification* tone versus an interrogative one, (3) the concept of the *3Rs*—ensuring that she had the *right people* in the *right roles* and that she influenced the *right conditions* for them to succeed, and (4) paying sufficient attention to both her verbal and nonverbal communication. Kathryn would not have been a good poker player, so a focus on her body language was key.

**Figure 2.2** Kathryn's Visual Leadership Metaphor® (VLM) #1.

*Drawing by Joe Williams*

| FRAME 1 | FRAME 2 | FRAME 3 |
|---|---|---|
| This leader is keeping many plates spinning on poles. | She now has even more plates spinning well on poles. | All the plates are spinning on their own, and this leader is now working on getting more plates up and running. |

In the early phase of coaching, a number of specific actions proved helpful to her making headway in all three of the coaching areas. These actions included: (1) her counting to 10 before reacting to negative information and thinking through how she wanted/needed to engage; (2) taking the "downs in stride" but without losing the root cause analysis of *why* and finding ways to solve business issues; (3) garnering more support from and engagement with her peers on key marketplace initiatives; (4) increasing high quality engagement with others (e.g., more one-on-one meetings with her direct reports, not doing emails in meetings, using a notebook in meetings to capture stimulating thoughts for follow-up later with specific individuals); and (5) giving people more "psychological paychecks" in the wake of work well done.

On a more pragmatic level—actions related to the time discernment coaching goal—Kathryn and her family moved to a home that was closer to the office, and she hired a full-time housekeeper. She also increased her delegation to others with the recognition that this was a development tool that could help them stretch. Further, based on input I gleaned from my board contact, Kathryn enhanced her executive presence by discussing business issues more deeply even at board dinners and by employing a less rapid-fire and more succinct communication style when presenting to them.

## Phase III: Coaching, Year 2

Early in the second year of Kathryn's coaching, the CEO gave her an outstanding performance review in which he emphasized her progress and discussed other possible roles that could help prepare her for greater leadership in the company. While I was aware that he had positioned her as his "emergency successor" with the board, this was not something she knew or that I could share with her. Instead I stated that, in my opinion, she had become a stronger CEO candidate and would continue as such if she maintained an integrated focus on what we called the "five boxes": strategy, structure, people, results, and rewards.

In conversations with the board, the CEO reaffirmed Kathryn's strong candidacy as a potential successor, and he followed through on my suggestion that he be more specific with her about his view on succession. He discussed the succession with her emphasizing his satisfaction in their level of trust, her ability to get the "tough things" done, and her learning agility. In gauging the coaching, he told me, "I like how you maintain an open communication loop with me. I know you can't share everything, but I think you're saying enough to be helpful to both of us."

### Additional Coaching Tools

Business pressures were increasingly difficult in every global sector, people performance issues were intensifying, and there was a growing concern about employee motivation. I introduced two tools to aid Kathryn's thinking and decision-making especially vis-á-vis the people reporting to her. I referred to the first as an exercise in *Perspective-Making* (see figure 2.3). The coaching intention here was to ensure that Kathryn integrated bad news about the state of the business with good news in terms of individual talents, company competitive forces, and her clear and optimistic view of the future. By doing so, she would be better able to keep people focused and motivated.

The second tool was a two-factor (results and behavior) exercise used to clarify her thoughts and decisions about whether or not she had the right people in the right roles (see figure 2.4). Since there was not a seasoned HR professional in the corporate HR role, it was more incumbent upon business leaders like Kathryn to address this.

By the end of the second year of coaching, we were discussing Kathryn's leadership effectiveness through the lens of what it takes to be a "remarkable" leader particularly the criterion of what I called "total brain leadership" (TBL). In my view, "These leaders apply their *what* and *how* leadership assets to win in a Darwinian global business climate. These are the courageous visionaries too impatient to wait and resilient enough to adjust when necessary...They are cutting bolder deals and gambling faster in a business atmosphere where the combination of anticipation, speed and execution rules."[15]

**Figure 2.3** Perspective-making—A Fundamental Leadership Responsibility.

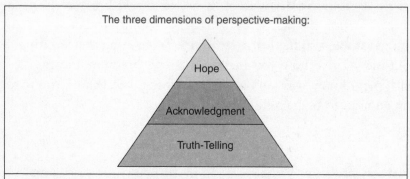

The three dimensions of perspective-making:

- TRUTH-TELLING—Stating reality as it truly *is*. Leaders present an accurate picture of current reality. They have the courage to confront the truth. They are persistently candid about what's *real now* including business results, business problems, business projections, and people performance issues/development needs. Leaders also have the courage and tact to confront any "sacred cows" in the company that could sabotage business success.

- ACKNOWLEDGMENT—Public comments about what's working well in the organization. Leaders capitalize on opportunities to affirm employees' good work, to celebrate success, and to build on aspects of the culture that ensure momentum, timely results, and competitive advantage.

- HOPE—Leaders instill hope in people by engaging in frequent and clear communication regarding all the reasons employees can feel optimistic and excited about the future. These messages emphasize strength of the strategic direction, specificity of objectives, realistic timelines, and robustness of the culture.

*IN TOUGH TIMES, THE BEST LEADERS MAKE PERSPECTIVE—*
*Emphasis is on HOPE*

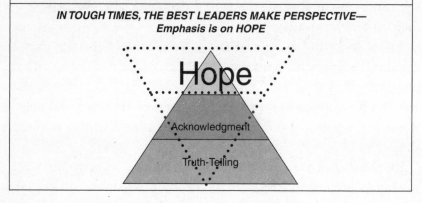

Kathryn needed to ensure that her strong left brain analytical and problem-solving preferences did not overwhelm right brain-based strengths involving empathy and relationship-building (as indicated earlier). We needed to minimize this as a leadership issue for as Kaplan and Kaiser wrote, "Leadership consists of opposing strengths, and most leaders have a natural tendency to overdevelop

**Figure 2.4** Two Factors for Assessing Employee Effectiveness

| RESULTS/BEHAVIOR | |
|---|---|
| 1<br><br>+ R<br>+ B | 2<br><br>− R<br>+ B |
| 3<br><br>+ R<br>− B | 4<br><br>− R<br>− B |

Key:

Quadrant 1: The top "high potential" people

- Both RESULTS and BEHAVIOR are strong
- **Major question:** "What do we need to do to keep them?"

Quadrant 2: The "question marks"

- RESULTS are not where they need to be but BEHAVIOR is right; usually highly loyal employees.
- **Major questions:** "How much time does this person need to get-up-to-speed?" (When person is new to role.) "Will this person be able to get-up-to-speed?" (When person has been in the role for awhile.) If the situation is fixable, "What do we need to do to get results on track?" (e.g., training, coaching, etc.) If the situation is not fixable, move person into another appropriate role.

Quadrant 3: The "saboteurs"

- RESULTS are strong but BEHAVIOR is a real problem; these people can be high maintenance, sour others with their cynicism, or otherwise erode consistent team performance.
- **Major questions:** "Is a behavior adjustment possible?" If so, "What needs to happen for that adjustment to occur (e.g., coaching)?" If behavior adjustment is not possible, "Is the person more trouble than he/she is worth?" If no, then retain person but step up performance management and make sure awards are aligned. If yes, move person out as soon as feasible.

Quadrant 4: The "dead wood" OR "recyclables."

- RESULTS and BEHAVIOR are both negative.
- Major questions: "Is this a temporary thing?" If so, "How quickly can an adjustment occur?" "What needs to happen?" If it's not just a flukey, temporary situation, "Is there another role in the organization in which this person can be successful?" If so, make it happen. If not, clear the way for a dignified exit.

one at the expense of its counterpart. This resulting imbalance diminishes their effectiveness."[16] The CEO also emphasized the need for Kathryn to integrate these two capabilities saying, "She's fast and brilliant, but I still need her to pay more attention to working well with others." This was a key factor in his giving her a corporate function to manage, that is, experiential learning as emphasized by McCall et al.[17]

In my ongoing conversations with the CEO, he described Kathryn's continued progress. He was pleased about their relationship and said she had become a better listener and was more self-disclosing about what was *not* going well in her business and functional responsibilities. By this time, he had also started to give her different external exposure (Wall Street, heads of state, US government officials). Things were obviously tracking well, she was feeling this, and thus her prior concerns about the seriousness of her candidacy for CEO had all but evaporated.

At the end of this year, we started to get more granular about CEO succession criteria. While we continued to focus on specific leadership competencies and behaviors, her interactions with the CEO, and her "performance events" with the board, I also urged a different level of *readiness*. Kathryn began to clarify her thinking and potential actions as related to critical business issues that would likely be facing the company at the time of the CEO succession. These included global economic conditions, industry consolidation, operational factors, business portfolio issues, potential legislative/regulatory change, and labor issues.

## Phase III: Coaching, Year 3

As we moved into year three, the CEO chuckled in one of my meetings with him, "It's now clear to me that she's going to be a CEO, but whether it'll be here or not is up to you." In this classic *truth in jest* moment, I chided him about it being our *joint* effort that included his interactions with the board. I also hastened to explore what was beginning to sound like his ambivalence about the succession. This had little, if anything, to do with Kathryn; I sensed it was more a function of his inner turmoil—a turmoil that would, unfortunately, remain unexpressed. He was an exceedingly private man when it came to his emotions. However, I could surmise that he was not doing well with his impending loss of the CEO role.

Regarding the psychodynamic of this particular loss of power, Sonnenfeld wrote, "[W]hen the time comes to step aside for newer, and almost always younger leaders, many high corporate officers are beset with fears…leaving office means a loss of heroic stature, a plunge into the abyss of insignificance, a kind of mortality."[18] Further, too young to retire completely, this CEO's lack of clarity about an engaging next life chapter seemed to exacerbate his ambivalence. Despite my efforts to explore these issues, in the end, I had to respect his boundaries, and I focused instead on encouraging his proactive exploration of future options.

With Kathryn, I urged her to: (1) not personalize the CEO's seeming "moodiness"; (2) stay riveted on achieving her major objectives (what we metaphorically named the "big rocks"); (3) not get trapped in the tactical (execution issues) at the expense of her having strategic impact; (4) remain tough on people performance and accountability issues; and (5) project calm and strategic clarity to the board. We also focused on her establishing a *reciprocal communication rhythm* with the board whenever she presented there. Related action steps included her making certain she heard an entire question before she started answering, her asking questions that conveyed her desire to satisfy and connect with her audience (*Did I answer your question? Does this lead us to any other related questions or topics that warrant discussion now?*). This concept of reciprocal communication had the dual intention of Kathryn projecting greater executive presence and increasing the board's comfort level with her.

## Phase IV: Coaching Consolidation

By the summer of the third coaching year, it was clear that Kathryn had progressed on all three coaching goals, and I reinforced this progress overtly as a way of ensuring she internalized lessons learned. Her own words confirmed progress made, "I've been behaving well—more balanced (not reactive) and thoughtful (reflective)." Further, the CEO sounded more satisfied with the depth and breadth of her strategic thinking and had requested she run a major strategic review for the company.

In our coaching meetings, I emphasized the need for her to relegate specific time for strategic thinking, to be crisp in her discussions of pressing business issues and her thoughts about potential solutions, and to be ready to capitalize on even impromptu discussions with the CEO. Further, in our conversations about people, Kathryn had become clearer about the need to promote and/or recruit "hybrid" individuals, that is, people with a mix of technical competence and commercial instincts.

In a year-end dinner with the CEO, he praised Kathryn for her continued good listening, driving results, bringing her market-facing instincts to the table, making good people decisions, and being respectful of him at board meetings. When I probed for what she needed to focus on next, he cited her delivering good business results, relating to the board in a clear, succinct and engaging manner, and her avoiding any appearance of an unhealthy competitive dynamic with the other internal succession candidate.

At the outset of the next year, Kathryn was deeply immersed in the company's strategic initiative and was scheduled to give a major presentation at an upcoming board meeting. While I knew she'd get the "what" (facts and data) right, I sent her written guidance regarding "how" she delivered the presentation.

In part my memorandum read:

> As you prepare for this Board meeting, we know you'll nail the objective content. So what follows here is some guidance about the subjective behavioral "stuff" that makes Board members feel comfortable with, as well as confident in, senior executives. Mea culpa if I'm being unduly redundant, BUT we cannot underestimate the power of this "feeling comfortable" factor. In the end, a CEO succession decision always hinges on this to some degree. So anticipate their questions, answer them as fully as possible, ask for clarification when you need it, use good body language, leverage your positive emotions (optimism) and manage any negative ones (impatience, defensiveness), stay attuned to both individual Board members and the collective, and project your full self (total brain leadership).

While the board presentation went quite well, I kept the spotlight on Kathryn's leadership—both the essential competencies

**Figure 2.5**  Seven Warning Signs of Executive Failure.

| | |
|---|---|
| 1 | Lack of clear direction |
| 2 | Failure to meet growth challenges |
| 3 | Complacency |
| 4 | Excessive change |
| 5 | Tolerating mediocre performers |
| 6 | Lack of delegation |
| 7 | Poor communication |
| * From RHR Executive Insights, Volume 23, Number 2, 2007. | |

(e.g., setting vision, strategic thinking, driving results, developing people, and having a macro view of the business) and what to avoid. Regarding the latter, we used the "seven warning signs"[19] of executive failure as a report card (tool) to gauge her effectiveness (see figure 2.5). Two areas received less than an "A" grade from Kathryn and thus warranted our continued attention on her: (1) not tolerating mediocre performers and (2) increasing delegation. Over the next several months, Kathryn would get tougher regarding people's accountability and continue to delegate more, as well as staying focused on using all the corporate functions to drive results.

By the summer of this year, the CEO had identified some compelling outside interests, and had decided he would retire at the end of the year. While his timing was a surprise, the board was ready for a new leader, and members had become quite comfortable with Kathryn. Further, she was especially well-equipped to succeed him given her market-facing capabilities and the board's expectation of further global expansion.

### CEO Succession Decision Made

One fall evening, the CEO invited Kathryn for a glass of wine—something he had never done before. Fearing bad news, Kathryn was stunned when he raised his glass and toasted her as the next CEO of the corporation. He said he admired her ability to make the often complex and obscure factors in their business relevant and understandable to both investors and customers. He also credited her with helping the company to achieve significant growth and said he saw her as the most likely leader to accelerate its continued growth.

### Coach Becomes Trusted Advisor

Kathryn was to assume her new role in several months for in the words of the CEO, "She needs some time to get used to the role." He asked me to continue as a trusted advisor to her as did Kathryn herself. To aid her rapid transition into the CEO role, I conducted a mini survey among other CEOs whom I knew and/or was working with to garner explicit guidance for her. I asked them: *What did you do in your initial days as CEO that most facilitated your successful transition into the job?* The four top themes I shared with Kathryn were: (1) getting out and meeting key company leaders throughout the world, (2) building strong relationships with board members, (3) building relationships with the largest shareholders, and (4) staying focused on—and never being distracted from—doing the right things for the company.

We also created a new Visual Leadership Metaphor® (VLM) as a tool for guiding her first year as CEO (see figure 2.6). Further, our conversations became more introspective in the weeks leading up to the actual succession. In one poignant moment, Kathryn raised the topic of confidence. After this meeting, I sent her an email that read in part:

> I offer you a few potentially helpful observations based on what I've seen and learned from other CEOs. First, no one is ever fully ready for this job. It takes at least a couple of years for a new CEO to get comfortable in and to take full command of the role. Second, the people around a new CEO will overtly or covertly test him/her—the challenge is to not rise to the bait, to not feel compelled to know all the answers, to draw upon his/

**Figure 2.6** Kathryn's Visual Leadership Metaphor® (VLM) #2.

*Drawing by Joe Williams*

| FRAME 1 | FRAME 2 | FRAME 3 |
|---------|---------|---------|
| It's the external crisis of 2008-09 and the world doesn't make sense anymore. The plan we had just won't work now. We thought we had a lot of good ideas about how to make money but everything's down the drain. | I'm clearly in construction mode now. There are cranes everywhere; we're tearing down some things, and we're building up other things that will set the future well. | I'm standing in the middle of many skyscrapers that are all aglow and working beautifully. Things are clearly robust, vibrant, and we know we can sustain this. |

her past experiences and mistakes, and to bring the "testers" into an atmosphere of full commitment and collaboration. I have no doubt that you have the right stuff to do this job—and to do it splendidly well.

Given the state of the global economy when Kathryn became CEO, she would have no "honeymoon" period but she was ready enough given her growth as a leader. In my view, she was destined to lead.

## DISCUSSION

While the coaching of internal candidates can be an aspect of a CEO succession planning process, its importance is exponentially greater in the absence of such an initiative in a company that had never had one. In this case, the dynamics of the coaching engagement were intensified further by the board's pressure on the CEO about his succession, the fact that the suggested coach had never consulted to the company, and that this coach was, in essence, being "parachuted in" by a board member. My heightened attention to establishing rapid credibility and to building trust with the

CEO, as well as to forming a strong rapport with the prospective coaching client, were key in the initial phase and eventual success of this engagement.

There was also an important consideration related to the *orchestration* of the coaching. It began with "doing my homework" by getting a thorough briefing on the company, the CEO, and Kathryn from the board member who recommended me for the assignment. Since he had been on the board for several years and I knew him well, I could count on the quality of his input, but I also knew I could only press so far given the boundary of confidentiality he had to maintain as a director. My not assuming the engagement was a "go" and scheduling a "no commitment" face-to-face meeting with the CEO in which I provided a list of other CEOs who were familiar with my work were also wise steps. This positive credibility screen cleared the path for an introductory "chemistry check" meeting with Kathryn. Given her openness, receptivity to coaching, and our quick rapport, the engagement commenced shortly thereafter.

Aside from the core of this work, that is, the techniques and tools used to aid Kathryn's progress and thus enhance her status as a CEO succession candidate, there was the ongoing challenge of managing my coaching "partnerships" with the CEO, the board member, the corporate HR executive, and another member of the CEOs staff, as well as with Kathryn. In this high wire walking, I needed to stay vigilant and guard against anything that would sabotage or otherwise disturb the flow of valuable collateral information I needed to aid Kathryn fully. The challenge, of course, was in knowing how to use this data in a manner that preserved the boundaries of both my role and the confidentiality as established at the outset of the engagement.[20]

Kathryn's progress on the identified coaching areas was a function of at least two key factors. The first was her strong intention to learn and to change certain leadership habits and behaviors. The second was that she accepted my interpretation of her "lopsided" leadership style[21] and believed she could be even more effective if she integrated her strong business and marketplace analysis capabilities with greater interpersonal effectiveness. My reference to this as total brain leadership[22] was a concept that resonated with her.

From a broad armamentarium of coaching tools, those that proved to be most useful included: (1) emotional intelligence as a learning vehicle to promote Kathryn's self-awareness, emotional containment, attunement to others, and her forming relationships that were not merely transactional; (2) mindfulness (intense listening to others and being fully present in meetings); (3) empathic resonance in her relationships with key others especially the CEO; (4) my advice on how to manage the mercurial temperament of the CEO, (not overpersonalizing either his lack of positive feedback or his more critical behavior); and (5) emphasis on her managing her own "branding" particularly in high visibility "performance events" with the board.

Further, it was of no small significance that Kathryn knew I would not be casting a "vote" regarding the ultimate CEO succession decision. In others words, she trusted the developmental intent of the coaching. I suggest that two other factors boded well for Kathryn's steady evolution as a leader. While these factors warrant continued research, the first was her gender neutral orientation to her career (*"Hey, let the gender thing go"*). Kathryn had never seen any barriers to her aspirations and from an organization perspective, her career goals were not sabotaged by what has been termed "second-generation gender bias."[23] The second was her husband's unwavering support and willingness to subordinate his career to hers.

Finally, the consolidation phase of Kathryn's coaching included a segment that focused on anchoring her path forward as CEO, as well as on reinforcing key lessons learned in the coaching. Her continued focus on executive presence and not letting her fierce independence interfere with maintaining strong relationships, particularly with the CEO, was central to her success. The best outcome of this CEO succession was not, in my view, compromised by the psychodynamic factors cited at the beginning of this chapter.[24]

## CONCLUSION

No corporation's decision is as replete with both opportunity and potential danger as the selection of its next CEO. In the best of circumstances, there is a comprehensive CEO succession planning process in place to guide the appointment of a leader who is greatly equipped to meet both current and impending business imperatives. However, when there is no such process in place, when the CEO is ambivalent about his succession, and when a consultant who is new to the organization is engaged to coach an internal succession candidate—this is akin to high wire walking without a net.

In such situations, the consultant is wise not only to marshal all of his/her relevant experiences but to form rapid "partnerships" with key individuals in the company who can provide essential collateral information. Further, holding collegial dialogues with trusted consultants who have had similar experiences can also prove helpful. It is hoped that the coaching of this CEO succession candidate—this high wire walk—provides insights to consultants who may find themselves in a similar circumstance, as well as to those whose coaching engagements are embedded in a robust CEO succession planning initiative.

For all that is revealed in any CEO succession coaching engagement, much can remain unrevealed especially as related to individual and organizational psychodynamics. The author's effort to remain vigilant about and responsive to the complicated psychodynamics of this particular situation helped ensure a sound outcome for the organization, its employees, and its shareholders. In this case, the coach walked a taut middle ground between helping Kathryn make progress on her development needs, and also providing her with enough psychological insight that she could effectively manage her relationships with an enigmatic CEO and members of the board. In addition to Kathryn's obvious business-based capabilities and success in accelerating growth for the company, the board's enriched comfort with her was pivotal to Kathryn's ultimate appointment as CEO.

Having ridden this sea with Kathryn, I am reminded that the executive coach/trusted advisor can play many roles as the waves of a CEO succession roll over an organization, the board, and the succession candidates themselves. These roles can include: swimmer, navigator, surf rider, fisherman, and life guard too. Perhaps the largest challenge then is this: knowing *when* to be *what*.

# Executive's Reflection

I am and have always been a very independent person. I have great pride in "getting there" on my own. I have had assessments and an occasional follow up with the consultants who deliver the tests or 360 to get feedback. These were basically one-way information sharing—this is what the tests or interviews said. Many times there were reminders of areas of strength to build on or improvement areas. And that was the sum total of the interaction. I would internalize it and set the tone and pace for how I would utilize it. Some experiences felt like I was relearning the same things. Some felt like it was based on dated information. Other times it seemed current and helpful. I was making progress. I never went back and reviewed any of it. I just kept moving forward.

When a board member asked me who I talked to about things—I stopped and realized that I internalized most of what I dealt with and had no outlets, no one to bounce things off of or hold the mirror up and ask the hard questions. No way to assess progress. Historically, I considered these intrusions.

Some months later, the CEO came to me with areas to think about in my development, like an outside board and an executive coach. I aspired to lead the company and maybe I would learn something to help me be more effective. So I met with Dr. K to see if I thought there would be benefit. Based on that meeting, I decided to try it for a year. That was almost seven years ago. We went through the testing and interviews. The feedback was much of what I already knew. But the engagement did not stop there. The engagement was deep and two-way. It wasn't just "do more of this" or "watch out for that." She added insight to the equation. She came at the topics in different ways. She went deeper to help me understand what was driving me or others. Yes, it included what I expected, too. She asked tough questions, pushed me in my areas of discomfort, gave me a sense of perspective based on her other experiences, gave me feedback on an ongoing basis, followed up with thorough summary notes and thoughts.

Her knowledge of business and psychology enabled a fuller discussion of real issues. In making change, why was it so difficult to make things stick? I had found a partner who focused me on the big issues and underlying drivers. And with that reinforcement, I increased my resolve for change and growth. The continuity was a critical part. This was someone who had counseled me through highs and lows.

During the transition when I was appointed CEO, she was the rock in a very rocky period. The Financial Crisis created huge issues in our industry globally, and I needed to bring a team together with a focus on what we could control. We had to come up with ways to generate cash in an environment where people were struggling with shutting down production and laying off people. We were working around the clock to create a plan. We had to let go of our historic processes and cycle times and focus on the short term. Every day, hour, week created a different opportunity and challenge. Having someone outside the fray with the background and history was a great help in keeping my energy on where it needed to be focused. We emerged stronger from the Global Financial Crisis and created new norms and priorities that have served us well in the ensuing years.

As time passes, the challenges change. Strategy, Execution, People are always the big three. Having a trusted advisor, someone who—no matter what the issue—is there to reflect, walk all the way around the issue with you, challenge, and most importantly make sure the elephant in the room is getting on the table quickly and dealt with effectively—this is invaluable.

# CHAPTER 3

# The Recovering Perfectionist

Wise beyond his years and already quite evolved as a leader when I met him, the subject of this case study represented a particular coaching challenge. This challenge centered on our discovering development areas that would truly capture and sustain his involvement. Working with this client, Jean Paul, was also an example of how unexpected business and personal events could nearly disrupt the career path of a gifted leader. These events, this leader's adjustment to them, and how his ultimate career aspiration was realized highlight a story of remarkable tenacity, resilience, and courage.

The work with Jean Paul is also an illustration of coaching provided in the context of a company-sponsored executive development initiative. In this sense, the case formulation was ready-made and straightforward: to assist talented leaders to evolve in the context of the company's established leadership competencies and behaviors.

This leadership development process, Leadership 3000,[1] had been designed and implemented a decade prior to Jean Paul's participation in it. It had been commissioned by the then CEO who was concerned about two interrelated issues: (1) limited growth given the maturity of the business portfolio, and (2) the lack of bold and entrepreneurial business leaders in the company. The two architects of this process were the corporate Director of Human Resources (HR) and an outside consultant, the author, because of her combined business background and training in clinical psychology. The participants were the top 70 business and functional leaders in the company, and the program spanned over two decades. To their knowledge, it was the longest continuous running leadership development process of its type.[2]

**Figure 3.1** Leadership 3000 Competencies and Essential Behaviors.

| Leadership 3000 Competencies | | |
| --- | --- | --- |
| **OUTSIDE-IN-PERSPECTIVE**<br>• Market-aware and customer-driven<br>• Strategic focus<br>• Global perspective | **SPEED TO MARKET**<br>• Bias for action<br>• Adaptive to change<br>• Creative problem-solving | **PURSUIT OF PROFITABLE GROWTH**<br>• Professional credibility<br>• Business acumen<br>• Persuasion and influence<br>• Safety performance<br>• People and performance management<br>• Interpersonal effectiveness |

| Leadership 3000 Essential Behaviors |
| --- |
| **COURAGEOUS LEADERSHIP:** relishes leading; willing to speak out, stand alone, influence open debate, probe unexpressed views, and leverage resident wisdom. The courage to confront any company "sacred cows," decisions, policies, and/or practices that could interfere with success. |
| **EMOTIONAL FORTITUDE:** ability to use self-awareness (of strengths and weaknesses), self-management (focus, discipline, tact, and diplomacy), attunement (empathic understanding of others), and relationship-building skills (relating to people in ways that are deeper than transactional need) to drive business results. Emotional resilience (can deal well with ambiguity, crises, adversity in all forms). Stays cool under pressure. |
| **ENTERPRISE THINKING:** playing-for-the-house. No silo mentality. Input into key decisions is focused on overall company objectives. Will put personal comfort aside to take on difficult new roles or additional assignments. More focused on building a great company than on personal ambition. |
| **PRAGMATIC OPTIMISM:** instilling hope about the company's future through consistent messages that emphasize rightness of the strategic direction, specificity of objectives and realistic timelines, company values, and effectiveness of executive leaders. |
| **STEEL TRAP ACCOUNTABILITY:** relentless drive for results. No defensiveness. No sad stories. No excuses. No blaming others. Making the necessary adjustments (in people, process, and/or strategy) if needed—and doing it quickly. Hard work alone is not enough—the results have to be there. |
| **TRUTH-TELLING:** stating the business reality as it *truly is* compared to established goals. Consistent candor and early signals about what's real *now* regarding business results, problems, projections, and people performance issues. Behavioral transparency and authenticity. |
| **TOUGH ON TALENT:** rigorous, relentless people appraisal and performance management. Tough scrutiny of current talent. Willingness to make hard decisions about people, to search outside for people who will fill major gaps, and to ensure the successful assimilation of new people into the company. Serious focus on deepening bench strength. Superb delegation, empowerment, and methodical identification and development of high potential talent. |

As indicated earlier, Leadership 3000 focused on both leadership competencies and essential leadership behaviors, that is, the *what* and the *how* of business leadership. Figure 3.1 represents the final iteration of the leadership competencies and essential behaviors used for the organization-based data-gathering. Of note is the fact that these same leadership competencies and behaviors prevailed through the duration of Leadership 3000. This influenced the emergence of a common language and clarity about what constituted the view of effective leaders in this company.[3]

This executive development process consisted of four distinct phases—not unlike such initiatives in other companies. These phases were: (1) data-gathering, (2) feedback, (3) action planning, and (4) follow-up. However, a set of *guiding principles* distinguished it from many other executive development initiatives. These principles can be found in figure 3.2.

Over time, two of these principles were especially significant to the enduring nature of this work. These were: (1) the CEO and boss as active participants in the action-planning and follow-up phases,[4] and (2) its being a boundary-less development process versus a contained and evaluative program. Further, a substantive follow-up phase, conducted several months after the action-planning phase, focused on progress made. Based on the participant's explicit action

**Figure 3.2**  Leadership 3000 Guiding Principles.

**Holistic development model:** a boundary-less *process* versus contained program that is focused on the whole person. After participants completed the four phases, they had ongoing access to members of their development "brain trust" that consisted of the CEO, their boss, the HR leader, and the external consultant, a consulting psychologist.

**Trust grounded in data confidentiality:** a developmental versus evaluative process in which all data generated was the property of the participants. Specific development areas and action plans were shared with the company.

**The power of psychological insight:** data-gathering included a life history, a battery of psychological inventories, and an optional spousal module in addition to organization-based leadership competency and behavior data.

**The conveyance of executive wisdom:** the CEO and boss participated in both action planning and follow-up meetings. The sharing of their work experiences, triumphs, mistakes, emotions, and other accumulated learning enriched action planning and ensured the avid engagement of participants.

plan, this progress was reviewed with his or her leadership development "brain trust" and additional ways to support the growth of these top high potential employees were explored. This robust follow-up contributed significantly to the staying power of Leadership 3000.

## Data-Gathering Phase

In my first meeting with Jean-Paul, I described the process, explained the boundaries of confidentiality, and answered his questions. These questions focused most on the sequence of events and the time commitment required of him. Along with the constant bouncing of one of his legs, the nature of his questions was an early signal about his impatience and urgency regarding not wasting time. I remember thinking to myself, "You better make this worth his while or you're going to lose him fast."

By the time I had completed the three-hour life history taking, we had started to form a connection and he seemed to relax into focused attention. I think he believed in my commitment to learn as much as I could about him, that is, that this was an *inside-out development process.* He also seemed to accept the premise that significant life themes could have implications for effective leadership.

However, he was more wary about the battery of psychological measures I gave him to complete and return at his convenience.[5] After explaining what each test measured, and the relevance of them for executive development, I still saw a question in his eyes. I promised, "I wouldn't ask you to spend time on anything that's not going to be helpful. You're going to wonder about some of the questions as you fill these out—but it's my job to weave it all together in a way that makes sense to you—and adds value to this process."

While Jean Paul still looked skeptical, he seemed willing to give the process a chance. A discerning and fast learner, I remember thinking we'd need to dig deep and make good linkages between insights and how they would help him accelerate his aspirations. Given the intensity of his ambition, his considerable charm and interpersonal fluidity were key in minimizing negative effects on others. However, it was clear that in his mind no one—or thing—was going to deter his march to the top. Beneath the surface of this refined and handsome gentleman, crisp in well-tailored suits and European shoes, was a disciplined warrior tenacious and confident to the core.

### Life History

Based on Jean Paul's description of his father as a "rational loner" and his mother as the "people-oriented one," it appeared that he was a great amalgam of both of their personalities. (I would see this later in his psych data.) Trained as a civil engineer, his father was also a French Army general, which meant they moved frequently as Jean Paul was growing up. It was not surprising then that he and his younger brother (by 16 months) were close and remained so throughout their adult lives. In Jean Paul's words, "He was the constant in my life." This was a clue about the importance of constancy and close connection with others that I would understand more fully later in my work with him.

Since science came easily, Jean Paul completed an engineering course in Paris and in the early 1980s completed a PhD in chemical engineering at the prestigious Sciences Po Paris. I got a glimpse of the pragmatic realist when he said, "I wanted to stay in Paris and play soccer so this is the only reason I have a PhD. It also made my relationship with my father even better because I became a semi-pro soccer player like he did!"

In a conversation about his soccer, the significance of his pragmatism emerged again. While the entirety of that conversation escapes me, its essence was about the greater value of leveraging a strength (his right foot, I think) versus wasting time trying to improve a weakness (the left foot). Surely, learning how to get maximum mileage from strengths would be a key aspect of his coaching.

### Key Career Facts

Jean Paul began his career in the research division of a global company. After working in Paris a few years, he was promoted to a worldwide marketing role in an industrial products group where he had an excellent mentor. The integration of technology, strategy, and customer relations came easily. He also had an important insight at this career stage, "I'm not a research bench guy; I'm too impatient for results to be a good scientist."

By the late 1980s, he had made a big jump into a North America-based marketing director role, but he was restless for more so when a recruiter called, he was ready to talk. He accepted a marketing role in France for a US-based industry leader. In his words,

> Things worked so well, I felt like I had been there forever. I worked really well with my boss, and I liked the company a lot. It was less hierarchical than my last employer which meant I could talk to anybody, and I was free to make most decisions.

I made a mental note about how important autonomy and close boss relationships were for him.

Within a few years, he was transferred to the United States where he was made the Research Director of one of the company's major businesses. As the company planned a major downsizing in the early 1990s, Jean Paul's humanism, emphasis on the importance of timely communication, as well as his pragmatism shone through. In his description of that difficult time for the company, he said:

> I tend to be more of a good soldier than others [*I wondered, His father's son?*]—so my attitude was if this has to happen, I have to make it happen quickly. I also wanted to focus on the survivors and get the team spirit going again. This meant a very high degree of communication about everything going on—almost on a daily basis. They saw I was caring and fighting to get jobs; the result was people saying they would follow me to the end of the world.

Clearly, Jean Paul put a high premium on communication. Over time, I would see how this undergirded his consistently motivational and even inspirational leadership style. When I probed this, he emphasized, "I rarely make a big deal of things. I prefer to handle problems face-to-face so if, for example, I hear a rumor that matters for the business, I'm going to get the people together and say, 'Here's what I heard, what's the deal?'"

### Big Aspirations

By the mid-1990s, Jean Paul was made head of North American sales for what was the third largest business in the company at the time. However, the combination of this role not really challenging him, how his family and he hated living in New England, and the political hassle with some of the people in this acquired business entity was getting him down.

When I asked him about his aspirations, he said in the short term he wanted to either run a business or be the business manager of a region. Already convinced of his enormous confidence and ambition, I was not surprised when he said he wanted to run Europe eventually or become the CEO. In his words, "I know I'll be at the top, but my biggest fear is that I'm not being prepared for one of those top jobs so I just can't stay in this one too long. I want to be calling the really tough shots, and that's not what I'm doing now."

I conveyed Jean Paul's restlessness to the CEO and my HR partner with the strong suggestion that plans be accelerated for his next assignment. I also thought that in terms of adult development stages, he was emblematic of what Levinson[6] termed the "boom" effect. "Boom" stood for *becoming one's own man* and occurred between the late thirties and early forties. For many, it can be a pivotal time in a career and involve decisions and changes intended to set the stage for the rest of a career. Clearly, the company needed Jean Paul to feel his future was there. More about this later.

### Development Areas—Digging Deep

What Jean Paul cited as his development needs were role-related: (1) building his network of business contacts ("This comes with one's job, and I've not been as exposed as I need to be"), and (2) running a business. After he said, "It's hard for me to know where to improve," I restated the point about leveraging his primary strengths, but I also knew we needed to get deeper fast.

I asked Jean Paul if he saw any barriers in the way he led. His response opened a path that we would walk on—and "work"—for many years thereafter. In his words,

Only my impatience and my silly drive for perfection. This makes me very demanding of both myself and others. I've learned that my impatience for things to be perfect can get in the way of anybody challenging me because I come so prepared and ready to defend my position. Also, I should really shut up sometimes; I can be so convinced that something is the right thing that I can't stop pushing it.

While it was early days for an interpretation on my part, I suggested that his intensely rational, impatient, always prepared, and perfection-seeking self could interfere with necessary relationbuilding especially with peers. His quick response was, "I need to watch that and my problem is also about coming to grips with my value judgment regarding what needs to be done." In the moment, I emphasized that everything Jean Paul said was the dark side of real strength and that his development would also be about titrating the intensity of certain behaviors.

## Feedback Phase

### Psychological Testing Data

Jean Paul's psychological data—and especially our discussion of it—highlighted a number of key insights that ultimately contributed to his growth as a leader. We wove together four resonant and interconnected themes: (1) perfectionism and impatience (for results), (2) strong preference for fact-based, rational decision-making (versus getting slowed down by emotional considerations), (3) his ambiversion behavior preference, and (4) his need to be loved (that played out as his wanting to have close connections to those with whom he worked—especially his superiors).

### Perfectionism and Impatience

While the intensity of Jean Paul's impatience and drive for perfection had been made clear in the life history-taking, the depth of this behavior pervaded his psychological data. It was fortified by his boundless energy and considerable boldness, too. I suggested that the combination of these factors could, at times, induce more stress in him (and others?) than circumstances warranted. I also emphasized that his tendency to maximize his own or others' mistakes, and to minimize self and others' successes was part of the dichotomous thinking pattern that characterizes perfectionists.[7] His reaction confirmed these points, "Sometimes I think I don't deserve the affection I get because with my perfection I can be really harsh on others and self-critical, too. I'm basically never happy with what I'm doing—it can always be better. If I could make progress on this, it would have a positive effect on my whole life."

Building on this important self-observation, I asked Jean Paul what *defensive* purpose his impatience, perfectionism, and critical behavior might be serving. He responded quickly, "I like power and success, but I also want to be loved. So this doesn't make sense does it because I hate when people don't feel comfortable around me. Is it my fear of failure that dominates everything else?" After probing this with him, I suggested that his perfectionism and impatience might be less about fear of failure and more existential. In other words, that because he defined himself exclusively by what he did, he believed he'd be loved primarily on the basis of his *achieving stellar results*. His response was telling, "Yeah, I need to lighten up on both myself and others. What I do will still be good." I emphasized this insight as the key to his behavior breakthrough regarding the adverse effects of his perfectionism and impatience.

### Preference for Rational Decision-Making

On the surface, his preference for fact-based decision-making was a core strength. However, it appeared that something that warranted our attention lurked below this. Specifically, Jean Paul found intense emotions unsettling and in his words, "I just don't do justice to emotions; I think it's a little ridiculous and weird. It's hard for me to get out the deeper emotions; I think people should just know how I feel about them, so why do I need to say the obvious?" While this was a theme I had heard from other male executives, I thought Jean Paul might have more emotional range that he could leverage in his leadership. In other words, his more intentional effort of linking head and heart in his communication with others would influence his being an even more effective leader.

Another development clue surfaced when he said, "I can be too quick, so people can be left behind regarding what I'm thinking. My quickness has gotten in my way with people, so I know there are times when I need to slow down a little." Yes, ensuring alignment—or in my language, his *slowing down to go fast*, would also increase his leadership effectiveness.

### Ambiversion Behavior Preference

The finding of ambiversion[8] in combination with the strength of his analytical assessment of situations explained his gift for connecting to others quickly. This was also a factor in his ability to relate to many different types of people. While many thought his rapid rapport with others was a function of his French charm, we discussed it as the elasticity of his behavioral preferences. In other words, Jean Paul could raise or lower his flame between extroversion and introversion depending on what a situation required of him interpersonally.

What I emphasized in the feedback was the importance—especially with new direct reports—of his at least mentioning that he could behave very differently at different times. In my view, he needed to make certain that they knew this difference in his behavior was intentional and not a function of anything negative like his being erratic or unpredictable. Further, I explained that an ambivert in a people-intensive role like his is usually "running on empty" emotionally at the end of most business days. Therefore, whenever he needed to carry on through the evening, for example, on a business trip, he'd be more effective at doing so if he had time to "refuel" in between. This could be a 15-minute nap, or quiet time watching the news, or a quick run—anything that did *not* involve face-to-face interaction with others.

### Need to be Loved

A strong inner tension emerged when we explored his seeming ambivalence about dealing with "authority" figures. Jean Paul was quick to comment, "Yes, I can have lots of trouble with a boss. It has to be someone I can learn from, admire, and have a friendship with—I need to feel a close relationship." His fascinating combination of pragmatism, confidence, and emotion was revealed when he said,

> When I don't have that kind of boss, I'm torn between respecting the person and my need for love. I'll tend to avoid a boss like that and not check in with him unless I really need to. If he loves me and I love him, I believe he can't hurt me and he doesn't have to fear that I'll hurt him.[9]

By now we had plenty of grist for the coaching mill. Further, shortly before the action-planning meeting, Jean Paul's father died. In the habit of speaking to his father weekly, this was a devastating loss that had a major negative effect on his usual upbeat mood. Thinking that it might be helpful for him to talk about it further with a bilingual bereavement counselor, I arranged for him to meet with one. This was wholly consistent with the holistic intent of Leadership 3000, and proved to be helpful to him.

### Organization-Based Feedback

This data was gathered by my HR partner and while Jean Paul was still concerned about his not moving fast enough in the company, this information guaranteed that that was going to happen. In a private conversation with me, the HR leader commented, "This is the strongest Leadership 3000 data we've gathered thus far. Jean Paul's a very complete package. Our major task is to make sure that the dark side of his many strengths don't create any problems for him especially with his peers."

His impressive array of strengths included: (1) natural strategic capability, (2) driving results, (3) great commercial instincts, (4) setting high performance standards for both self and others,

(5) preparedness, (6) relationship-building based on trust and commitment, (7) motivational ability/charismatic impact, (8) skill in finding win-win solutions, (9) steadiness/resilience in the face of adversity, and (10) a global and multicultural approach to the business.

The indications for Jean Paul's development tracked with the psychological findings. These included his: (1) perfectionism—tendency to overtax himself and/or his organization, and (2) impatience—a tendency to write off those who couldn't keep pace with him. The need to increase his finance knowledge was also cited.

## ACTION-PLANNING PHASE

My HR partner sent the following message to the meeting participants (the CEO, Jean Paul's boss, and myself):

> This meeting is the culmination of the Leadership 3000 data-gathering phase and the beginning of development planning. It is a very unique conversation, and one that will be of particular importance to Jean Paul. The responsibility for ongoing performance and development reviews, feedback, and coaching rests with the direct boss. This meeting will provide an opportunity for establishing the direction and plans that will guide this process for the next two years or more.

Attached to this memo were the lists of Jean Paul's strengths and improvement areas as they'd been distilled from the integration of the psychological and organization-based data-gathering. Jean Paul's development document, written after this meeting, included coaching with me as a key action. He wanted to explore the underlying emotional aspects of his development areas. Regarding the finance improvement area, he planned to attend an executive education session at either Harvard or Cornell.

Leveraging his strengths found him being more intentional about advancing the success of a new business platform for the company, trusting his intuition in combination with strong analytical problem-solving, turning around the R&D organization of this new business, and deepening his relationships both inside and outside the organization—including with key customers.

## FOLLOW-UP PHASE

Our coaching work over the next year identified a number of key actions for Jean Paul. These focused most on the overarching and seemingly resistant area of perfectionism. These actions included his increased delegation to and empowerment of others, and his recognizing and practicing the difference between expecting *excellence* versus *perfection*. Through our discussions, he seemed to recognize the burden of his perfectionism and its associated issues that included: (1) his strong need to be in control, (2) his self-induced worry, (3) how he was unfairly judging people who were not as driven as he, and (4) how his inability to say "no" to top management increased already high levels of stress within himself and his organization.

As our work continued, other actions would yield development value, too. These included: (1) his not letting his desire for speed and/or his aggressive ambition become an issue with peers, (2) remembering that he was especially powerful when he combined his analyses with his ability to speak from the heart, and (3) continuing to model his version of pragmatic optimism.

We also recognized the importance of his learning to relax and making enough room for others' input. Further, after the CEO made a comment to me about how some people found it hard to understand Jean Paul given his thick French accent, I urged him to work with an English language consultant, which he eventually did.

### *Career Landscape Improves*

After grappling with a thorny political climate in his business, Jean Paul was promoted to a worldwide operations and technology role. He described the role as the job he "dreamed of" and was especially pleased that the business had a dotted line to him. His contentment was palpable, "I'm feeling much more at peace now and the company has done a lot for me financially by pushing me faster, so I'm not wondering anymore about how well I'm doing."

### Key Insights—Mastery, Loss, Constancy, and Tangibility

In the wake of this promotion, a helpful insight emerged regarding his perfectionism. He stated, "I realize now that I'm more this way when I don't feel that I have mastery of a situation, and then when I feel I've moved up the learning curve, it eases off. I need to keep thinking about this because this kind of stress just wastes too much energy." ("Bingo, I thought to myself—his underlying pragmatism may actually trump his reflexive perfectionism.")

Perhaps of even more significance was a connection we made between his perfectionism and *loss*. As I was probing the underlying basis of his competitive instincts, Jean Paul commented, "I can see now that my competitive instinct is so strong and makes me push so hard in my career because of things I've lost on the personal side by not being in France. This means that work becomes the constant for me." When I made the interpretive comment, "Like how your brother was the constant when you were little," he says, "Yes, having something constant is really really important to me and being great at work is key." Of note also was the constancy of his wife and how her level-headedness and calm were an ongoing source of particular support for him.

Probing these insights further, we discussed how his impatience really spiked when things didn't go well because in Jean Paul's words, "Yes, because this is the way I define myself." ("Bingo again, I thought.") While he agreed when I remarked that his ego ideal was that of a *winning warrior*, he also said, "My biggest problem is that I can't *see* my contributions to things."

This gave me the opportunity to convey an important leadership insight: that the essence of leadership at his level was to set direction and to *orchestrate* what others did; therefore, there wasn't anything tangible for him to see anymore. I urged him to think about "tangibility" differently. For example, he could consider it in terms of all that he'd done to (1) expand his business in Asia and to (2) influence the culture of the business in which he was working at the time. Jean Paul's response was encouraging, "I really view this next year as a critical shift regarding my making the transition from the tangible to the intangible."

Not wanting to miss the opportunity to use metaphorical thought as a tool in helping Jean Paul beat back his perfectionism, I sent him a poem by Antonio Machado that appeared in a book by David Whyte.

> Last night, as I was sleeping
> I dreamt—marvelous error!
> that I had a beehive
> here inside my heart.
> And the golden bees
> were making white combs
> and sweet honey
> from my old failures.[10]

### Career Trajectory Continues

Within a few years, Jean Paul was made the President and COO of his rapidly growing business and soon thereafter in 1999, he was appointed a corporate Vice President. Also in that year, the company CEO succession was completed. This was good news for Jean Paul as the new CEO was, in fact, one of the executives who recruited him to the company and remained both a mentor and a friend. He had also been a Leadership 3000 participant whom I knew well.

Through this period, Jean Paul and I discussed numerous staffing challenges including managers who might succeed him and the tough decision of firing his CFO. With the hiring of a more gifted financial executive, Jean Paul, in fact, had an informal opportunity to take his finance knowledge to the next level.

### A Career Disappointment

By the end of 2001, Jean Paul had identified his successor and fully expected that his family and he would make their much-awaited return to France. But the European region job went to one of his peers instead. Jean Paul was despondent, "This was my last hope to get back to Europe at a good time for my family and under a great set of circumstances."

While I knew that the board was concerned about his running his business from Europe, this consideration did little to ease the intensity of his disappointment. This was more than apparent when he said,

> Obviously, the CEO changed his mind but he didn't speak to me about it. I wish I had been involved in the decision. I'm still focused on running the business and putting on a good face but I really have to weigh career and family very seriously now. People are asking me why I didn't get the Europe job; I've never asked for anything, but this was really important to me and my family.

I sought and he gave me permission to speak to the CEO about it.

In my conversation with the CEO, I conveyed Jean Paul's deep disappointment but, as he asked me to, I held back the fact that he had a tempting opportunity elsewhere. Instead, I said that in my opinion he could become a retention risk, and I urged the CEO to set up a special conversation in which he could clear the air. He needed to explain fully what his reasoning was regarding the Europe role and, to the extent possible, indicate what Jean Paul might expect career-wise in the near term. Their conversation went well.

Within a few years, Jean Paul received the European region role as well as top responsibility for the business platform he had helped build for the company. There were myriad talent issues for him to manage and for some, we used Leadership 3000 as a focused development tool.

### Personal Tragedy Strikes

A few years after moving back to Europe, one of Jean Paul's two sons was diagnosed with a life-threatening illness. While I had supportive conversations with him and he appeared to be doing a good job of keeping this in perspective, I could see the severe emotional impact of this frightening personal event. At one point, he said, "If this doesn't get stabilized so we know he'll survive, I will give up my career—none of this will matter." Fortunately, there had been a medical breakthrough in the treatment of this illness and Jean Paul's son was going to be able to manage it with medication.

### *Coach Becomes Trusted Advisor*

It was in this time frame that I became more of a trusted advisor than coach to Jean Paul for he had made great strides with his Leadership 3000 development agenda. Now we focused on numerous perplexing issues including his struggle with the corporate CFO (a very demanding, volatile, and, at times, unreasonable person), ongoing talent management problems in his business, and how the CEO was expecting a 24/7 work ethic of Jean Paul and other members of the CEO's leadership team.

### *CEO Succession on the Radar*

By the middle of 2007, the CEO had gotten serious about his own succession, and it appeared that Jean Paul was the leading candidate. When the CEO asked me if I thought Jean Paul was interested, I indicated that he very much was and urged the CEO to lean in harder with his mentoring, to create more opportunities for Jean Paul to interact with board members, and to provide different external exposure for Jean Paul.

By the summer of that year, I leaned in differently, too, that is, increasing our focus on this ultimate aspiration. For example, I used a technique called the Visual Leadership Metaphor® (VLM)[11] to focus on his readiness to be CEO. Jean Paul's VLM revealed just that (see figure 3.3).

In this time frame, I emailed Jean Paul a quote from a CEO client in another company. Given how Jean Paul's leadership had evolved, I thought this quote would resonate well, "Leadership is about connecting two points in the longest distance in the world—the one between the head and the heart." He wrote back, "This is a great quote. It fits what I think and try to do." We remembered how we had touched on the integration of head and heart a few years earlier; its utility seemed as important now as ever.

Over the next year, we continued the Leadership 3000 work with people in Jean Paul's business. I could count on his being especially strong and directive in the action-planning meetings. At the same time, I noticed that the CEO was looking and sounding disconnected. Several months later, I learned that that was when he

**Figure 3.3** Jean-Paul's Visual Leadership Metaphor® (VLM).

Drawing by Joe Williams

| FRAME 1 | FRAME 2 | FRAME 3 |
|---|---|---|
| I'm leading the way I feel I need to lead in the situation. My effort is to connect the people and I want to do this in a natural and intuitive way. There are no rules or set expectations about how to be. | I know where I want to go. I can see the path forward. | I'm leading a big organization. I'm with people I like and I'm running it in a way that makes it a fun place to be. I'm making things happen without a lot of focus on who is who in the hierarchy. |

had started to grapple with events that ultimately lead to the sale of the company.

### Stunning Event—A Reversal of Fortune

By the time of the sale, Jean Paul had been named President and COO of the company, that is, the defining signal of his being the top internal CEO succession candidate. But this was not to be. While he was appointed CEO of a significant enterprise within the acquiring company, in less than a year he would retire from that entity. Soon thereafter, another well-respected company in his industry would accelerate the retirement of its CEO in order to recruit Jean Paul into that role.

The retiring CEO of this company wrote to the employees there, "Jean Paul is an exceptional talent among peers, a truly global manager with an impeccable record of achievement in large, complex manufacturing companies. The breadth and depth of his experience is extraordinary as is his proven ability to achieve profitability and growth during the full economic cycle."

Toward the end of his first year as CEO, Jean Paul had already started to think about his succession—even knowing it was at least several years away. While there was a short list of possible internal candidates, we anticipated inevitable twists and turns as we started to work on the readiness of his successor. In the meantime, it was going to be fascinating to watch someone whom I viewed as a truly "remarkable" leader[12] take this company to its next level of growth, as well as operational excellence.

## DISCUSSION

In this case we see that when executive coaching is embedded in a company-sponsored leadership development process, there is a cluster of key relationships that must be managed for the work to maintain traction and realize a positive outcome. At their best these relationships are woven into a highly visible and collaborative partnership. In the work with Jean Paul, this partnership involved the CEO, the corporate Head of Human Resources, and the consulting psychologist who navigated the development process. In this instance, a "positive outcome" involved intertwined and mutually inclusive objectives: his company preparing its top CEO candidate, and Jean Paul achieving his ultimate career aspiration.

In addition to his many natural leadership competencies and behavioral assets, a number of psychological insights, action steps, and the committed presence of his coach/trusted advisor helped ensure his ongoing effectiveness as a gifted business leader. Through the coaching Jean Paul learned to channel his perfectionism, to integrate head and heart in his decision-making, and to slow down to go fast thus helping others keep pace with him. In summary, his ability to both leverage his strengths and minimize the darker manifestations of them contributed to his overall power as a leader.

## Conclusion

This executive coaching case study has focused on the challenge of how to engage an already accomplished leader in a meaningful developmental effort. It illustrates that regardless of the quality of data gathered in an executive development initiative—the data are just the beginning of the story. This story, replete with growth-promoting insights for Jean Paul, follows the path of his career and personal highs and lows. Witnessed by his executive coach and eventual trusted advisor for over 15 years, these highs and lows were managed with equal doses of learning, affirmation, and support. And forming beneath it all was an enduring relationship of particular trust and candor.

As this work unfolded, the challenge for the consulting psychologist moved from merely engaging her client to a number of thornier considerations. Since these are likely considerations that other consultants may encounter when working with senior executives—the potential instructive nature of this case is amplified. These considerations included the consultant maintaining a critical thread of constancy with her client, pacing a series of insights that would have meaning and lasting impact for him, not losing objectivity about this immensely talented and charming executive, and keeping their trust even in the face of knowing he had become a retention risk for the company.

Finally, in the execution of his responsibilities as CEO of a global company, it appeared that Jean Paul would achieve his overarching objective: to leave the company in even better condition than it was in when he became CEO. There would be significant value creation given the force of his combined strategic, operational, and inspirational leadership capabilities. It might not be absolutely *perfect*, but it would make him happy—very happy.

# Executive's Reflection

I started working with Karol in 1995. I must say that I was very conflicted when I was first told about the process. I was certainly very excited to be selected to participate in this corporate program but also fearful of what I was getting into. Once the initial discussions, questions, and tests were completed, the real process began. It was exciting, often challenging, but above all it required a willingness to learn, grow, and allow myself to be vulnerable. Being vulnerable and "uncovered" were enormously challenging for me. I was too guarded to fully engage initially.

I was able to transcend the feeling of being vulnerable rather quickly. I understood that this process was for "me." The sole objective was to make me better. It was between Karol and me, nobody else. Her caring behavior and thoughtful approach to the process made being vulnerable a natural stage. A trusting and lasting relationship was born and my fears were gone.

This brings to mind the best football (as we call it in Europe) coach I ever had. I was a teenager preparing to play at the national level. His advice for me was, "Let's focus first on your strengths where you are more skilled than other players. We will concentrate on these things that differentiate you from other players, make them even more differentiating and deal with your weaknesses later."

To some extent Karol started off our work together in the same manner: seeking to understand what I was doing well and why. The objective was first to acknowledge these strengths and then reinforce them. I had had some success in my career but did not really know why. I could not leverage my skills beyond what I was doing instinctively. This was by far the hardest part of the process for me. Being a perfectionist, I was unable to see that there were things I was doing well. I would brush off any praise and try to move to where I needed to improve. Recognizing my qualities was an essential step and key to my growth, but was it ever hard. I had always found it so much easier to move to the next step of learning where to improve and change; there I was in my natural element!

It is strange at times to look back at all these years. TBL, EQ are now part of my everyday language and what I look for in the people around me. (TBL and EQ are two leadership concepts I learned from Karol. TBL is an acronym for "total brain leadership," that is, the ability to integrate left brain analytical strengths with right brain interpersonal capabilities for maximum leadership effectiveness. EQ is commonly used to represent emotional intelligence and the key dimensions of this concept— self-awareness, self-management, empathy, and the ability to form/sustain relationships that are not merely transactional.) These are critical elements in the development of tomorrow's leaders, as they were for me. These concepts were a foreign language to me 15 years ago; yet they proved to be critical to my development. Change will come from the least expected places, proving that self-growth alone would never have allowed me to achieve what I did through these years of partnership. I changed throughout this process with Karol, but I never lost who I was.

I remember this debate within myself. It is hard to explain why but the following example has impacted me deeply. Maybe it is because it was the first breakthrough in a long development process that took me to places I was not expecting. I could never decide if I was an introvert or an extrovert. I would find myself being very outgoing on some days, the "life of the party," and other days I would withdraw, not communicate, be distant, and could be viewed as aloof. People would have a very different picture of me depending on when they had met me and under what circumstances.

Karol's explanation of the concept of "ambiversion" put this in perspective for me. I learned that I am neither a strong extrovert nor a strong introvert. Rather, I'm a combination of both, which means I can size up a situation and make a choice about how I need to "be" in it. I learned that this is a leadership strength that, in Karol's words, meant I had significant "behavioral elasticity" that enabled me to adapt to different situations very quickly and to handle them effectively. This is especially valuable to me as I travel through different regions of the world intent upon connecting well to the local employees. This is one of many examples of how learning to understand myself turned what I thought was a flaw into a strength that had a profound impact on my future behavior. I realized that not only do I feed off of other people's behavior and personalities, but I can adapt to and function in the environment created by these differences. As a result, people are generally very comfortable with me and relate to me easily.

I believe that the business world we operate in today requires the broadest possible range of leadership skills. I can't help occasionally wondering who I would be without the work I did with Karol, but I most certainly would not be in the chair I sit in today doing what I do and participating in the development of tomorrow's leaders.

# CHAPTER 4

# The Duality Within

Every executive coaching engagement is its own adventure involving the complex interplay of many factors. These factors include how the coaching was initiated, the executive's interest in the coaching, his or her career aspirations, the company culture, and chemistry with the coach. This interplay is exponentially complicated when, as with this engagement, the coaching is focused explicitly on a struggling boss-subordinate relationship in a company where coaching had not been used at the senior executive level. In this case, an Asian American woman reported to a Frenchman in a male-dominated culture that placed little emphasis on leadership development.

The contextual variables were intensified further by the fact that the coached executive was the highest ranking woman in a business management role. Further, her career progress depended not only on her forming a stronger working relationship with this boss but also on her resolving long-standing business issues—issues that male peers before her had not solved but whose careers prospered anyway.

## PRECOACHING

### *Initial Contacts with the Company*

This engagement was initiated in an email from a new Human Resources (HR) Vice President in a multinational company. We had had a collegial relationship when she worked in a global organization where I had coached many senior executives. She believed that executive coaching could be a valuable development tool and, in fact, the coaching of this prospective client, the President of a global business unit, would be a "pilot" at that level in the organization.

In our initial phone contact, I pursued more information about the context than I did about the executive. I needed to gauge the likelihood that this executive coaching "experiment" could be positioned well, that is, to the leader's potential benefit, and that I'd have the inside partners (executive's boss and HR) I needed to guide my work effectively.[1]

I learned that the company was over two hundred years old, had more than one hundred thousand employees worldwide, and its annual gross revenue exceeded $40 billion. It was led by an executive team of all French men most of whom were engineers. Understandably, this was a culture in which solving problems and getting things done were prized above all else. While the prospective coachee, Rachel, was in the United States, the boss was based in Paris so my HR contact questioned the likelihood of his partnering with us in this work.

I also learned about my prospective client's demanding scope of business responsibility: over one thousand employees in numerous facilities spread throughout several countries. Rachel had been with the company for over a decade with impressive accomplishments in an array of roles that included strategy and planning, eBusiness, IT, and another business unit. However, for the first time, she was reporting to someone younger than she—and someone with an abrupt and intensely analytical leadership style. In addition to the strain in the boss relationship, her own empowering leadership style was, in the words of the HR person, "not always recognized or appreciated in this culture."

After the HR person said, "I have a personal investment in making her successful given her unique combination of strategic, conceptual and leadership strengths," we discussed how to ensure the coaching got positioned as a development resource versus being perceived as a remedial intervention.[2] We agreed that the next step would be my face-to-face meeting with her boss, a business executive on rotational assignment through human resources.

In my meeting with him, he emphasized two reasons for Rachel's coaching: (1) an improved relationship with her boss (a "French rising star"), and (2) the resolution of certain business issues. Regarding the former, he described the boss as "terse, remote, and austere in his interactions with others." He confirmed that it was unlikely that I would be able to establish an engaged rapport with him, and he advised that we wait for the "right moment" to introduce me. Regarding the struggling business, he said the issues were deep, long-standing, and had proven too difficult for talented leaders before Rachel was in the role. I made a mental note that she might be getting held up to a higher performance standard than her male peers—but I'm getting ahead of myself.

He emphasized that the biggest risk at this juncture in Rachel's career was to "plateau at this level." When I emphasized the need for the coaching to get positioned carefully with the boss, he said he would help ensure the boss's understanding of its developmental intent, and would assist in my having a "live" meeting with him.

### First Meeting with the Prospective Client

While I indicated that this meeting was a no-commitment, mutual "chemistry check," Rachel quickly conveyed an interest in our working together. In retrospect, I think her recognition that she needed rapid help with her boss primed her receptivity. At our handshake, I was reminded of something else the senior HR professional had said, "She's a small person with a lot of quiet authority." In our first 15 minutes, I experienced the steady, clear flow of her story. I learned that she was South Korean, in her mid-forties, and had an impressive pedigree of education and experience. These included a degree in engineering, an MBA from The Sloan School, consulting at Booz-Allen, and several successful roles in her current company. Rachel not only expected to do well, she was fixated on realizing the fullness of her capabilities. As we discussed the importance of self-actualization,[3] I detected doubts—or at least some shadow of self-questioning—that I would later understand as the beginning of her realization of a deep inner conflict.

There was an impressive coherence between her natural beauty and executive persona—tastefully groomed, articulate, and quick-minded. She was born preloaded with the capacity to excel—although, as indicated earlier, questions had begun to emerge. In her words, "Realistically, I probably only have one more move here." While her fear of plateauing was palpable, "one more move" in the company did not sound compatible with her inner drive. I sensed there was something other, more compelling, bigger—something for which she yearned but was not fully able to express.

When I asked her *why coaching now*, she mentioned the relationship with her new boss but in another poignant moment said, "To be successful in this company requires me to behave in ways that are different from who I actually am." After probing this, she said her coaching goals—in addition to an improved relationship with her boss—were: (1) a better understanding of what motivated her, (2) learning how to adjust her leadership behavior for success in this company's culture, and (3) finding more joy and happiness in her life.

Noticing that she seemed somewhat daunted by the possibility of behavior change—change she would have to make to continue to succeed in this culture—I showed her a behavior change model (see figure 4.1). She was encouraged by the notion that sustained

**Figure 4.1**   Behavior Change Model. © Copyright 1992, K.M. Wasylyshyn, Psy. D., Philadelphia, PA.

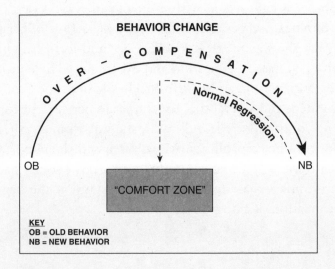

behavior change necessarily involves some degree of regression. By this point in our discussion, I knew she was intentional about new learning, had the potential to change, and that the timing was right for coaching. I also thought our chemistry was good, and at the end of this meeting we agreed to work together.[4] While I held a reservation about the extent to which senior executives in this culture could recognize and/or receive any changes she might make, I was optimistic that the coaching could be a pivotal career experience for Rachel, and that this might have meaning for the company as well.

In their discussion of how to best position the coaching with Rachel's boss, the two HR professionals decided to give Rachael and me a few months to work together before contacting him. Presumably, some progress would be apparent to her boss and at that point, my face-to-face meeting with him would be more productive.

### Case Formulation

A number of forces influenced the conceptualization of this case. First, I would have to carefully manage realistic expectations of the coaching. The company expected that Rachel would (1) improve her relationship with her boss, and (2) resolve certain long-standing problems with her business. I needed to be clear that coaching could help with the former expectation—especially if HR helped influence my having adequate communication with her boss. The latter expectation was really beyond the remit of my capabilities as an executive coach—with the exception of my influencing Rachel's timely decision-making and ensuring she had the right people and structure in place to support business success.

Second, through my relationship with the HR vice president, I would need to remain hypervigilant about the culture and its potential adverse effects on the coaching. In this alpha male milieu, most of the top leaders were engineers who valued problem-solving and results over all else, possessed little emotional intelligence, did not invest in leadership development, and probably (I surmised) did not have an accurate understanding of the value of executive coaching. Even worse, I feared they would reflexively place anyone being coached in the remedial category.[5]

Third, while Rachel accepted the company's view of her coaching agenda (I suspected there might be some degree of capitulation on her part), she also held her own set of expectations—expectations that clearly signaled the beginning of deeper considerations about her career and overall sense of contentedness, that is, being able to lead as her authentic self. I would have to manage these in the context of her behavior change commitment.

Fourth, I would have to monitor potential countertransference (based on my own early career experiences), as well as my beliefs about fairness and the advancement of female executives in the workplace. I could not let any of this blur my objectivity or bias my work with Rachel.

## Phase I: Data-Gathering

Since Rachel's travel schedule was so demanding, the first coaching meeting was designed to achieve maximum engagement.[6] A half day was set, and I began with something unexpected—eliciting content for her Visual Leadership Metaphor® (VLM). The VLM is a tool used to anchor the coaching, as well as to gauge its progress (see figure 4.2). I asked Rachel to describe herself in the most visual terms possible and in three different time frames: (1) her current view of herself as a leader, (2) her transition state as a leader (progress made in the coaching), and (3) her future or desired state as a leader (having achieved her coaching goals).[7] Rachel's portrayal of herself as evolving from a highly hands-on maestro to the leader of a world-class orchestra was a stunning metaphorical representation of the leadership growth we would be challenged to pursue in the several months contracted for the coaching.[8]

We continued Phase 1, data-gathering,[9] with my taking her life history. I also gave her a packet of psychological measures[10] explaining the purpose of each and underscoring that in our next meeting, I would review the results of these measures integrated with the major themes from her life history. I also emphasized that at the end of that meeting, we would reach final agreement on the specific

**Figure 4.2** Rachel's Visual Leadership Metaphor® (VLM).

*Drawing by Joe Williams*

| FRAME 1 | FRAME 2 | FRAME 3 |
|---|---|---|
| This is an orchestra that can, at times, make brilliant music and then at other times the music is not good at all. I'm on and off the podium as the maestro. There are certain instruments that I can play myself and I do—showing them/ demonstrating something so they can play better. There are certain other sections where I don't know the instruments at all so I can't demonstrate how they need to be played. I'm much less sure with this part of the orchestra so I need to find different ways to get what's in my head across to the players in this section. | I'm having to learn more of the instruments I'm not comfortable with—I have to learn the different language of other instruments. If I do this then I can communicate, demonstrate, and reinforce ways to do things differently. I may have to be more direct and find different means, different ways to make myself clear—to communicate, to describe the music I'm hearing in my head. | This is now a world class orchestra. There's a critical mass of leadership in each section and they see and hear the music the way I do. It's the final phase of mastery that I've helped the orchestra get to. It can now successfully try different sounds and different interpretations. I can easily interject something new and things easily keep moving forward. |

areas that would be focused on in the coaching phase. Further, I explained that the coaching phase would be followed by a consolidation phase in which key lessons learned would be distilled as a tool for her ongoing leadership effectiveness.

The boundaries of confidentiality were also discussed—as they had been in my initial meeting with her. Specifically, that all of the life history and psychometric data were completely confidential, that is, these were tools for our use only to quickly surface relevant information for her self-understanding and growth as a leader. Further, that the specific content of our coaching meetings was also confidential. What would be shared with the organization would be the coaching areas, my observations about her engagement in the coaching, her progress, and—with her permission—thoughts about steps her boss could take to further leverage her strengths and/or progress as a leader.

Before I began the life-history taking, I asked her if there was anything we missed in our initial meeting. Her answer punctuated the importance of her work identity. In her words,

> I should tell you about my husband and the nature of our rela- tionship. He's a closet handyman and I'm the bigger earner. He never complains about anything and would have preferred to be a graphic designer instead of an attorney. He loves to cook and he loves to play with the kids. He derives meaning from life in a very different way than I do. He works hard just for the joy of working. For him the girls, our family—these are always first. But for me well, there are really moments when I can easily say that work comes first.

A brief conversation ensued about their complementarity as a couple. I would only later appreciate how significant their respec- tive preferences were for her—and ultimately, for their happiness as a family.

### Life History

I believed that Rachel's ability to "better understand" herself would be informed by the thematic material from her life history.[11] I have maintained that "the details of how an executive navigated through each life stage provided clues about possible fixations or regres- sive tendencies that had potential adverse implications for effective leadership."[12]

Most significant in Rachel's early history was the dominating presence of her mother who demanded excellence. As the quintes- sential "tiger mom,"[13] Rachel's mother expected her to be a driven achiever and expressed her disappointment both through verbal and physical means (i.e., spanking) whenever Rachel fell short of expectations.

Rachel's father provided some emotional balance in that he was not as harsh emotionally, but he too held high expectations for her achievements. By early adolescence, she was focused on attending

Ivy League schools where she continued to excel. Also of note was the fact that her father's entrepreneurial pursuits may have spawned Rachel's interest in running her own business—an interest that would keep surfacing later in her career.

Based on her life history themes, I emphasized the points that had specific implications for her as a leader. These included: (1) her ability to trust others would be contingent upon their performance, (2) her single-minded goal orientation, while predominantly a strength, could also be a double-edged sword in that results would always trump relationships, (3) her identity was primarily dependent upon career success, and (4) mentoring others, while not a priority now, could help ignite her next growth spurt as a leader.

Interestingly, she described having children as the "most courageous" thing she'd ever done because her mother devalued this. For Rachel, becoming a mother had positive collateral effects that might not have happened otherwise and that, in my view, contributed to her growth as a leader. These included her ability to give and receive affection, the importance of tuning into the needs of others (empathic resonance), and a heightened sense of, in her words, "the speed of life." How these major life history themes dovetailed with the highlights from her testing feedback (see later) made the task of identifying the key areas for the coaching phase that much easier.

## PHASE II: FEEDBACK

Rachel's superior cognitive ability was surely no surprise. Certainly, her strength in analytical reasoning and problem-solving was significant and, no doubt, played a major part in her having achieved success in a company that placed a major premium on this. Rachel's striving for achievements dominated her profile. Most prominent were the intensity of her results orientation, high performance standards for both herself and others, competitive instincts, ability to tolerate frustration, strong ethics and integrity, discipline, ability to control impulses, and a pragmatic sense of optimism.

Rachel's emotional constriction was also no surprise in light of her early history especially how her mother's affection was so contingent on her achievements. For Rachel, achieving her goals transcended making time for close relationships. As a leader, she would be less inclined to mentor others, thus her relationships would be primarily transactional. She would expect others' emotional resilience, be reluctant to get involved in their problems, and be guarded in expressing her feelings.

### Coaching Areas Identified

As indicated earlier, the synthesis of Rachael's major life themes with the psychological data informed the identification of the coaching foci. Of note is the fact that these tracked well with the input from HR, as well as with her own statement regarding expectations from the coaching. The three coaching areas were set as follows: (1) building a more positive relationship with her boss—one in which she would make a proactive effort to "connect" with him to foster their reciprocal rapport, (2) becoming a more effective leader in this hierarchical culture, and (3) increasing her joy and happiness. This third would, later in the coaching, be recognized as something more than a natural quest for happiness. We would discover that it stemmed from an internal conflict that we would name her *duality within*. More about this insight later.

## PHASE III: COACHING

Despite the demands of her travel schedule, our monthly meetings (one and a half hours in length) stayed on track, and we had email "conversation" when necessary. Initially, we focused on emotional and social intelligence, that is, using this as an important coaching tool for the goals related to both her boss relationship and ongoing leadership effectiveness. Light bulbs started going off quickly for Rachel as she became more thoughtful about the contrast between how she had been and how she was now trying to adapt to both her boss and the culture. The essence of her development effort was to be more attuned to others' needs/concerns, and to be less transactional in her relationships.

### Maintaining Contact with the Organization

As a matter of course, I sent an email to my HR contact before meetings with Rachel asking if there was anything I should know from the organization's perspective. A few months into the coaching, the HR VP sent me a message saying that Rachel's boss had told the top HR professional that he was "seeing improvement." This created the opportunity for him to deliver on his promise to tell the boss about the coaching (positioning it as a strong development tool), and to open the door for me to meet with the boss the next time he was in the United States. A breakfast meeting was set (three months after the coaching had commenced). I began my mental rehearsal of what I wanted to accomplish in this meeting.

### Holding Up the Mirror to the Client

In coaching meetings before this breakfast, I held up the coaching mirror to Rachel about her behavior, that is, what could be getting in the way of her even *making an effort* to try to build a better relationship with her boss. I gave her specific reading material on my concept of *remarkable* leadership[14] as a way of influencing her thinking about the value of integrating her powerful left brain (analytical) capabilities with less developed right brain (interpersonal) behaviors. Rachel's learning about the four dimensions of emotional intelligence, captured in the memorable acronym SO SMART® (see figure 4.3), stimulated her important reflection of *who I really am as a leader versus how I need to be in this culture* (more about this later).

I also modeled *empathic resonance*[15] in our coaching meetings by: (1) acknowledging the "whip lash" she was feeling trying to thrive in this culture; (2) continuing to urge her to think about *her* version of managing up while still managing people in a manner that was consistent with her values and beliefs as related to empowerment; and (3) emphasizing how her *attunement to others* or her version of *empathic resonance* could yield dividends as she tried to motivate others and achieve difficult business objectives—especially in Europe (2012) where things were seriously tanking.

**Figure 4.3** SO SMART®—Emotional Intelligence.

| Four Dimensions of EQ | |
|---|---|
| **Self-Observation (SO)**<br>• Awareness—of one's emotions<br>• Accurate assessment of own strengths and weaknesses<br>• Self-confidence<br><br>Core ability: Perceiving emotions | **Self-Management (SM)**<br>• Self-control—can channel emotions effectively<br>• Discipline<br>• Resilience<br>• Motivation—bias for action<br>Core ability: Managing emotions |
| **Attunement (A)**<br>• Focus on others<br>• Empathy<br>• Awareness of organization dynamics<br><br><br>Core ability: Using emotions | **Relationship Traction (RT)**<br>• Authenticity<br>• Influence and persuasion<br>• Consistency<br>• Connecting to others<br>• Collaborative teamwork<br>Core ability: Understanding emotions |

### The Boss

My HR colleague briefed me more fully about him before the designated meeting. He had the highest education pedigree in France, and a set of interrelated behaviors that underscored his lack of emotional intelligence.[16] She described him as super analytically smart, political, ambitious, competitive, and self-centered. When I probed further, it was clear that his narcissism was primarily in the service of getting his ego needs met.[17] While he was married and had four children, she said his work-family integration was not good and she laughed upon telling me how he preferred to solve math problems in his spare time.

She also commented, "He has no idea how to use HR as a strategic partner and will play along with us only as long as he thinks the coaching of Rachel will help him." The blinking yellow light in my head turned red when she mentioned that he had told the top HR person that Rachel was "not strategic." While I thought this was mostly a function of his stereotypic thinking, I also knew that the view of women as "not strategic" was still a gale force wind in business that obstructed their advancement.[18] I anticipated an uphill slog with him—and was not disappointed.

### Meeting with Boss

I went into this meeting with three objectives: (1) to influence his perception of coaching as a *developmental* resource, (2) to convey my opinion of Rachel as a high potential asset well worth the company's investment, and (3) to get his candid assessment of her. I would emphasize her strengths to leverage, as well as her development areas—especially improving their relationship. I would also look for the right moment to give him some explicit guidance for his side of the relationship (e.g., encouraging what she's doing right and increasing their collaborative problem-solving on current business challenges, thus leveraging their potential for complementarity and his getting a closer look at her strategic capability). I held a dim hope for igniting his active collaboration in the coaching—but I was not rewarded.

The person I met matched my expectations: serious, smart, intense, arrogant, and an uptight introvert. Foregoing ice-breaking conversation, he inquired about my background and then got down to business. He had a host of "concerns" about Rachel that included: (1) her not being quick enough to make key personnel changes, (2) the lack of progress in the troubled business, and (3) her inability to "tell a compelling story," when she presented to senior management.

In expressing his view of the struggling business, he said (1) people in it were fearful of changing too quickly and, (2) they were not creative enough to identify a new direction. Regarding his comment about "story-telling," he said, "If you're a good strategist, you should be able to tell a good story; so conversely, if you're not, you don't tell a good story." Learning that he'd really not given Rachel any of this feedback, I urged him to do so, and he indicated he would at an upcoming meeting in Europe.

I was encouraged when he acknowledged Rachel's good leadership of another business in her portfolio. He praised it as well-organized, growing, and responsive to the competition and that she was managing expectations effectively. However, he did not seem to appreciate my effort to establish a balanced view of Rachel by juxtaposing her real general management capabilities with the demands of a struggling business numerous others before her had failed to resolve.

When I inquired how she was doing in her relationship with him, he said, "She's trying to be more proactive in her interactions with me versus always waiting for my direction." He also offered that he wanted her to be more forthcoming about what was going on in her businesses, and to be more discerning about what she brought to him for consideration (less tactical).

### Boss on the "Ideal" Direct Report

Because I was after the most explicit input I could get about their relationship, I asked him to describe the "ideal direct report." He said it would be someone who (1) had the potential to succeed him, (2) didn't need much direction, (3) was highly strategic, (4) would hire the best people, and (5) would develop others ("because I'm not good at this"). This input was double-edged. On the one hand, it revealed what he valued most in a direct report. On the other, it contained a disappointing level of managerial abdication that he did not own fully, and this would necessarily delimit the growth of anyone reporting to him. I recognized that his way of leading was transactional to the core, and that he was incapable of respecting the way Rachel led others. I suspected that he might even have been derisive of her preferred empowering leadership style.

In an effort to keep trying to build our collaborative rapport, I sent him an email after the breakfast: "My job is easier when I can have an open dialogue with the boss. We started that today—thank you. I'll look forward to talking to you again in Q4 if not before." He responded, "It was nice to meet you. If I forget, don't hesitate to send me an email." (I did but he did not respond.) Taking a cue from my HR partner, I sensed that he did not believe that Rachel's coaching was going to help him so he remained disengaged.

### Feedback to Client—Key Insight Emerges

I began my next coaching meeting with Rachel by conveying what her boss had said about an "ideal" direct report. I characterized this as good *grist for our coaching mill* and she agreed. I emphasized that he sounded unaware of the progress she was making with her troubled business and that she needed to take responsibility for ensuring his accurate perception of her efforts. His comments about her "story telling"—or lack of same—proved to be an important insight that influenced different behavior on her part especially in her subsequent presentations to senior management.

The written summaries I sent Rachel after each of our meetings proved to be a strong coaching tool. They served to punctuate highlights from our discussions—and also gave her a resource she could revisit as a way of reinforcing both her learning and change efforts. The summary segment that follows illustrates my effort to distill the coaching meeting insight about business "story telling."

### Excerpt from Coaching Meeting Summary, August 2012
#### Your Presentations

*I think an important insight got uncovered. You've been thinking that he's focused on how your decks are not "slick" enough when what he said to me focused on your ability to tell a compelling story. Further, he emphasized that a true strategic thinker should be able to tell a story to senior management in a manner that is persuasive and conveys his/her passion about/commitment to the business he or she is running.*

*As you and I discussed, there's something key here for you in terms of your "getting out of yourself." In your words, "He is right, I could get more rigorous about building a compelling business story line."*

*You also said that among key executives there he does the best job of telling a compelling story. It would not hurt for you to mention this to him, as well as your intention to learn more from him about how to do this well.*

In this pivotal session, I also put other key points on the table—points synthesized from the meeting with her boss that I believed might aid her in establishing a stronger relationship with him. These included: (1) her communicating to him how aggressively she was pushing on certain business issues; (2) her displaying more active leadership—not appearing "too remote" from the business; and (3) her being more discerning regarding what she brought to him for discussion, that is, staying at a strategic level.

Still trying to forge collaborative engagement with her boss, I sent him an email about how these key points had been discussed with Rachel thus laying the foundation for their face-to face meeting in a few months' time.[19] His response was a brief (terse?) "Thank you."

### *A Sudden Surprise*

Toward the end of the coaching phase, Rachel revealed that her company, in an effort to generate cash, had decided to sell the most successful business in her portfolio. This excited and aroused Rachel's entrepreneurial instincts, and the company was amenable to her purchasing the business. She quickly put together a combination of her own and external funding to do the deal. The prospect of her owning and running this business was the most passionate I'd seen her since we met. What she felt—and what I could confirm based on the coaching thus far—was a coalescence of her education, career experience, and leadership skills. While this boded well for her taking this courageous step in her career, I wanted to influence her balanced reflection.

### *Client's Insight Increases*

It was year-end and as Rachel left for a family skiing vacation, I urged her to consider *why this now* in terms of the business deal. Not surprising, the opportunity to run her own thing—in her own way—was the crux of it. Given this clarity, I advised her to concentrate on (1) ensuring a smooth transition for her business team, and (2) managing her relationships with senior executives within the company until the deal was completed. In one prophetic moment I emphasized, "These deals can get complicated—and protracted. It's not over 'til it's over."

In January of the next year, we reviewed what she had prepared for the annual performance review discussion with her boss.[20] Clearly, as I had feared at the outset of the coaching, it appeared that she was being held to a higher performance standard than were her male peers. After she met with her boss, she wrote in an email to me,

He says I'm on a short list for his job or one like it; however, it's contingent on my turning around this one business. So I'm deemed to have runway, but I need to 'earn it' in this job when some of the mess I'm trying to clean up now was created by someone in the role before me. The double standard between French and non-French is not so unusual here.

This, of course, heightened her interest in the aforementioned business deal.

## Phase IV: Consolidation

Within months, she learned that the CEO had changed his mind about selling the business—cash had been generated through the sale of other parts of the corporate portfolio. While disappointed, Rachel also appeared somewhat relieved. This happened right at the consolidation phase of our work. Based on her excitement about going entrepreneurial and then her seeming sense of relief when the deal fell through, I made an interpretation about her "duality within." This proved to be pivotal in the final phase of the coaching.

### The "Duality Within"

The *duality within* interpretation helped Rachel recognize that the financial security of her family still trumped any entrepreneurial interest. The following excerpt from a coaching session summary proved to be catalytic for Rachel's thinking about her path forward.

Excerpt from Coaching Meeting Summary, January 2013
**The Duality Within**
If I were writing an essay about you, the full title would be: "The Duality Within: A Business Leader's Struggle Between Financial Security and Pursuing Her True Aspiration." You've made a number of compelling comments that support this essay's title:

> *I realize I'm becoming more of a portfolio manager than being truly intimate with a business which I really like better. I'm not so sure that I can find this here.*
> *Everyday I'm making a decision against myself because the way I would do something is not the norm here.*

> *I know that staying here would be weak and wrong for me but I do it because it's the safe thing. Maybe it's really more financial than I realized.*

While the insight about this *inner duality* is new for you, what is *not* new is *your desire for something more—and especially your desire to run something in a manner that's consistent with your values as a leader.* I think the sense of relief you experienced when the deal was scuttled came from the financial security place within you—but this is not an accurate indicator of your true *aspirational self.*

As we discussed, it may well be time for you to move from what you described as a "passive-reactive" pattern vis-á-vis your career to a pattern of "overt pursuit." This can involve both your stepped up effort within the company, and your leveraging external pathways as well. Remember that the realization of a strong aspiration includes three key elements: (1) a plan, (2) good timing, and (3) the desire to achieve it. The most critical element—especially in terms of managing the anxiety related to change and/or risk—is desire. This is why you need to think deeply about your duality within. Your resolution of this will strengthen your resolve/fuel your desire (*I deserve more*) and accelerate your efforts to pursue what you really aspire to—wherever that may be. Finally, I believe you are poised for a breakthrough—and *you* are more master of this than you may think.

My effort to influence Rachel's proactive thinking/planning about her career was supported by the HR contact who was beginning to question seriously whether or not Rachel would advance further in the company. Further, in one of my last conversations with her, she highlighted culture factors that indicated Rachel's progress in her coaching was shrouded in a fog we could not clear. These factors included: (1) her boss's tepid support, (2) the company's long-standing gender bias, and (3) the fact that Rachel's leadership style was still not a match with the command and control version of the French executive team.

Rather than playing messenger or challenging my neutrality any further, I urged that the HR person have a candid conversation with Rachel, which she said she would do. Because Rachel's own questions about her potential happiness in the company had now bubbled hot to the surface, I also urged her to speak to HR and then to have a follow-up conversation with her boss. It would be important for the company to have the opportunity to "save" a disillusioned executive if that was what it wanted to do. If not, candor would be in the best interests of both the company and the individual executive.

In our last two meetings, Rachel and I reviewed her three coaching objectives to gauge progress made. Yes, she had made some headway in her boss-relationship, but we knew he wasn't her champion, and he had never become engaged in the coaching. Yes, she had also made progress on leading her team and making key personnel changes but she was never going to lead in the preferred hierarchical mode of her male French superiors. In the end, I believe she became inured to the intertwined contextual realities of those objectives and began to seriously question her willingness to "adapt" in this milieu. Through the twists and turns and surprises of this coaching adventure, it was the progress she made on the third objective—finding more joy and happiness in her life—that may have mattered most. She was poised to use the insight about the conflict between her being the primary financial support of her family, and her pursuing another career path.

## DISCUSSION

In this executive coaching "experiment," I was retained by the company to help a valued executive improve the relationship with her boss. The other stated objective of her resolving long-standing issues in one of the business she was managing was, I stated at the outset, beyond my capabilities other than to influence her decisions regarding key people in that business. Given the minimal involvement and eventual unresponsiveness of her boss to my efforts to engage him, it was difficult to make more than incremental progress on the objective involving their relationship. However, something else, something of lasting significance happened for the client as a result of the coaching. Through an insight-oriented coaching approach, Rachel was helped to identify and to reflect upon what we came to call her *duality within*, that is, the inner tension between her ego ideal (true aspiration) and practical concerns (financial security of her family). Rachel reached this insight through the sequenced use of a variety of coaching tools including the key psycho/social aspects of her life history, psychological testing data, her VLM, the written summaries from her coaching meetings, and my interpretive observations. Further, the candid input from my HR colleague proved invaluable in terms of clarity about intractable culture factors that did not bode well for Rachel's advancement in the company.

Once in touch with her *duality within*, Rachel could more realistically examine her career choices and plan accordingly. She could be more focused and aggressive about pursuing what she really wanted—either in her current company or not. Further, she seemed liberated by the realization that if she could not find happiness there, it would be in the best interests of both herself and the company to consider other options—and something entrepreneurial seemed likely.

## Conclusion

Coaching came at a pivotal time in Rachel's life. At this writing, I do not know what the next chapter of her career will be but I believe she is destined to lead. Her deepened self-awareness and willingness to explore her *duality within* was the silver lining in the coaching; it should help inform good decisions *for her* going forward. For the executive coach, this engagement was a reminder that there are times when we must hold simultaneously—and as objectively as possible—the seemingly disparate expectations of the organization, and those of the individual being coached. In these instances, we can hold up a double-sided mirror, and while the outcome of the coaching might not be anything that either the company or the executive expected—through the honesty reflected in this work—we can influence a more contented future for both.

# Executive's Reflection

I work for a large global industrial company I'll call "S." I am the highest ranking female line executive with full P&L responsibility for approximately $600 million and twenty-five hundred employees. I joined Company S in 1999 and was successively promoted through several different assignments. In 2012, the company sponsored me to work with Karol to further develop my business leadership skills.

I have always been a hardworking, disciplined, and driven person with aspirations to lead others. I find deep satisfaction in building teams and then working together to do more, better, faster. I derive satisfaction and happiness when I can lead "my way" with my values. I'm less satisfied when "my way" and my value system conflicts with the norms of my work environment. Given management changes in recent years, I found myself in a context where the frequency and scope of this conflict became increasingly greater.

The work with Karol helped me to examine fully my value system and leadership style. We began by identifying the people and experiences in my life that shaped who I am. First and foremost, my parents instilled in me the values of hard work, sense of responsibility, and integrity. As first generation immigrants, with minimal funds, language skills, or network, they successfully established roots as a family in a new country. To this day, no matter how hard I work, I cannot measure up to the work ethic of my parents. Through their sacrifice, they gave my sister and me a safe, loving home and the opportunities for great education and careers. The way they led their lives and how they interacted with those around them is rooted in integrity.

Given my upbringing working hard, being honest, open, empathetic, and sharing with others are important values to me. I expect everyone on the team to practice the "Golden Rule" (i.e., do unto others as you would have them do unto you; put yourself in the other person's shoes first, etc.)—which is my definition of integrity. In business, I like operating as a "flat" and informal organization where people can quickly go to the source of information or knowledge regardless of their position in the organization. I try to foster an environment where people can openly debate and advocate their views with their minds (i.e., data) and hearts (i.e., their beliefs), passionately. I prefer an environment where decisions are made relatively quickly using the 80/20 rule of facts and analysis (80) and what your gut is telling you (20). I want people to work hard because they are passionate about what they do and find joy, satisfaction, and pride in the environment in which they do it. And as a result of all of those elements, I aspire to lead a team driven to excel and win.

I have grown in many ways during my years in Company S. I've acquired new skills, met wonderful people, formed deep friendships, and had the opportunities to contribute in numerous ways. However, as I've become more aware of the type of organization I want to create and lead, at times I feel constrained and conflicted because the "norm" of the company is not fully aligned with my value system and the behaviors I seek in an organization. This company is hierarchical and information flow up and down the organization is managed carefully. Controversial views are not always readily shared and much of the presentation and discussion in meetings is very much geared toward the highest ranking person in the room. At times people are not motivated by passion and beliefs but rather by receiving an accolade and the next promotion. As I continue to mature as a business leader, and as my scope of responsibility continues to increase, I have become more sensitive to the importance of alignment of my values and behavior and those of the broader organization to which I belong.

This self-awareness as a leader became greater as a result of my work with Karol. By overexamining contexts and specific cases of difficult situations, as well as successes and accomplishments in my work environment, I became more explicitly conscious of how my behavior and mindset can impact outcomes—both in positive and negative ways. Karol gave me specific advice on different ways to frame and think about difficult problems and also new approaches for communicating with and influencing my boss and others around me. She helped me realize that although I may at times have to modify my "natural" behavior in "managing up," I can still keep my values "intact" when leading my teams.

Karol also helped me to understand much more deeply who I am as a person and to relate my behavior and values to the people and experiences in my life. Our discussions of who I am as a whole person—a wife, mother, daughter, and a business leader—helped me to reach a stronger equilibrium and comfort about Me. By making an explicit connection to my personal history and those who have influenced me, Karol helped me to realize the power of those experiences and to motivate me to improve who I am as a leader by gaining new experiences, as well as continuing to build and strengthen relationships in ways that help me to live my values.

As a result of my coaching, I have a better understanding of what drives me, my natural leadership style, and the values with which I want to shape my organization. My next career challenge will be to figure out how I can create a work environment in which I continue to become a stronger and more impactful leader while being true to myself. I will need to figure out if I can create that context within Company S and if so, what I need to do more of and less of to affect such changes. I will also need to assess if there are other environments outside of this company that will offer a more natural fit with who I am as a leader and what efforts and risks are entailed in such alternatives. Karol helped me to realize that I experience the most satisfaction and happiness when I can lead my way. So my journey as a business leader going forward will be to not only work hard and achieve results but also to find happiness by leading My Way.

# CHAPTER 5

# The Demon Slayer: Conquering a Dark Side of Deference

The subject of this case study was among the first participants in a company-sponsored leadership development initiative that focused on its top 70 executives and spanned over two decades.[1] This is an atypical executive coaching engagement in that it involved different phases of intensity spread over many years. Further, it concluded with the author having served in the capacity of *trusted advisor* for several years leading up to this leader's career retirement—but let me not get ahead of the sequence of events.[2]

In the mid-1980s, the CEO of this global manufacturing organization was concerned that the company portfolio consisted primarily of mature businesses that could not produce rapid growth. He was also concerned that most of his top business leaders were the product of a company culture that he described as "hierarchical, approval-seeking, and overly polite." Recognizing this as a central factor retarding business growth, he charged his top Human Resources (HR) executive with the creation of a development process that would help groom a generation of bolder, entrepreneurial leaders.

The HR leader believed certain leadership behaviors, especially courageous decision-making, bias for action, boldness (versus approval-seeking), and deepened self-awareness, would need to be emphasized if this program was to be successful. Given this behavioral emphasis, he chose as his external partner a consulting psychologist (the author) who was clinically trained and who also had a business background. This collaboration resulted in a leadership development process that was originally named Leadership 2000.[3]

**Figure 5.1** Leadership 2000 Leader Competencies.

| Ability to earn trust and support among superiors, colleagues, and subordinates |
| --- |
| Ability to form a realistic vision for the organization |
| Ability to communicate a vision and inspire commitment/quality performance |
| Toughness and drive to overcome obstacles |
| Ability to size up opportunities/problems and take effective action |
| Managerial and administrative competence |

**Figure 5.2** Leadership 3000 Guiding Principles.

| |
| --- |
| **Holistic development model**: a boundary-less process versus contained program that is focused on the whole person. After participants completed the four phases, they had ongoing access to members of their development "brain trust" that consisted of the CEO, their boss, the HR leader, and the consulting psychologist. |
| **Trust grounded in data confidentiality:** a developmental versus evaluative process in which all data generated was the property of the participants. What was shared with the organization were the specific development areas and action plans. |
| **The power of psychological insight:** data-gathering included a life history, a battery of psychological inventories, and an optional spousal module in addition to organization-based leadership competency data. |
| **The conveyance of executive wisdom:** the CEO and boss participated in both action planning and follow-up meetings. The sharing of their work experiences, triumphs, mistakes, emotions, and other accumulated learning enriched action planning and ensured the avid engagement of participants. |

Its first generation of competencies—as defined by the CEO and his Corporate Management Development Committee—can be found in figure 5.1.

Conceptually, this work was influenced by the HR leader's strongly held belief about sustained executive development. In our first meeting he said:

> We need to go inside out. We need to assess the whole person not just one's profile of leadership competencies. We need to have real relationships with these people and they need to know themselves and understand what influences their behavior in good

times and bad. Their accurate self-awareness is essential for continued learning and personal growth. Continued learning and personal growth are essential for the development of world class leaders.[4]

This conceptual spark for Leadership 3000 led to four principles that guided the creation and implementation of this work (see figure 5.2).

## A Memorable First Meeting

By the time I met Ravid in 1987, he had held a number of finance jobs since joining the company in 1972. He had received his first business unit leadership role a few years earlier and was doing admirably well. Raised in India, he received his bachelor's degree (mechanical engineering) in Mumbai and his master's and MBA degrees in the United States.

I was struck by the combination of his quick mind, humility, intensity, and pride. A comment he made in this meeting would stay with me because it reflected his underlying sensitivity and initial apprehension about our work together. In his words, "I have a fear that the company may be looking for a certain executive profile, but I think it's important that people be able to maintain their differences and have sufficient freedom to be different and to have different perspectives. Heterogeneity in the leader ranks is an important thing for a company if it is to grow."

Ravid's comment caused me to focus on the fact that he was the first senior Indian executive with whom I'd worked. Even though he had spent his entire business career working for an American company, I wondered about the extent to which his orientation to business might be influenced by certain cultural subtleties and nuances to which I needed to be attuned. However, it was the 1980s, so I was not successful in my effort to find other consultants who had worked with business leaders from India so I read what I could find. In the end, my HR partner was the most helpful in underscoring factors that be believed mattered most to Ravid: self-empowerment, pride, and a focus on establishing customer intimacy.[5]

My own belief in the importance of a heterogeneous mix of executive leaders at the top—in combination with Ravid's intention to learn and belief in the value of introspection—would ultimately influence what he described as a "life-changing" experience. This experience was founded on our mutual trust and my careful orchestration of the four Leadership 3000 phases: (1) data-gathering, (2) feedback, (3) action planning, and (4) follow-up.

## Data-Gathering Phase

The data-gathering phase consisted of a full life history, a battery of psychometric measures,[6] and organization 360 data that was based on a customized interview protocol.[7] This interview protocol covered the company's leadership competencies, and at a later stage of Leadership 3000, also included the company's "essential leadership behaviors" (see figure 5.3).

## Feedback Phase

The feedback phase consisted of two meetings—one in which life themes and psychological data were integrated, and another in which organization-based data were mined for development clues along with information from the first feedback meeting. The coherency between Ravid's life history, psychological, and organization-based data led to a clear identification of the areas for focus in the action-planning stage.

### Organization-Based Data

Ravid's "self" and "other" ratings were quite consistent. He was strong on all of the leader competencies with the exception of (1) sizing up opportunities and (2) administrative competence on which his ratings were average. The first was a function of his limited time in a business unit leadership role (this would increase significantly as his career unfolded). Regarding administrative competence, like most of his peers, this was not ever likely to be much of an emphasis but he was sufficiently detail-focused that nothing major fell through the cracks. He also made a point of having strong administrative support.

The qualitative analysis of Ravid's 360 data revealed a number of significant strengths. These included his quick analytical ability, capacity for work, logic and analytical problem-solving, and ability to relate well to customers (strong "negotiating" capability). Other data that warranted our attention included perceptions that approval-seeking could erode his speaking truth to power, dread of revealing any deficiencies, sensitivity about being treated fairly (concern about cultural bias), and tendency to play things too close-to-the-vest.

### Psychological Data

Many behavioral strengths indicated Ravid's likely continued success as a leader. These strengths included what I interpreted as "ambiversion," that is, the elasticity of his behavioral repertoire that, in concert with his accurate "read" of situations, was a key aspect in his relating so well to customers. As Grant stated, "Ambiverts... naturally engage in a flexible pattern of talking and listening... and are likely to express sufficient assertiveness and enthusiasm to persuade and (they)... are more inclined to listen to customers' interests and less vulnerable to appearing too excited or overconfident."[8]

By temperament Ravid was serious, quiet, and reserved. He was also pragmatic, exceedingly accountable, and earned success through his powers of concentration and thoroughness. A constellation of humanistic, affiliation, achievement, and self-actualization factors underscored his natural inclination to manage and mentor others.

The cautions for Ravid behaviorally appeared to be interrelated and primarily a function of his early socialization—particularly his deep-seated deference to and respect for authority. Therefore, he could dwell on perceived criticism and be overly sensitive to his superiors. He might struggle in silence to resolve issues rather than raising a controversial topic that could potentially irritate or disappoint others. Wanting to please his bosses, he might not take bolder actions quickly or trust his intuition before he had some signal from them that he was on the right path. It was also clear that he needed to be tougher in his performance feedback to others, disliked ambiguity, and that he masked a fierce competitiveness with his well-mannered sociability.

After weaving the highlights of all the data, we settled on two major development areas: (1) confidence as related to his not avoiding conflict, being less approval-seeking, being less sensitive to criticism, and giving tougher feedback; and (2) the pursuit of business opportunities—his being bolder in expressing and pursuing his thoughts and ideas especially with senior management.

### Client's Reaction to Feedback

After the feedback discussions, Ravid sent me a letter in which he wrote, "As you know, I walked into this process somewhat apprehensive and have come out of it feeling very positive. However, I realize that the process of behavioral change and evolution in other areas will be a slow and deliberate process. Meanwhile, I hope that my superiors, colleagues and collaborators will be patient with me."

Over time, Ravid came to realize that it wasn't about people being more patient with him. In fact, the CEO and other senior executives believed his ongoing success was inevitable. In a private conversation the HR leader told me, "We were wise to choose the people we did to 'pilot' this process and they have given it a running start in terms of credibility. I'm especially pleased about Ravid's participation. It's meant a lot to him personally, he's been a strong advocate, and my money says he's got a shot at the top job."

## Action-Planning Phase

The action-planning phase was based on a "live" planning discussion attended by the participant's development "brain trust"—the CEO, the boss, the HR leader, and the consultant.[9] Shortly after receiving Ravid's letter, I facilitated his action-planning meeting for which he had prepared a summary of his Leadership 3000 action areas and some beginning thoughts about how he would address them.

Two major themes emerged in this meeting: (1) the need for Ravid to lead more forcefully, that is, from the strength of his convictions about how his business could grow, and (2) the need for his boss to play his ambassadorial role in conveying Ravid's growth to others as well as intensifying his mentoring efforts. Regarding the mentoring effort, he recognized that Ravid would be helped by his putting seeming "political" events in perspective, that is, minimizing the potential for Ravid to overpersonalize them.

### Coaching Conceptualization

Since Ravid was based in Europe, my opportunities to meet with him were limited; however, I had annotated his development plan in a way that I thought would help increase his continued development. Yes, he would seek less approval and take the bold decisions sooner as related to the growth of his business. Yes, he would be more forthcoming with both his concerns and views that departed from those held by senior management. And yes, he would be more direct in giving difficult performance feedback to those who reported to him. But, in the end, what aided Ravid's growth as a leader was less about granular action steps and more about the affirmation he received through this process—and how this affirmation helped liberate his willingness to apply the fullness of his capabilities.

I also reinforced the strength of his "difference," his impressive mix of strengths, and how he compared most favorably to senior executives in the company—as well as to others elsewhere. I could say this with confidence given my experiences with executives leading other global companies. In short, my conceptualization of this case centered on helping Ravid clear away any psychological debris that muted the force of his power and potential—especially as it related to his pattern of deference to authority. Metaphorically, we discussed this as his need to *slay his deference demon*.

Within a year, Ravid was promoted to a major leadership role in another Europe-based business. In his year-end holiday card to me he wrote, "I want to take this opportunity to thank you sincerely for the time you spent with me last year. The exposure and experience in this program have turned out to be one of the most valuable things I have ever done."

## FOLLOW-UP PHASE

In the follow-up phase, the same "brain trust" reassembled to discuss Ravid's progress on plan and to offer further development guidance. For Ravid this included coaching focused on the behavior *how* dimension of leadership. By the mid-1990s, we referred to this as emotional fortitude and several publications by Goleman proved instructive.[10]

Within a year of the original action-planning meeting, it was clear that Ravid had made considerable progress. He was leveraging his strengths, and his two development areas had about faded from consideration. In the follow-up phase meeting, a new development objective was identified: increasing his formal communications skill so he would be more effective in large group settings. The HR leader facilitated Ravid's working with the company's external communications consultant to address this need.

In an effort to accelerate Ravid's progress in this area, I sent him an outline of points that he could convey to his communications consultant. I emphasized the potential of his being: (1) more emphatic in the expression of his views, (2) more at ease making comments about the future (versus just staying focused on quarterly results), and (3) more inspirational regarding the company's future prospects—prospects that he, in fact, would propel. Specifically, with the CEO and a few other key top leaders in the company, Ravid would expand the company's presence in Asia considerably. He would also help build a new business platform that significantly accelerated the growth of the company.

Ravid continued to build his track record of business success, and a few years later he was promoted to Vice President, a major accomplishment in this company. This significant promotion was the prelude to much that would come thereafter—including the next phase of my work with him.

## Second Phase of Coaching

### *A Step in the CEO Succession*

This second phase of coaching with Ravid started several years after his participation in Leadership 3000. We began this phase by debriefing a report that had been written by the HR leader. This report was based on discussions he had had with a number of senior leaders in the company including the CEO, as well as with Ravid's peers and direct reports. We understood this as the HR leader's role in guiding what was the company's low-key and internally driven CEO succession planning process.

I was struck by a number of Ravid's comments. He was pleased that the report was an endorsement of his capabilities overall and that there was no "ceiling" for him. In his words, "I've really been discovering myself the last couple of years." Of particular note from a behavioral perspective was his comment, "I feel liberated from my fear of the unknown and from that need for approval."

He cited a number of factors in his growing sense of liberation. These included his: (1) ongoing business achievements, (2) growing financial security, (3) insights about himself as a leader, (4) having become a vice president, and (5) progress he'd made integrating work and family priorities. His concern about the interaction of work and family issues had been a kind of sidebar issue that we didn't discuss openly with the others in the action-planning meeting. However, I was mindful of this tension in his life, and it appeared that his and his wife's participation in the Leadership 3000 optional Spousal Module had been helpful (see later).

The HR leader described Ravid as a man who had become "truly comfortable with himself." We both agreed that the challenge for him now was to continue to reveal more of himself more quickly. Through my ongoing conversations with Ravid, I helped him see that there was no longer a need for him to play things so close-to-the-vest. Further, we knew that his ability to meet the demands of an increasingly Darwinian marketplace would require him to channel his leadership behavior in ways that helped him make rapid and inspiring connections with others.

In concluding his report, the HR leader cited three development foci for Ravid: (1) executive impact—more straight talk and holding people accountable; (2) inspirational leadership—expressing more passion, warmth, and heart; and (3) outside involvement—joining a corporate board and becoming more active in industry groups. This third area was soon to be addressed, and by the end of his corporate career, Ravid would have served on a number of prominent for-profit boards. The other two areas were already receiving our attention, and progress on them would be amplified by input from the CEO.

### A Jump Start

After Ravid and I had debriefed the HR leader's report, our work was accelerated further by a meeting with the HR leader and the CEO who provided a number of compelling coaching points. In his words, "Ravid has said the hardest thing for him to do is to disagree with me or his boss in Europe, but we both *want* this. The issue for me is about passion—his speaking passionately about what he believes needs to happen for the business."

In encouraging Ravid, the CEO noted how he'd been a "major change agent" in his last two roles by both turning around a business and helping set a clear path forward for the European region. He encouraged Ravid's outside involvements including in the industry's major association. And finally, he noted that Ravid could do much to position the company in what was then referred to as the "Pacific region." This would, over time, become one of Ravid's major legacy contributions to the company.

As this meeting ended, the CEO said, "You're doing an incredible job. There's been a real change in you as a confident leader. What I'd like to see happen now is for you to start moving toward being more of a spokesman for the whole company—for you to move from being a member of the gang to being the leader of the gang."

When the CEO asked Ravid if there was anything else he could do to support his ongoing success, Ravid said, "Yes—give me a prod when I'm being too deferential." Obviously, this was also a clue for me in the coaching. Integrating the input of both the CEO and the HR leader, my coaching goal now was to tap into Ravid's competitive instincts and exhort his greater candor and boldness. I emphasized that if he wasn't as candid and bold as he needed to be, he would run the risk of losing the CEO succession race. At this point, it looked like the succession decision was down to two internal candidates—and he was clearly one of them.

### The Spousal Module

Harkening back to the "holistic" intent of Leadership 3000, I had convinced the HR leader to include an optional spousal module for those executives who wanted to involve their marital partners.[11] Ravid and his wife chose to participate knowing that the information generated here was completely confidential. Through the convergence of the data from their individual interviews, important family issues were surfaced and helpful action steps were identified to address them. This appeared especially helpful to Ravid's wife, who like other spouses of senior executives carried the weight of significant family and business/social responsibilities related to their husbands' careers.

### Surprising Celebratory Event

Around this time, I was invited to Ravid's fiftieth birthday celebration. This invitation was a pleasant surprise for me and a bonus for my husband, a lawyer, who happened to have the restaurant owner where the party was being held as a client. The room was lively and crowded with many personal friends, family members, and a small sprinkling of work-related colleagues. At one point, Ravid took a microphone and said he was especially grateful to three people whom he considered as central in his career progress and happiness. He cited the CEO and his boss for their continued confidence in and mentoring of him. I could not have been more stunned—and gratified—when I was mentioned as the third.

### A Stunning Request

As the CEO succession issue heated up, it was clear that there were two leading internal candidates and, as indicated earlier, Ravid was one of them. The other was a peer who had started in the R&D side of the organization. Like Ravid, he had had a steady career trajectory that included significant functional, operations, international, and business management experience. Unlike Ravid, he had aspired to become CEO since he first joined the company. While I knew Matt fairly well (he had also participated in Leadership 3000), I had had less interaction with him in recent years.

About a year before the CEO succession decision was to be made, Matt called with a stunning request. He said, "Ravid and I have been talking about this whole CEO horse race, and we're wondering if you'd be willing to meet with us for a corporate 'marital therapy' type of engagement?" I said I would but with the caveat that I'd never done anything like this before and couldn't be sure of its value. Matt said they trusted that I knew enough about each of them, the CEO, and the culture to be helpful as they grappled independently and collectively with the mounting pressure of the succession and how it had become such an open topic of speculation in the company.

My HR partner also thought this was a good idea, and he continued to build his own rapport with both of them. Given the magnitude of the succession issue, I was most focused on helping these two very talented albeit very different executives reinforce their potential for preserving a positive relationship in the wake of the CEO appointment. At the time, I believed it would be in the best interest of the company for both of them to be on the executive leadership team.

Further, the CEO was aware that in the Leadership 3000 boundaryless model, I might have ongoing contact with Leadership 3000 participants—including Matt and Ravid. He also knew that whatever interactions I had with the participants—even these two—would remain in the "development" category. In other words, while he and I would discuss the capabilities of various participants, I would not be asked to "vote" when it came time for the succession decision. Matt and Ravid understood (and trusted) this as well.

There were three or four meetings with Ravid and Matt—meetings of incredible candor and tension, too. Obviously, they were both intent upon becoming CEO and recognized their respective strengths and experiences that qualified each for the job. Both recognized too that his tenure as CEO would likely be enhanced if the other was still in the company—assuming the ego of the "loser" could recover from the disappointment, and he could settle into a supportive and productive working relationship with the new CEO.

My strategy in these discussions was threefold. First, I wanted each to express why he thought the other would make an excellent CEO. I believed this honoring of their respective strengths could have staying power over time. Second, I wanted each to "think aloud" about how he might partner with the other in the event he didn't become CEO. I believed getting granular in this way might start paving the path of their collaborative working relationship. And third, I strove to get them to discuss how they might deal with each other during moments of real strategic or operational difference.

In other words, as in a traditional marital therapy,[12] I wanted to assess and get them to experience their likely capacity for compromise. I believed that this capacity for compromise, in combination with mutual respect and trust, would be a sine qua non for their fruitful working relationship.

Simultaneous to my activity with Ravid and Matt, there were numerous performance events arranged by the CEO in which they presented to the board. There was also a global managers' meeting in which they both made presentations on their respective visions for the future of the company. While I was not present, several people commented on how Matt read from a script while Ravid was more engaging in speaking from an outline.

### CEO Decision Made

A few months prior to the CEO succession decision being announced, Ravid and Matt agreed that they would come to my office for a champagne toast on the day of the announcement. When the day arrived, Matt contained his disappointment well, and Ravid seemed to be in a state of relieved contentment. In a business press interview soon thereafter Ravid was quoted, "I

**Figure 5.3** Leadership 3000 Essential Behaviors.

| |
|---|
| **Courageous leadership:** relishes leading; willing to speak out, stand alone, influence open debate, probe unexpressed views, and leverage resident wisdom. The courage to confront any company "sacred cows," decisions, policies, and/or practices that could interfere with success. |
| **Emotional fortitude:** ability to use self-awareness (of strengths and weaknesses), self-management (focus, discipline, tact, and diplomacy), attunement (empathic understanding of others), and relationship-building skills (relating to people in ways that are deeper than transactional need) to drive business results. Emotional resilience (can deal well with ambiguity, crises, adversity in all forms). Stays cool under pressure. |
| **Enterprise thinking:** playing-for-the-house. No silo mentality. Input into key decisions focused on overall company objectives. Will put personal comfort aside to take on difficult new roles or additional assignments. More focused on building a great company than on personal ambition. |
| **Pragmatic optimism:** instilling hope about the company's future through consistent messages that emphasize rightness of the strategic direction, specificity of objectives and realistic timelines, company values, and effectiveness of executive leaders. |
| **Steel trap accountability:** relentless drive for results. No defensiveness. No sad stories. No excuses. No blaming others. Making the necessary adjustments (in people, process, and/or strategy) if needed—and doing it quickly. Hard work alone is not enough—the results have to be there. |
| **Truth-telling:** stating the business reality as it *truly is* compared to established goals. Consistent candor and early signals about what's real *now* regarding business results, problems, projections, and people performance issues. Behavioral transparency and authenticity. |
| **Tough on talent:** rigorous, relentless people appraisal and performance management. Tougher scrutiny of current talent. Willingness to make tough calls on people, to search outside for people who will fill major gaps, and to ensure the successful assimilation of new people into the company. Serious focus on deepening bench strength. Superb delegation, empowerment, and methodical identification and development of high potential talent. |

never aspired to be a CEO. I just worked to do the job in front of me as best I could and after 13 jobs and 18 bosses, my time came."

It didn't take long for the Ravid and Matt "camps" to converge and for people to get on with addressing the pressing business issues at hand. About a year after his appointment, Ravid held a world-wide leadership conference; and at the end of it, he amplified the ongoing Leadership 3000 work with a set of "essential behaviors"

**Figure 5.4**  Leadership 3000 Competencies Revised.

| OUTSIDE-IN-PERSPECTIVE |
| --- |
| • Market-aware and customer-driven |
| • Strategic focus |
| • Global perspective |

| SPEED TO MARKET |
| --- |
| • Bias for action |
| • Adaptive to change |
| • Creative problem-solving |

| PURSUIT OF PROFITABLE GROWTH |
| --- |
| • Professional credibility |
| • Business acumen |
| • Persuasion and influence |
| • Safety performance |
| • People and performance management |
| • Interpersonal effectiveness |

(see figure 5.3). Further, by this time, the leadership competencies had been revised (see figure 5.4).

The year had gotten off to a good start for Ravid. At this conference, he announced an important acquisition, that all business targets had been met the previous year, and that shareholders had seen a significant increase in the company's value. What was not going as well was the working relationship with Matt. While he insisted that he had made peace with not being made CEO, he struggled mightily with the boundaries of their respective roles. Despite Ravid's patience and my best efforts, Matt's ego never fully accepted his loss and he ultimately left the company. He needed to pursue his long-held aspiration: to become a CEO. This was an aspiration he would not realize.

## THIRD PHASE

### Consultant Becomes Trusted Advisor to the CEO

Over the next several years, Ravid and I maintained a relationship in which I continued the Leadership 3000 work and also provided him with what I referred to as spontaneous "feedback moments." By now, the trust and working rapport was so natural between us that I could do this knowing he would receive the feedback in the support-ive spirit it was intended. He knew, as Saporito[13] aptly pointed out, that as CEO he was not likely to get the candid input he needed.

For example, I once initiated a conversation in which I told him people were concerned about the immense workload he was carry-ing and how, at times, that made him appear less attentive in the moment. His response led to constructive action, "I need to sim-plify the reporting lines so I have fewer reports—because it's true, I just don't have enough time for all of them!"

Seven years into his tenure as CEO, the company had undergone significant changes as it expanded into new technologies and sold off businesses. Sales had grown by 50 percent and earnings had tripled. Expansion into Asia had gone exceedingly well—with the company far outpacing its industry competitors in this regard. By this time, Ravid had also begun to think about his succession that would likely occur within the next three–four years. We had con-versations about various high potential people at the time but one person, in particular, was emerging as the most likely candidate. He was running a new business platform for the company that was influencing explosive growth in Asia. I urged Ravid to increase his mentoring time with this individual—whilst being careful not to ignite the competitive dynamic he found himself in years before.

### A Centennial Anniversary—and a Startling Event

Almost ten years into Ravid's tenure as CEO, the company cel-ebrated its one-hundredth anniversary, and it was acquired by a giant in the industry. Naturally, the events leading up to this out-come, an outcome that Ravid and his most trusted colleagues tried mightily to fend off, were physically and emotionally exhausting. On the morning of the announcement, he sent me an email that read in part, "[I]t has been a roller coaster ride, but under the cir-cumstances, it is an excellent outcome for the employees, the future of our business, and certainly for our loyal shareholders." While he positioned his potential successor and other gifted leaders well with the acquiring entity, we doubted that any of them they would remain with that company. And we were right.

## Discussion

From a methodological perspective, the work with Ravid unfolded in three distinct periods spread over many years. The first period was based on the four phases of an executive development initiative called Leadership 3000. The second involved executive coaching as part of a CEO succession process. And the third involved the coach's role as "trusted advisor" to her client after he became CEO. In this capacity, she continued the Leadership 3000 work, integrated all she had learned about him into meaningful bits of timely feedback, and ultimately, in the wake of the company being sold, helped guide his retirement from corporate life.

From a consulting perspective, there were three overarching factors that contributed to the long-standing nature of this leadership development initiative and, by extension, to the consultant's ongoing work with the subject of this case. These factors were: (1) the CEO's imprimatur of Leadership 3000 and his active involvement in it, (2) the consultant's close collaboration with the company's top Human Resources leader, and (3) a development model committed to working with participants as holistically as possible. Further, *one* model with a consistent set of leader competencies and essential behaviors was used for the duration of the work (over 20 years) thus establishing a familiar semantic and understanding of what "leadership" looked and sounded like in this company.

But in the end, what most distinguished the work with Ravid was our relationship in which I was committed to his seeing what he needed to see about his capabilities—capabilities waiting to be released from his inner emotional container of deference that constricted his full effectiveness for a time. This was what he signaled at his fiftieth birthday celebration when he mentioned me as a helpful force in his life. In that moment, the inexorable importance of the executive coach/trusted advisor relationship with a senior executive was honored and revealed. Leadership models and competencies notwithstanding, at this level of leadership, little compares developmentally to safe and shared looks into the mirror when the executive can be vulnerable and the coach can give courageous feedback with equal doses of candor, encouragement, and compassion.[14]

## CONCLUSION

### *Company Postscript*

In the wake of the company's being sold, an assessment of over half of the Leadership 3000 participants was conducted by an outside evaluator as an aid in making key business role appointments. Compared to peers in the acquiring company, they were assessed as being "significantly above the industry benchmark." Further, the lead consultant observed that these leaders were remarkably more aggressive and "nonhierarchical" than he had remembered leaders in this company as being and that the company was the "best CEO University" he'd ever seen. While his comments were bittersweet for Ravid and me, we also felt proud and knew the former CEO and our exceptional HR partner (now deceased) would have been as well. Together we had achieved our objective of changing a leadership culture.

### *Personal Postscript*

In the wake of the company being acquired, my conversations with Ravid focused on his retirement transition. I shared a five-factor model to aid his reflection and planning (see figure 5.5). Based on my experiences with other C-level executives, I knew that Ravid's

**Figure 5.5** A Five-P Model for Retirement Planning*

| |
|---|
| **Purpose**—What do I want to do and/or get involved with that will provide a real sense of meaning in my life now? |
| **Place**—Where do I really want to live now? What locations(s) will be most compatible with my desired lifestyle? |
| **People**—Who are the people with whom I want to spend the most time? |
| **Physical**—What do I need to do to ensure my physical well-being? |
| **Prosperity**—What more might I need to do to ensure my long-term financial stability? |
| * For some executives, i.e., those who are craving a greater spiritual component in their lives, there is a sixth factor that can be spelled "phaith" thus making it a "Six P Model." This involves a different type of introspection that may lead one back to a religious practice—or not. It matters not what "it" is; rather, the importance is the identification of this need and then a targeted response to it. |

biggest challenge initially would be with the "purpose" dimension. He would feel compelled to stay busy and would receive numerous requests for his involvement that he needed to scrutinize carefully choosing only those that really mattered to him. He would also have to discover a new life rhythm with his wife who had a host of her own expectations about the next phase of their life together. All of this would necessitate some trial-and-error, and I emphasized that he would not likely be in his new rhythm for at least three years. Finally, given how I had come to know him, I expected that Ravid would never be fully retired, and that his commercial instincts, resources, time, and his distinctive "difference" would likely merge and be channeled in ways that reflected his growing philanthropic priorities.

# Executive's Reflection

I was among the first participants in a company-sponsored leadership development process focused on top high potential individuals. This work was initiated at the request of the CEO then (mid-1980s) because we needed to match our leadership bench with our strategic game plan. Specifically, we needed to change our rather insular culture to one that was more diverse in keeping with the global markets we were trying to enter and in which we wanted to be a competitive force. We needed leaders who had both strong business skills and the social intelligence for us to expand on a global basis.

The holistic program created and implemented by Karol and our corporate HR Director also resonated with my fundamental belief about leadership: it requires emotional and social, as well as cognitive and business skills. It is honed by life experiences, natural talent, and teaching. No one is born a leader, in my view, and no one gets it right the first time. This program ran for over 20 years and it focused on a combination of ten leadership competencies and behaviors. These were: strategic focus, bias for action, customer satisfaction, business acumen, persuasion and influence, interpersonal effectiveness, organization development, global perspective, creative problem-solving, and integrity.

What distinguished my work with Karol was the collaborative nature of each step in the process. She used both organization-based data-gathering focused on leadership competencies, and psychological testing to identify behavior traits that resulted in a comprehensive picture of development areas. Further, she involved my boss, as well as the head of HR, in the action planning and development follow-up discussions.

What did this mean for me or allow me to see and develop? It's not easy to put such a long and comprehensive process in recipe form because it was not a "start and stop" process. (I maintained contact with Karol for over 20 years.) I think I started to see myself in a different way—more holistically. I started to watch myself in more deliberate and discerning ways so that I could make adjustments in my behavior or in my reaction to what others were telling me or perceiving from my own communication.

There were two especially key points that emerged from my 360 feedback with Karol. The first echoed feedback that I had already had from my major mentor in the company, and it was that some perceived me as having "an agenda for advancement." This was a perception that he thought could hurt me, so I set to modifying it. The second was the perception that I valued humility in a public sense almost to a fault—to the point that I would not voice my opinion or viewpoint in a meeting; and while I would do so afterwards, that could be less effective or compelling. This too would be something I'd make progress on developmentally. With Karol's coaching, I came to think of it as overcoming my own demons.

In overcoming my own demons, one of the most telling changes I made was in how I managed difficult encounters. Before the work with Karol, I might have either avoided likely confrontations entirely or have allowed the difficulty to go on beyond what was wise. After my reflection on the feedback I received about this and the coaching, I became better equipped emotionally at facing each interaction or issue. This included my dealing with tough and potentially adversarial encounters sooner, adopting strategies and positions that allowed me to be more effective at hearing and resolving differences, and setting boundaries and standards that I thought were appropriate for my peers and for agendas with my superiors.

My other major change was in offering my opinions where I thought they were appropriate or important to the discussion. While I had been concerned before about appearing arrogant, I became viewed as a more active and significant contributor. If I weren't, people I respected told me, I wouldn't have even been in the room.

Another comment I would make about my work with Karol and her work with other leaders in the company generally was that it offered a scorecard you could keep on yourself. It was a scorecard with all the hits, walks, errors, and strikeouts that an executive could encounter. It was also a trust process strewn with sometimes harsh realities, candid assessments, and relentless self-management. In the end, I believe, if you were honest with and true to yourself—and to the greater good of the enterprise—you became something akin to the servant leader. This is someone who is able to set direction, inspire and empower others, and at the end can say "thank you" for the tasks people completed or the tenure that was served.

The results of this development work, tabulated over 20 years, showed marked improvement in the ten areas cited earlier and our business results showed we were in the top ranks when compared to our industry peers. We benefitted in other ways as well. From a primarily North American and Euro-centric product and manufacturing base in the 1980s, by 2008 more than half of the company's earnings were tied to Asian and other non-US markets where we had established a solid manufacturing footprint and vibrant customer base. Further, total shareholder return (TSR) outpaced industry competitors and overall market performance during the last 5 years before the company was sold in 2009 achieving a TSR of 17.3 percent compared to the S&P 500's 4.8 percent. This was an amazing achievement due in no small part to leadership team members and the competencies and behaviors they brought to their roles and assignments in executing our strategy.

Finally, there was a telling postscript that involved the quality of the senior business leaders in the company. In an executive evaluation process requested by the acquiring company, our leaders were assessed as being particularly talented as compared to those in the acquiring entity. I believe much of their success was due to their work with Karol, especially her focus on social and emotional competency and its importance in their navigating well through both uncharted and uncertain waters. This was surely true for me.

CHAPTER 6

# A Midlife Reinvention

At its core, this case involved an executive's existential struggle between the successful person *he had become* versus the person *whom he really longed to be*. I discovered quickly that what made Max feel truly passionate in his work hovered over like a thousand fireflies. And like the June fireflies, these moments came and went—but not without leaving just enough light for him to be haunted about the possibility of a very different future. Increasingly, he could envision himself stepping away from his corporate role and toward what he believed he was destined to do. As his executive coach, I was challenged to keep this in perspective as we worked on the areas his boss, HR Director, and he all believed would enhance his effectiveness as a leader in his *current* role.

Further, events conspired *with* us to fuel a story of particular courage for him—and learning for me. In short, over a few years, I would have the privilege of both (1) helping him make changes that reinforced his strengths as a leader, and (2) aiding him to initiate a significant shift in his career. Challenging and poignant in its twists and turns, this case exemplifies the alchemy of the leader/coach relationship, how to manage expectations of a boss, and the extraordinary courage of someone who faced himself in his coaching, and then launched a major midlife reinvention.

## THE REFERRAL/COACHING AGENDA-SETTING MEETING

Max was referred for coaching by the Human Resources Director in the North American sales organization of a global manufacturing company. This was the largest business unit in the company and Max had recently become a Senior Vice President with significant sales responsibility. The HR professional described him as a "rising star" and the highest ranking African American leader in the company—an admired "role model" for many.

Of note is the fact that I had been consulting to this organization for nearly 20 years and had had many assimilation-into-new-role engagements here. In the coaching agenda-setting meeting, Max's boss praised his quick and conceptual thinking but also said he needed to focus on the clarity of his communication and "not jump tracks too much." The HR Director emphasized the need for Max to navigate the "political" landscape by making sure he formed all the key relationships now that he was in a corporate role.

Since this company was familiar with my four-phase coaching model (data-gathering, feedback, coaching, and consolidation), expectations regarding our respective roles, and the boundaries of confidentiality, the coaching agenda-setting meeting moved quickly to the identification of interviewees for Max's 360 data-gathering. This was a representative sample of 19 people who included Max's boss, his peers, and a number of current and former direct reports. The interview protocol was customized to elicit data in the identified coaching areas—with an emphasis on his communication style and cultivating key stakeholder relationships. Most interviews were conducted "live," and I had the advantage of either having worked with or previously interviewed the majority of the respondents. In other words, I could count on the quality of the information that would emerge through this data-gathering.

### A Telling Debriefing Conversation

In debriefing the coaching agenda-setting meeting with Max, he agreed with the development areas cited in that discussion; however, he said something of particular note. In his words, "It's going to be a combination of what they said about what I need to do now in this role *plus* watching you as a coach." While I didn't spend much time probing this in the moment, Max's interest in my coaching model and style proved to be a major consideration later in the coaching.

I was also struck by how he described his work, that is, his having "happened" into a sales and marketing career that "just kept going." He advanced quickly, completed global assignments, and became a senior executive in this industry-leading corporation. He was also an especially talented mentor who had influenced the careers of many employees. He actually preferred this activity to anything else he did saying with a mischievous grin, "I think I'm really a closet HR guy."

In the moment, I failed to realize how prophetic this comment was or how it linked to his interest in my coaching approach. In retrospect, I believe I let my usual optimism about new possibilities be trumped by pragmatic considerations. I mean really—was a successful business executive approaching his fifties going to throw it all over for something else? Well, I was in for a great object lesson in personal change and resilience—but I'm getting ahead of the story.

Another thing that struck me about Max was the force of his presence. While he was tall and powerfully built, he was also readily accessible, charming, and his distinctive brand of humility could border on amusing self-deprecation. He was worldly without conceit, playful but not inappropriate, super smart but still able to listen. His words tumbled in a cascade of humor, wit, and free association that made the laughter easy and mutual. Max sparkled and cared about driving results, but my early impression was that he cared more about the relationships that he could nurture—and the people who would love him back.

I realized how different Max was interpersonally from most of the other senior executives in his company—executives who were decidedly more staid and starched than he. I already knew it would be difficult for Max to feel an affinity for the leaders with whom he was expected to establish rapport now. I knew that if they were to walk in a park together, Max would hear the birds singing while most of them might only see the benches.

## DATA-GATHERING PHASE

In a four-hour meeting, I took Max's life history starting at birth. As with other clients, this conversation was a powerful jump-start for the coaching in two ways. First, it punctuated my commitment to discovering specific life themes that had implications for his leadership. Second, the depth of this conversation helped fuel a trusting connection and empathic resonance between us. The message to Max was: "I am fully present and I am making an effort to see you—to really see you."

Max was the third of four children and the only one to go to college. Since his father was a career enlisted man, they moved around the United States and also lived in a number of off-shore locations. Max was often the only child of color at various grammar schools where he had his first experiences of racism. In his words, "I got called the 'N' word and that really hurt my feelings then, but I realize now it was an experience that's helped me a lot. It helped me to learn how to cope, and so now I can readily deal with all types of people." I noted Max's ability to reframe negative experiences, as well as his emotional resiliency.

Max said he was much like his father whom he described as "extremely hard-working, impatient, intolerant, driven, a worrier, open, direct but not affectionate, and externally insensitive but internally highly sensitive." Max's mother worked outside the home but also did much to create an atmosphere there that was supportive and focused on "sacrificing for the kids." While she was "open and down-to-earth," Max also emphasized that she was "guarded" like his father, and he joked that she didn't hug him enough. In his words, "Yeah, I could have used some more affection. I was definitely more of a sensitive child than I showed." This was an important clue about Max's affiliation need—a clue I didn't register fully until later in our work together.

In high school, his natural leadership ability began to emerge, for example, in his presidency of the Black Students Union and being captain of the track team. Max first went to a junior college and then transferred to a well-respected private school in California. While he majored in science and ultimately completed a PhD (pathology), in his words, "I realized science was a good hobby but not the right vocation for me, so I started doing other things like real estate and wrote new goals for myself."

When Max spotted an ad in a science magazine for a job that was a combination of science and business, he remembered thinking,

"This was written just for me!" Hired into a sales role by that company, it was a good fit for Max from the outset. During this time frame, he married and his two children were born. He had a rapid career trajectory on the commercial side of the company given the integration of his science background and business acumen. In his words, "I was becoming more of a business person, and while I was doing well, there was an awakening for me about the 'political' stuff. I never much cared for it—that wasn't me." This was another clue about Max that I would put into perspective only later in the coaching.

By the mid-1990s, Max would have succeeded in key roles in Europe and Asia, as well as in North America. His visceral and connective leadership style invariably helped him establish what he termed a "true performance culture" that also focused on people's individual career aspirations. His creation of a "career enhancement" program was "a big deal" in the company, but it was even bigger in the scheme of Max's future aspirations.

When asked about his short-term aspirations, Max said he wanted another global role or to run a business unit. However, he also repeated what he had said after the coaching agenda-setting meeting, "You know, I'm a secret HR guy and what I'd really like to do is be a global developer of people—a super good match-maker helping people get into roles they'd be happiest in and do good for the company, too." After probing the seeming conflict between Max's wanting a big commercial role and his "secret" HR aspiration, I realized the former was the psychological residue that he needed to clear before pursuing anything else.

At the end of the history-taking meeting, I introduced the Visual Leadership Metaphor® (VLM) by asking Max to describe himself in three stages of leadership. Specifically, how he saw himself currently as a leader, how he would see himself as he made progress in coaching, and his future view of himself given success in coaching. I explained that this would be a tool for us to gauge his coaching progress (see figure 6.1 for his VLM).

While Max said he wanted to run a business, it was clear from his VLM that the most compelling aspect of that was aiding the development of others. Max's "match maker" (see frame 3 of his

**Figure 6.1** Max's Visual Leadership Metaphor® (VLM).

*Drawing by Joe Williams*

| FRAME 1 | FRAME 2 | FRAME 3 |
| --- | --- | --- |
| Implementer — the person who's making something happen. Metaphorically, it's like the person who's getting the right people (men and women) on the bus, and the wrong people off the bus. Everybody is doing the role he/she needs to be doing— everyone is in the right seat. | Captain of a boat — there are a number of people (men and women) in a boat and I'm at the helm. We're moving fast, we're having fun, and we're definitely going some place— we have a destination and we're on track for getting there. I'm over-seeing the trip and we're excited about where we're going. | Match Maker — I'm like a traffic cop at a very busy intersection. I'm keeping the flow going right … making sure everyone is going where he/she needs to be going. I'm making those connections for people in a way that's right and really meaningful for them. |

VLM) was code for his long-held albeit contained desire to focus his career on coaching and talent management. This, in combination with Max's comment in our first meeting about wanting to watch me as a coach, signaled the intensity of this career aspiration.

## FEEDBACK PHASE

### *Test Results*

Taken as a whole, the results of the battery of psychological tests[1] underscored Max's significant strengths as a sales executive. These included his superior analytical reasoning and appetite for problem-solving, fluid and engaging personality, outgoing and open orientation to others, and strong emotional intelligence. Clues for development included his underlying anxiety, impatience, and a degree of disorganization that prompted him to say, "I really need to de-clutter."

By the end of our feedback discussion, it was clear that Max needed to be in a role that was fast-paced, complex, and interesting enough to ensure his focused attention. Not surprising, it was also clear that he felt uncertain about his future. In his words, "It's good to be a Senior Vice President, I guess but this role is just not exciting for me. I don't have a plan for the future, and I don't do well when I don't have a plan, so I'm a little more all over the place than usual." In that moment, I could have probed what he meant by a "plan"—but we would get to that later.

### Organization-Based (360) Data

This organization input highlighted Max's distinctive strengths and key development areas. The top strengths were strategic vision, innate intelligence, bias for action, relationship-building (authenticity and integrity), his focus on getting the right people in the right roles, and (surprise, surprise) people development. The development areas tracked with what was said in the coaching agenda-setting meeting: (1) focus—not spreading himself too thin, less multitasking, (2) better time management, and (3) political savvy—building relationships with key senior stakeholders in the company.

Given the integration of all the data, we agreed that the coaching would concentrate on three interrelated areas: (1) focus—his staying riveted on key business objectives (not overcommitting, saying "no" more), (2) executive presence—increasing this through clear and influential communication, and (3) relationship-building with other senior executives.

### Case Formulation

While Max's progress on the identified coaching areas would increase his effectiveness as a leader, he was, in fact, quite ambivalent about his current role, and he was also at a critical crossroads in his career. I would have to monitor this tension, ensure traction with Max in the coaching, pace necessary truth-telling with him, and manage the boundary of confidentiality I had established at the outset of the coaching.[2]

I thought the best path forward initially was to stay focused on Max getting settled in his current role, his building a solid rapport with his new boss, and my helping him develop new habits that would enable him to be even more effective. Fortuitously, my long history consulting to his company included the coaching of his boss. Surely, this would give Max and me much grist for the coaching mill.[3]

While the parameters of this coaching engagement were clear, I knew, given Max's underlying restlessness and limited opportunity to advance further in the company (there were few business unit leader roles), that he would benefit from additional coaching beyond the time frame of the initial contract. I believed it would be in the best interests of both Max and the organization if he had a safe and objective place in which to weigh his considerations about the future. This meant that I would have to influence the paying sponsor to extend the coaching engagement.[4]

This last point warrants particular attention because it raises a tricky consulting issue. What do you do when there's a gap between a client's aspirations and available career opportunities in the company? With Max, I knew his interest in running a business unit would likely not be realized despite his growth in coaching. There were at least three or four other executives who aspired to the same goal—including his boss. I also knew, as indicated earlier, that this interest was more of an "unfinished business" objective for Max in his corporate career than it was a true aspiration.

My approach to handling this issue would have to center on an ongoing collaboration with the boss and HR professional. While guarding confidentiality, I would convey Max's restlessness for his next role. Of note was the fact that Max was a much beloved and respected senior executive in the sales organization. Therefore, if the company recognized him as a retention risk, it was preferable for him to be well-supported in his career planning efforts so that if he chose to leave the company, this occurred in the most positive way possible. I believed this would enable me to extend the original coaching contract.

Finally, given Max's underlying sensitivity, I would need to dose the coaching with my positive expectations as a way of reinforcing his optimism about the future—both short and longer term.[5]

## COACHING PHASE

### *Specific Actions Yield Progress*

At the outset of the coaching, Max and I agreed that a set of inter-related actions would set the stage for the rest of our work. He recognized that his highly intuitive and spontaneous approach would not serve him as well in his SVP role—and especially not with a boss who was considerably more methodical and organized than he. I urged Max to: (1) ensure clarity of objectives, accountabilities, and timelines; (2) develop a better follow-up system; and (3) provide more lead time when planning team activities.

After Max said, "I need to have a brutal focus," I introduced an exercise I call *The Driving Force*.[6] This coaching tool was positioned as an aid for his staying focused on his most pressing business priorities and his saying "no" to any requests that would siphon time away from these priorities. Over time, this proved to be a helpful coaching tool—except when it came to requests he received for informal career mentoring. These he could not resist—another signal about his real passion at work—but we were still not quite ready to address this.

### *More Actions*

Key actions that came out of the 360 feedback included: (1) his having monthly face-to-face meetings with his boss to ensure alignment on objectives and concrete results, that is, his not confusing activity with results; (2) the need to step away from his previous regional role and grasp the multi-regional responsibility of his new job; and (3) monitoring his pace to ensure better work-personal integration. On this last point, a number of people had expressed concern that Max not "burn out" given the travel demands of his SVP responsibilities.

### *The Working Alliance*

During the next several months, our working alliance solidified, and Max gained important insights with implications for his leadership effectiveness. As in any coaching process, the working alliance between coach and client is central to a positive outcome. Three meta factors—traction, trust, and truth-telling—significantly influence this working alliance.[7] The data-gathering, including content from the coaching agenda-setting meeting, helped ensure traction through the clear identification of coaching goals. This was amplified further by Max's intention to learn and by the VLM that depicted specific phases of the coaching and its ultimate goal.

Further, my rapid connection with Max, making it safe for him to be vulnerable, and maintaining the boundary of confidentiality, as stated at the outset of the coaching, all contributed to a high trust factor. Finally, truth-telling was provided in an empathic manner that ensured Max heard what he needed to hear about his three coaching areas. Later, explicit truth-telling conversations about a potential career change influenced his courageous decision-making.

### Key Insights

Four insights in particular had enduring effects during the first year and a half of the work with Max.

#### Insight #1: The "Rejected Outsider"

While probing why he continued to overcommit (coaching goal: maintaining focus on key objectives), Max said, "I have a real fear of saying 'no.' I don't want to be acting like a big deal, and I don't want people feeling rejected." Helping Max reframe "acting like a big deal" to "acting like the senior executive I am" was helpful. On a deeper level, we examined his greater affinity for the "little guy," and how this affected his self-perception, and even had implications for the coaching area of building relationships with senior executives. I said, "If you don't feel like a senior executive, if you are harboring negative thoughts about being this, you will sabotage the likelihood of your building these necessary relationships."

What also emerged was Max's concern about the potential of others "feeling rejected." I suggested that this might be a projection based on his own early history of having been the "rejected outsider." Making this link seemed helpful in the moment but given the parameters of the coaching model, I question if it had as much impact as would have been the case in a clinical intervention in which we would have mined this insight more deeply.

*Insight #2: Need for Affirmation*

Despite all of Max's many talents and distinctive capabilities, he was prone to periods of self-doubt. Even after weaving together key themes from his life history, the psychometric findings, and his impressive career successes, his confidence could falter and optimism about the future would wane. Not ready to tackle the underlying existential issue yet, I stayed in the present asking, "What's really getting in the way of your being fully confident? This doesn't make sense in the presence of all your talent and accomplishments."

Max responded, "When I get tired, I can think crazy thoughts and I can really let self- doubts creep in. I think that executives are not really honest with each other here, and also senior leaders don't acknowledge people very much—so you can feel like you're left in limbo."

I underscored that for most people their defenses against self-doubt, for example, let down when they're tired. Since Max had a lifelong pattern of masking his underlying self-doubts and sensitivity, I also emphasized how this emotional containment could build and erupt into episodes of vulnerability. Further, in the safety of the coaching relationship, we discussed how his sensitivity was spiked in this corporate atmosphere where he felt increasingly alienated. Privately, I reflected that our working alliance was thriving given his possible positive maternal transference, that is, his coach as the mother who was indeed "hugging him enough." There was no "limbo" in our relationship.

*Insight #3: Need for Affiliation*

Max began one of our coaching meetings with a quote from Pulitzer Prize–winning journalist Walter Lippmann, "Ignore what a man desires and you ignore the very sources of his power." In discussing this with Max, I gained a deeper understanding of the importance of his relationships. Max's life was a vibrant fabric woven tightly on the strength of him as a husband, a father, a colleague, and a friend. Affiliation with others mattered mightily for Max.

In pursuing what Max really desired to do next, we recognized the possibility of a middle path or bridge between his current sales leadership role and his going entrepreneurial. This would involve his seeking an opportunity to run a business elsewhere. When such an opportunity actually occurred, perhaps I should not have been surprised regarding Max's reticence to leave his current employer. Clearly, I had underestimated the strength of his affiliation need.

*Insight #4: Interaction between "Being Different" and Self-Actualization*

As the coaching progressed, and especially as we were working on the executive presence issue, Max often asked me what I thought of various senior executives in his company. While I was circumspect about whom I had worked with, I knew that these questions were, at least on some level, related to his underlying anxiety about whether he measured up or not. In one of the more humorous examples of this, Max asked me if I thought he should be replacing his Timex with a "power watch." I didn't answer that question directly, but I did notice that some weeks later Max was wearing a more expensive timepiece.

At one opportune moment, I offered the interpretive question, "Do you think there's something about your early years that may be muting your sense of power now and your belief in becoming self-actualized?" This opened a fruitful discussion when for the first—and only—time we touched on race.[8] Max reflected aloud on his negative childhood experiences of being the "different one" and how that might have implications for the present. It was complicated—and while we never had a full conversation about it—he agreed that his psychological introject of "being different" had adverse effects on his maintaining a steady state of self-confidence.

## COACHING PHASE

### *Input from Boss and HR*

Despite the combination of insights, tools, and actions that contributed to Max's progress in coaching, I wasn't certain that his star was still rising in the company. In conversations with Max's boss and HR partner, they both noted his progress but also mentioned how he continued to overcommit himself—especially to anything that involved people's careers. I knew this was code for "Max is not driving the results we need him to be driving," so I aggressively probed his pattern of overcommitting.

Max's response brought us right back to the beginning, "My passion at work—what gives me the greatest sense of purpose—is about helping people with their careers. I wish I could be the Chief People Officer!" Staying true to the coaching agenda, I tried to integrate Max's passionate interest with the demands of his current role. I emphasized the need for him to: (1) make tough people decisions, (2) do the necessary blocking and tackling so his people could drive sales results, and (3) accelerate his efforts to, in his words, "touch their souls so they don't just feel like cogs on a wheel."

### The Most Significant Insight

In the second year of the coaching, Max gained what appeared to be the most significant insight in his coaching. Knowing that he was an avid golfer, I said I thought he was at risk for hitting a plateau in the company if he didn't stop "under-clubbing" when he was with his boss. This interpretation influenced Max's decision to "step up, not back" in his interactions with not just his boss but with other key senior executives as well.

This interpretation also ignited a pivotal coaching conversation in which Max said, "Wow, that's it! My lifelong pattern has been about me under-clubbing! I'm really old enough now to stop and think more about what club I'm using versus the club I *need* to be using."

To reinforce this powerful insight, I sent Max an email immediately after that meeting which read in part: "I urge you to 'work' with the golf under-clubbing metaphor. This insight will prove useful as you continue to gain mileage in your executive presence development area. It can also be insurance against behavior regression, i.e., a tool for you to keep your phantoms at bay."

## Consolidation Phase

By the middle of year two in the coaching, we moved into the consolidation phase of the coaching. Max had A's on his Coaching Report Card[9] in the areas of (1) focus on key objectives and (2) building key relationships. He gave himself a B+ on executive presence in terms of his more crisp and clear communication. It appeared he would make further progress in this area given his commitment to: (1) *breathing* as he spoke, (2) minimizing his bad verbal habit of saying "you know" too much, (3) completing a thought before jumping to another, and (4) his creating enough space for others to insert their thoughts.

Max also believed he had moved into the third frame of his VLM. However, by the end of this second year, he was still preoccupied with what he really wanted to do in his career. His ongoing existential concern was reflected in statements such as, "Yeah, this is going well, but am I really having all the impact I could?" And, "What's my purpose? What's the meaning of my work?"

### Sudden Turn of Events

Right at the end of the second year of coaching, one of Max's former bosses—someone who had left the company for a major role elsewhere—offered to make Max the General Manager of a global business unit. Max was interested, and I knew this was awkward territory that had to be navigated carefully with due concern for both Max and his company.

For Max, I wanted to assist in his making a wise decision, that is, not jump to another job because he was unhappy where he was. For the company, I needed to influence Max's having the necessary conversation with his boss, in particular, so he could have a chance to counteroffer if he so chose. Further, Max would need to communicate appropriately with his sales organization and to make a dignified exit if that was what he ultimately decided to do.

I gave Max something called the *Stay-Go Exercise* as a tool for his assessing the pros and cons of his staying or leaving his current employer (see figure 6.2). When it was clear that Max was ready to "go," I helped him prepare for the conversation with his boss whom I knew was not going to be caught off-guard because I had

**Figure 6.2** Stay-Go Exercise.

**Exercise instruction:**
1 To make this exercise as relevant as possible to your current situation:
   o Read all the factors
   o IGNORE factors that do not apply
   o Add new factors under the "Other" section—factors that match your current situation
   o Make a copy of this exercise *before* you fill it out. You may want to have someone who knows you well fill it out independent of you. Comparing your respective ratings should prove useful.

2 Rate each factor on a 1–5 scale, with 5 as the highest rating. For each relevant factor, place a rating in *both* the **Stay** and **Go** columns.
   For example, if you think the *Relationship with Boss* factor is very negative, you would put a 1 or 2 under **STAY** and a 4 or 5 under **GO**.

   Conversely, if you think the *Opportunity to Learn* factor is quite positive, as compared to another company, you would put a 4 or 5 under **STAY** and a 1 or 2 under **GO**.

3 Add the scores you've placed in both columns. A big difference (more than 10 points) in the **STAY-GO** ratings is a clear signal in favor of the **STAY** or **GO** option, i.e., the column with the highest score.

4 If there is not a big difference in the **STAY-GO** ratings, this indicates a caution for you to reflect carefully and make sure you do not make an impetuous decision.

Rate factors on a 1–5 scale, 5 being highest

| Factors | Stay | Go |
|---|---|---|
| Autonomy—level of empowerment | | |
| Creative latitude—freedom to pursue/apply one's own ideas | | |
| Daily level of stress | | |
| Desire to pursue something different altogether (e.g., MBA, law school, another career objective) | | |
| Intellectual stimulation | | |
| Job security | | |
| Money (current) | | |
| Money (future potential) | | |
| Pace of work—fast, medium, or slow | | |
| Peerage—relationships with peers foster real collaboration | | |
| Potential for bigger role in the organization | | |

*Continued*

**Figure 6.2**  Continued

| | | |
|---|---|---|
| Power—ability to influence boss and others | | |
| Professional legacy—work provides opportunity to mentor, teach, influence others | | |
| Recognition—stature, respect for work done | | |
| Relationship with boss—effects of this in terms of mood, morale, motivation | | |
| Relationships (colleagues, staff) | | |
| Resources—staff and other resources needed to meet job objectives | | |
| Self-actualization—becoming all one can be | | |
| Span of impact | | |
| Travel—enough opportunity to travel; travel is not excessive | | |
| Visibility to senior management and the board | | |
| Work environment/location—comfort, positive aesthetics, reasonable commute | | |
| Work-personal integration; negative effects of role on personal life | | |
| *Other factor (if any)* | | |
| *Other factor (if any)* | | |
| *Other factor (if any)* | | |
| **TOTALS** | | |

conveyed Max's career unrest to him many months earlier. I later helped Max craft his resignation letter.

In one of our last coaching meetings, Max brought me a gift. It was a wooden plaque with a golden golf ball placed over two crossed golf clubs. The inscription below read, "For My Life Caddy, guiding the way 'off the course' in selecting the right club, shaping the shot, and finishing the putt." It seemed to be an especially fitting way to conclude the consolidation phase of his coaching.

### POST COACHING: A NEW BEGINNING, AND BRIDGE TO THE FUTURE

Max and I contracted for me to support his assimilation into his new General Manager role. While he did well, he wasn't content. In his words, "I was in the wrong seat on the bus." Both Max and his management realized this, but their emphatic message to him was *we want you on this bus, so what else would you want to do here?* Max worked with a senior human resources professional in the company and attempted to create a role that was focused on building people development processes in the organization. However, the company was really not ready for what Max had to offer, and he decided to leave. In his words, "I just didn't want to stay and slug it out to fit into that role." He was now ready to pursue his reinvention in earnest.

At that point, I referred him to a career management consultant so he could start crafting an exit plan that included his getting a good financial package from his current employer and creating a focused plan to pursue his next career chapter or, as he once put it, "How I'm going to escape from corporate."

This was both an anxious and intoxicating time for Max. Within a year, he decided to establish a consulting practice focused on leadership development and career management. He attended coaching courses, wrote promotion materials, and used his sales skills to develop an initial flow of business. While I was no longer working with him, he stayed in touch often seeking advice about his coaching activities and business development efforts. While he would experience the inevitable pangs of starting a new business, the fireflies became a constant.

### DISCUSSION

The most challenging aspect of this case was meeting the agreed upon objectives of the coaching engagement, that is, not letting them be overwhelmed by Max's emerging interest in a striking career change. His signals about being a "closet HR guy" could not have been clearer, nor could his aversion to the political dynamics of his corporate life have been stronger. In short, our work unfolded in two distinct phases spread over a two-year time frame.

In phase one, we focused on Max making progress in areas that helped him be more effective in his senior corporate role. The challenge in phase two was to manage the coaching focus in a manner that (1) helped him make sound decisions about his future, and (2) was understood and supported by Max's boss. This necessitated my close and ongoing collaboration with both the boss and his HR Director—up to and including Max's decision to leave the company.

Phase two of this coaching necessitated enough trust in the relationship with Max that I could press hard about the soundness of what he was envisioning as his path forward. Was he in an existential crisis given the seeming plateau he had hit in his company? Did he need to do another big corporate job? (He did.) Was he really willing to step off the corporate track and launch a mid-life reinvention? (He was.)

Increasingly, it became clear that the combination of Max's many strengths and personal characteristics made him well-suited for the career and leadership coaching he had long yearned to pursue doing as a consultant. These factors coupled with his passion for the work, track record of success in advising others informally about their careers, and his sales background boded well for his making this turn in his career. Further, it appeared that significant insights revealed in the coaching would abet his successful career transition. Specifically, he had made progress in resolving feelings of being the "rejected outsider." He had placed his needs for affirmation and affiliation in perspective and it appeared these would be better met in his new career. And he had placed himself on a path that would likely lead to his desired self-actualization. Max would, in my view, not underclub his career reinvention. Instead, he would integrate all of his life experiences and insights in a manner that would reward others—as well as himself.

## Conclusion

This executive coaching case study underscores the responsibility of a coach to the sponsoring organization—especially when the engagement is pulled into an unforeseen direction by the force of the coached executive's underlying objectives. Given Max's charm, candor, and emerging urgency about pursuing the work he believed he was destined to do, it was a challenge to keep the coaching focused on the leader development issues as framed by the company. In the end, a combination of factors prevented the coaching from derailing, and resulted in a satisfactory outcome for both Max and the company. These factors included: (1) the firm sequencing of the issues "worked" in the coaching (company foci first and then Max's career aspirations); (2) the coach's close collaboration and transparency (while still respecting confidentiality) with both the boss and HR partner; (3) adequate time (an extended coaching contract) to make progress on the initial coaching areas, and to influence his subsequent career decisions; and (4) the pacing of deep personal insights and use of interpretive questions.

While the boss would have preferred Max remain with the company, he understood Max's decision to leave and run a business unit elsewhere—as he harbored that same aspiration. What he could not have anticipated was Max's *next* career move—the one that would take him out of his career closet and into the light of an even more compelling aspiration. Rarely had I witnessed such a midlife turnabout. Some years after his "corporate escape," as he called it, Max and I met for coffee, and I heard his existential contentment when he said, "I love the song I'm singing now." Max had escaped *into himself*—a full set of golf clubs at his ready disposal.

# Executive's Reflection

"It's like a valuable caddy helping a golfer to get around the course and do well." That is the way I describe the coaching experiences I have had with Karol. I had the opportunity to work with her in different stages of my career, but the initial engagement occurred as I moved into a national and more complex senior leadership role at a major multinational organization. The challenges included an increased scope, leading a larger team with a tenfold increase in headcount, as well as navigating the nuances and dynamics that exist in a headquarters role. The coaching support provided me with a structured and safe sanctuary that proved to be invaluable as I made the transition.

After a base line determination of my strengths, traits, professional liabilities, and our initial discussion sessions, the developmental priorities became crystal clear. Our sessions worked well because discussion was safe, objective, and highly relevant to my actual work experiences. The importance of truth-telling and authenticity rang through each session and continues to ring constantly with me as one of the most critical factors for effective leadership. Subsequent sessions led to more self-reflection, greater self-discovery, and ultimately an increased sense of self-awareness. Taking some of the nuggets gained and applying them in various real-time work situations fueled our discussions.

Some development needs were easier to address, such as prioritization and time management, but others were harder to understand and subsequently were more challenging to address. An example, and an important development need that was identified was my tendency frequently to "hold back." In certain situations, instead of taking a bold position, or stepping up to be heard, I would refrain from stretching beyond my comfort zone. This attribute could result in a myriad of negative professional consequences for an executive, so we explored potential reasons or triggers for this tendency in order to address it.

After some initial tap dancing around the sensitive topic of race, our ability to have candid discussions allowed us to consider the environment of my childhood. Until high school, I had, in fact, always been in the setting of being the only, or one of a very few, African Americans in a majority white setting. Did I condition myself over the years to try to blend in and not stand out or not be too different from everyone else? Did that experience have a professional impact in my adult life? Although deeper analysis might provide more definitive answers, having open discussions were helpful in addressing the issue, and I made notable progress stepping beyond what was comfortable to me—with being bolder in general.

As a result of this coaching engagement, I made changes that I believe resulted in greater contributions to many decisions related to the business performance and employee engagement in the organization. In addition, self-reflection has become a valuable tool for me to slow down the pace for evaluation, perspective, and self-control, as well as for planning. A key realization was that sometimes one has to slow down to be more effective.

After 21 years with this company, I accepted a broader and more challenging position as a General Manager for another large multinational company. I continued to work with Karol as she supported my efforts to navigate through the unfamiliar waters of a foreign role. The progress made from the coaching support in my prior position proved to be useful early in my new assignment. The emphasis that the coaching placed on choosing the right priorities was helpful as there were multiple challenges from the onset. My prior coaching had conditioned me to keep my focus on items with the greatest impact and to weigh rigorously the benefits of impact versus activity. With a robust workload, as well as a constant stream of meetings and people requiring my attention, the time management coaching enabled me to be a more effective leader; to be more in command and more disciplined, too. The progress I made on being bolder made my new role more manageable since I had several new functional areas of responsibility as well as a greatly expanded scope of accountability in the organization.

Without a great deal of knowledge or experience in the field, I had to step up to lead a large cross-functional team with confidence, which the coaching had prepared me for. The coaching and reflecting provided me with the self-confidence ultimately to acknowledge and accept that the skill set required for the highest level of performance in that role was not the optimal fit with my skill set or my professional interests. Despite the multiple learning experiences, exposure to new functions and successful contributions made, I decided it was more prudent to leave the position after two years versus continuing to try to squeeze a "square peg into a round role." This action was a huge return on investment for the coaching I received. I was now not only emboldened to step up and stretch beyond what was comfortable, but I was ready to begin a journey seeking professional authenticity.

The pursuit was to combine my natural strengths, and the skill set that I developed over a 25-year career as a contributor and leader, with my passion for talent development in a way to help leaders (especially new and emerging leaders) and their teams deliver higher performance and to be all that they can be. With an uncertain path and endpoint in front of me on this journey, it was the many sessions of coaching that continued to pay dividends. Knowing and trusting my strengths, conquering fear, being as authentic you can be, and focusing on the right priorities were a few of the guiding principles that helped in the journey. As Karol continued to provide coaching and guidance which blended into mentorship, I established an independent company focused on organizational health to advise, coach, and teach leaders and their teams to deliver higher performance. Many of the principles and methods used during my coaching tenure with Karol have become a part of my operating principles.

# CHAPTER 7

# Fighting the Force of Old Habits

This case involves a senior leader's efforts to change the force of old habits, thus making him a stronger CEO succession candidate. The engagement unfolded over four years: (1) the initial phase of coaching, (2) the middle phase, (3) a consolidation phase, and (4) a final coalescence of his learning and behavior change. The work was enriched by the active participation of the organization's CEO and another external consultant who guided leadership development initiatives for members of the CEO's leadership team in this financial services company.

Further, the working relationship among the CEO, external consultant, coached executive, and coach was characterized throughout by high levels of collaboration and transparency. Given the quality of their partnership, this engagement may be considered as a model for leveraging corporate investment in executive coaching.

## THE REFERRAL

This executive coaching referral is an excellent example of how social interaction can lead to a business opportunity. At a year-end holiday party, I met a partner in a strategy development firm who was consulting to Remington, the company in this case. Sometime later when the CEO asked this strategy consultant for the name of a senior executive coach, he remembered our conversation and called me. Since the referral matched my experience, I sent him my resume, which he forwarded to the CEO. When the CEO and I spoke, he described his CFO whom he saw as a strong internal candidate to succeed him but he would need to develop his leadership ability further to be ready for the demands of the CEO role. We agreed that I would have an introductory "chemistry check" meeting with Walt, the CFO.

## INTRODUCTORY "CHEMISTRY CHECK" MEETING

Walt was right out of central-casting—he resembled the tall, handsome, fit, and impeccably groomed candidate for president, or senator, or surely for CEO. While reserved by nature—a factor of great significance throughout the coaching—he also possessed a certain warmth that peaked through his focused intensity. After I answered his questions about my approach and experience, I gauged his interest in the coaching by asking, "Why coaching now; how might this be helpful to you?"

Walt's responses indicated varying degrees of self-awareness, ambition, and readiness for coaching. In his words,

> The CEO benefited from coaching before he was appointed to his role, and I'm always open to new learning. Frankly, if faced with the choice, I'd rather continue to be a highly successful CFO than a mediocre CEO—as I firmly believe that anything worth doing is worth doing well. I think the primary focus for me is going to be emotional intelligence (EQ) because I want to better connect with people and display more empathy, too.

This tracked with the conversation I had had with the CEO and with my initial impression of Walt. Then he added, "I believe I need to have the answers whatever role I'm in; I take this on my shoulders. Having the right answers is really key." This behavior was also confirmed by the external consultant who would later design and implement the company's CEO succession planning process. He saw Walt's need to have all the answers and/or to always comment on issues—versus listening more deeply—as a limiting leadership behavior. He believed that Walt needed to learn how to sit back and be more thoughtful and deliberate especially in leadership team meetings when substantive issues were being debated. Walt's description of his behavior reminded me of a Socrates quote about how great leaders must give up the force of their habits. I knew that if I was to work with Walt, we would have to explore his leadership habits, and seek to modify them with behaviors that would strengthen his potential for becoming CEO.

What I didn't appreciate fully at the time was the extent to which the force of Walt's habits helped him defend against underlying fears of failure. While he had actually put it right out there in essence telling me, "I would rather be good at this (CFO) than fail at that (CEO)," I didn't catch this in our first meeting—but surely would later.

The "chemistry check" went well, and within a few days Walt called to say the coaching was a "go." The next step would be an "agenda-setting meeting" that I would facilitate among the CEO, the external consultant, and Walt. As a prelude to this meeting, I had a teleconference with the external consultant, Ian, in an effort to learn more about the Remington culture and other relevant facts related to the coaching.

## COMPANY CULTURE AND OTHER RELEVANT FACTS

Ian gave a thumbnail description of Remington as highly traditional, serious, analytical, cautious, and caring. While he said leaders—including the CEO—were prone to some degree of micromanaging, I would not have to worry about my boundary of confidentiality being compromised. However, he stressed that the CEO would expect a regular flow of information that would guide his reports to the board regarding Walt's progress and readiness to succeed him. I concurred, and also emphasized that I did not expect to cast a "vote" about Walt as the CEO choice. This had important implications for my level of trust with Walt whom I saw as my client and Remington as the paying sponsor.

Ian also shared information that he had included in a recent report to the board. He had highlighted Walt's significant strengths and also stressed a need for the development of his leadership behavior. He believed Walt had great potential to become CEO but only if he made progress on *how* he led. He needed to be more self-aware and build closer relationships with all key stakeholders—including board members. This behavioral dimension of leadership was not to be underestimated in its importance at Remington. Given my own research and writing, I understood this completely.[1]

### First Interaction with the CEO

A "live" conversation with the CEO a few weeks before the designated agenda-setting meeting was especially enlightening and set the stage well for everything to follow. I was struck by his intensity, warmth, clarity, and comfort with his own vulnerability. Emblematic of what I have described as a "remarkable" leader, he integrated left brain analytical ability with right brain conceptual strength, appeared to have strong EQ, and his ego was surely in the service of his company.[2]

He was both engaging and forthcoming saying that his retirement "clock" was somewhere between two and four years. To a significant degree this timing would depend on the readiness of a successor. While he praised Walt's intelligence and business acumen, he echoed Ian's comments about the leadership "how" issue. As our meeting ended, he said, "It would be great if Walt could succeed me but only if he develops his leadership capacity. My concern is that he doesn't appreciate the magnitude of the gap. He was shaken when I first spoke to him about it, but he said it was something he could address." I knew I would have to probe this "gap" issue in the upcoming agenda-setting meeting; both Walt and I needed to gauge the extent to which his focus on the intellectual and technical demands of the CEO role was occurring at the expense of his grasping the importance of the leadership *behavior* dimension.

### Agenda-Setting Meeting: A Strong
### Collaboration Takes Shape

With the CEO, Walt, and Ian present, I facilitated a discussion that included a description of my coaching model (data-gathering, feedback, coaching, and consolidation), time frame (12–14 months), our respective roles, the boundaries of confidentiality, and the areas for coaching. We agreed that rather than my gathering 360 data upfront, I would draw this organization-based information midway in the coaching as a way of assessing Walt's progress.

The discussion of the areas that needed to be addressed in the coaching was encouraging but also candid and specific in ways that seemed to surprise Walt and was additive for me. As in my first meeting with him, he said he needed to develop his EQ so he interacted with people in a "more personal and influential" manner. Ian agreed but was also quick to amplify Walt's development agenda. He emphasized the need for Walt (1) to deal with problematic personnel issues more quickly instead of putting "spin" on them as "not so serious," and (2) to form more collaborative working relationships with his peers thus increasing their readiness to follow him.

The CEO was equally candid. He told Walt that the board wanted a different kind of relationship with him, that is, one that didn't make them feel like they'd "invaded his space" when they asked him questions. He said Walt's presentations could be too dense with technical detail and that he could come across as condescending and pedantic instead of being well-attuned to his audience. The CEO pressed on with, "You're not yet showing the level of maturity that we need to see in a CEO." When Walt asked if the situation was insurmountable, the CEO said, "Not at all—if you make the necessary changes in your leadership behavior."

This brought the moment for me to probe the "magnitude of the gap" issue. The CEO said, "It's sizeable. In terms of succession, on a scale of 10, I'd like Walt to be a consensus of an 8–9 among the Board members but right now, he's only a 5–7. The big question, as I've stated, is all about leadership behavior —the confidence he projects as a leader and the way he connects to people." Walt responded by saying he was a good learner and looked forward to addressing the issues in his coaching.

In my concluding comments, I emphasized how well-aligned the CEO and Ian were in their view of Walt's development need and that Walt's progress, that is, his adapting his leadership behavior, would pivot on his giving up leadership habits that were no longer serving him well. These habits included the way he had been presenting to the board and the transactional manner in which he related to others. I acknowledged the strong collaborative effort we were forming, and I encouraged the CEO and Ian to provide Walt with (1) positive reinforcement when they observed specific instances of progress, and (2) constructive feedback when/if they witnessed his lack of progress and/or any regression.

## DATA-GATHERING AND FEEDBACK PHASES

The data-gathering phase began with an effort to learn as much as I could about Walt in as efficient and rapid a manner as possible. I took his life history (starting at birth) and gave him a battery of psychological measures.[3] In an extensive feedback meeting a few weeks later, I integrated this information in a manner that focused on his leadership behavior.

Based on the thematic material in his life history, I discovered the underlying basis of his reserved nature. I could surmise how this behavior influenced the quality of his work relationships, as well as perceptions of him as a leader. His father was an academic, highly analytical, introverted, and stoic in nature. While his mother was more outgoing, she maintained high standards for Walt and his younger brother, insisting that there was always a "proper way" of doing things and that they needed to stay focused on their accomplishments.

It was not surprising to learn that Walt did very well in school, always getting high grades and never being a disciplinary problem. He gravitated toward subjects that involved facts and numbers, and he was also a good athlete who played soccer his entire life. He observed, "Since I was reserved and shy, I was a tad delayed socially, but I always knew where I stood on a sports field." Embedded in this comment was a clue about his deeply competitive nature—something Walt said he had learned to modulate over time. However, I wondered if Ian's comment in the agenda-setting meeting about Walt needing to be more mindful of his peer relationships connected to a remnant of Walt's intense and individualistic drive to compete.

Walt studied engineering at an Ivy League school, and he later received an MBA from another prestigious university where he graduated near the top of his class. After success with a few major employers, he joined Remington as CFO. The culture of this smaller company felt right, he respected its leadership, and he could envision completing his career there.

The psychometric data supported Walt as a strong candidate in the CEO succession process. This data tracked with Ian's findings especially in terms of Walt's significant innate and analytic reasoning strengths. However, there were two points that warranted particular attention. First, Walt was eager to please and preferred to avoid conflict. In my mind this finding helped clarify the point that Ian had made about how Walt could "spin," that is, minimize the seriousness of issues in his team. Second, his emotional intelligence tested as higher than average. This indicated that the development issue was not about the need to increase EQ as much as it was about his using the EQ he had. It appeared that Walt's reserved nature masked the fullness of his interpersonal capabilities; we would have to focus on getting him *out of himself.*

### Case Formulation

It was clear how Walt's major life history themes and the habits that flowed from them had worked well for him. However, I would need to help him see them as strengths in excess, that is, as potential barriers to achieving his current career aspiration. In addition to his reserved nature, other themes that would have to be explored included his: (1) preference for figuring things out himself, (2) needing to always have the right answers, and (3) his quest for perfection. I would need to help Walt see that the intensity of his self-imposed performance standards could trump the give-and-take of team-based leadership—his CEO's preference, and a highly valued leadership behavior at Remington. These performance standards could also diminish Walt's empowerment of members of his own (finance) leadership team.

I would weave together what we had heard from the CEO and Ian in the agenda-setting meeting, Walt's major life history themes, and the psychometric data to arrive at the foci for the coaching phase. I would use two specific coaching tools: (1) the Visual

Leadership Metaphor® (VLM), and (2) a coaching report card to track our progress on established coaching goals. And finally, I would leverage fully a close collaboration with the CEO and Ian to ensure that Walt and I were always working with a flow of key collateral information from the organization. Surely their input would help me gauge Walt's efforts *away from* old habits related to interpersonal reserve, perfectionism, and deference to authority (more on this later).

## COACHING PHASE

### *The Interaction of Insights, Actions, and Tools*

Walt and I had agreed on three foci for the initial coaching phase: (1) leveraging his emotional intelligence (being more attuned to others and less transactional in his relationships), (2) managing others (ensuring the right people in the right roles and dealing with staff conflicts in a timely manner), and (3) conveying his strategic thinking (ability to go beyond tactical issues) to the CEO in particular.

At this juncture, I introduced the Visual Leadership Metaphor®,4 another tool I had created for anchoring and tracking coaching progress. I asked Walt to describe how he viewed himself currently as a leader, how he would see himself at his next level of leadership effectiveness, and how he would be leading in the future— assuming his coaching success.

Walt's VLM language and imagery were an accurate depiction of the journey we needed to travel in the coaching (see figure 7.1). I was encouraged by his sequence of (1) *resident expert,* (2) *go-to-guy on the court,* and (3) *coach/manager.* If Walt could evolve into frame 3 of his VLM, he would have made major headway as a leader. In other words, he would be closer to approximating the mature executive presence the CEO said Walt needed to project.

In the coaching phase, Walt and I met face-to face (one and a half hours monthly) for a year, had email "conversation," and I maintained frequent contact with both the CEO and Ian. Further, one of the most important ongoing actions I urged for Walt was his spending as much time as possible in one-to-one meetings with the CEO.

**Figure 7.1** Walt's Visual Leadership Metaphor® (VLM).

*Drawing by Joe Williams*

| FRAME 1 | FRAME 2 | FRAME 3 |
|---|---|---|
| I'm a professor/teacher, the resident expert who's turned to for help with difficult business issues. | I'm like Michael Jordan here—he was the best at what he did on the court and he wanted to coach but he couldn't take himself away from being the go-to guy on the court. | I'm coach/manager here—clearly leading the team, setting direction, motivating people for success, and helping them do their best. |

This frequency would be critical to Walt's conveying the progress his boss expected to see as a result of the investment in coaching.

### Insights

A number of significant insights emerged during the initial phase of Walt's coaching. These interrelated insights were as follows: (1) his perfectionism was a real problem for someone at his level; (2) his aversion for taking anything "half-baked" to the CEO blocked the iterative communication the CEO preferred; (3) his discomfort with ambiguity spurred his "jumping to the end game" in senior team meetings rather than his staying in the questions the CEO was raising for discussion (not solution); and (4) his needs for control and to avoid failure fostered a stiff presentation style, that is, he missed opportunities to "connect" with his audiences—especially board members. These insights highlighted the habits that Walt needed to break.

As can often happen when an executive is being coached, his or her antennae are sharpened in ways that generalize to the personal sphere. For Walt an experience with his son produced a breakthrough insight. In his words, "I went on a retreat with my son, and I learned what a burden it is for him trying to live up to the expectations of a father who always does everything well." We discussed the generalizability of this insight to his relationships at work, and I pointed out that the more *empathic resonance* he had for others, especially in a culture like Remington's, the more effective he would be. I shared a quote from Goleman that emphasized this point: "The fundamental task of leaders is to prime good feeling in those they lead. That occurs when a leader creates resonance—a reservoir of positivity that frees the best in people. At its root then, the primal job of leadership is emotional."[5]

### Actions

There were numerous specific actions discussed in the coaching meetings—actions that if taken consistently could help Walt produce new and better habits. These actions included his: (1) replacing his pursuit of perfection with expectations for achieving *excellence*; (2) ensuring iterative dialogues with the CEO on important business topics; (3) being an active, open participant in leadership team meetings versus jumping to problem-solving or being overly focused on tactical details; and (4) distilling the technical content of his presentations and focusing primarily on ways to foster interactive engagement with his audiences. I also pointed out that he had a habit of rubbing his hands together in a manner that made him look anxious—not the best nonverbal language for the executive presence he wanted to project!

### Tools

The tool of greatest significance for Walt was the discipline of the coaching meetings in which he could think aloud about his development progress and ongoing challenges. Listening to how various events were unfolding at Remington, I served as an objective sounding board highlighting Walt's progress, encouraging his sustained efforts, and citing missed opportunities, too. I remained vigilant for insights that would help accelerate behavioral change, and I captured each meeting's discussion in a detailed written summary for Walt's further reflection between our meetings.

Figure 7.2  SO SMART®—Emotional Intelligence.

| Four Dimensions of EQ | |
|---|---|
| **Self-Observation (SO)**<br>• Awareness—of one's emotions<br>• Accurate assessment of own strengths and weaknesses<br>• Self-confidence<br><br>Core ability: Perceiving emotions | **Self-Management (SM)**<br>• Self-control—can channel emotions effectively<br>• Discipline<br>• Resilience<br>• Motivation—bias for action<br>Core ability: Managing emotions |
| **Attunement (A)**<br>• Focus on others<br>• Empathy<br>• Awareness of organization dynamics<br><br><br>Core ability: Using emotions | **Relationship Traction (RT)**<br>• Authenticity<br>• Influence and persuasion<br>• Consistency<br>• Connecting to others<br>• Collaborative teamwork<br>Core ability: Understanding emotions |

Not surprisingly, another major tool was Walt's learning about EQ and its four dimensions that had been conceptualized in the memorable acronym SO SMART® (see figure 7.2). Throughout the coaching, Walt was encouraged to use the EQ he had by identifying his own emotions, focusing on those of others, expressing his feelings, having empathy for the issues and concerns of others, and forming relationships that were not so process-driven.

Using Walt's Visual Leadership Metaphor®, at the start of a coaching meeting, I frequently asked him, "What frame do you see yourself in now as a leader?" He also graded himself monthly on a personalized coaching report card that focused on his three development areas. Further, given feedback that Walt still needed to be more succinct in his board presentations, I supported the CEO's suggestion that he work with a communications consultant, which he did. The videotaping segment of this consultation proved to be quite helpful.

And, of course, another tool that fostered Walt's growth was his face-to-face time with the CEO. As indicated earlier, the importance of this frequent interaction could not be overstated. I urged Walt to insert himself into his boss's busy travel schedule, to express his strategic views, and not to be unduly deferential in their meetings. To do so, I insisted, would prevent him from conveying his progress and broader leadership capability. However, I was not convinced that Walt carried through on this, and I learned later in the coaching that my concern was warranted—but I'm getting ahead of myself.

## COACHING

### Middle Phase, Time for Input from the Organization

Six months into coaching, Walt and I created an interview protocol for the 360 data-gathering I'd be conducting in the organization.[6]

Figure 7.3  Interview Protocol—360 Data-gathering Questionnaire.

| | |
|---|---|
| 1 | What leadership strengths would you like to see Walt leverage further? |
| 2 | What weaknesses, if any, does he need to focus on/improve to be fully effective as a leader? |
| 3 | 1–10, how aware do you think Walt is of his strengths and weaknesses? |
| 4 | 1–10, how aware do you think he is of the impact of his behavior on others? |
| 5 | 1–10, how effective is Walt at using his emotions—both positive and negative—as a tool for achieving results? |
| 6 | 1–10, how tuned in is Walt to the needs, concerns, issues of others? |
| 7 | 1–10, if you have had a chance to observe him make a presentation to a larger group, how effective was he in terms of connecting to his audience? Any suggestions for how he might be even more effective? |
| 8 | 1–10, how effective is Walt at building relationships with people in all key stakeholder groups? Do his relationships tend to be more transactional or personal? |
| 9 | 1–10, how would you rate his strategic thinking ability? Give me an example of Walt at his strategic best? Give me an example of a time when he missed an opportunity to behave and/or influence an issue in a more strategic way. |
| 10 | 1–10, how would you rate Walt in terms of his managing people effectively? What does he do particularly well? What does he need to improve as a people manager? |
| 11 | Any other observations? |
| 12 | If you were to offer Walt one piece of advice, advice that would enable him to be even more effective than he is now as a leader, what would you tell him? |

These questions can be found in figure 7.3. The protocol was designed to elicit specific information related to the three coaching areas. The sample of respondents included a few board members in addition to Walt's boss, peers, and direct reports.

While the feedback indicated Walt's progress, it also revealed themes consistent with his development agenda. These themes were: (1) the need for him to worry less about being right/having all the answers and more about putting his best strategic thoughts forward; (2) his not letting conflict fester in his organization; (3) increasing his formal communication skill; and (4) enhancing his executive presence by being an active listener, showing more vulnerability, and displaying the simultaneous engagement of both his head and heart.

Walt took the feedback well, and I redoubled my efforts to get him to be overt about his coaching as a way to help close the gap between the progress he'd actually made versus the lag in others' perceptions of that progress. Specifically, I encouraged him to: (1) express his gratitude for the candid input people had provided, (2) tell them what he had learned, (3) convey how he was going to use the feedback, and (4) invite people to provide in-the-moment feedback—especially when/if they saw him regressing into old habits.

### Another Habit to Break

Of note was the fact that after Walt's wife read his feedback report, she commented that he was more emotionally intelligent than people realized—especially in terms of empathy. Her comment, in combination with the EQ psychometric finding, led to an important insight about Walt's habit of *compartmentalization*. In other words, it appeared that Walt behaved differently at work than he did in his private life.

I commented, "Development progress is a lot easier when it's about releasing a behavior that's already there versus trying to build in one that's missing. I'm convinced that you're not using the EQ you've got." The path forward was clear: Walt needed to break the habit of compartmentalizing his behavior. If he could generalize the EQ he displayed in his personal life to the work setting, he would accelerate his developmental progress.

## Serendipity

A few months before the coaching wrap-up meeting, Walt was feeling encouraged by progress made. His most telling statements included: (1) "I don't feel like I have to be the subject matter expert," (2) "I'm thinking more about influencing issues than jumping to solutions," (3) "I'm choosing my words more carefully and trying to connect to audiences better," and (4) "it's about my stepping back and helping my direct reports evolve and develop." And then something serendipitous happened that further fueled his proactive thinking about leadership and his behavior changes.

The CEO and his leadership team attended an offsite leadership retreat in Gettysburg. After this moving experience, Walt reflected in a coaching meeting, "It's all about the power of relationships, isn't it? We saw the contrast of leadership styles at Gettysburg and the fact that one single style is not the answer. We saw that leaders are just people like the rest of us; they're not on a pedestal and they don't need to be perfect. What's key in leadership is adapting to the needs of different people."

This was a coalescent moment in the middle phase of Walt's coaching. He got it on an intellectual level. We would continue to press hard on the emotional level, specifically his integration of the *what* and the *how* of leadership. I referred to this as "total brain leadership" (TBL).[7]

### Middle Phase, CEO Ratings on CEO Succession Criteria

Further evidence of Walt's developmental progress was provided by the CEO who rated him on five primary CEO succession criteria. Walt received "high" ratings on his understanding of the company and on his leading in accordance with its principles. He was rated "good" on his interactions with all key constituencies and vision/ strategy formulation. His one "satisfactory" rating was on team development and people management.

This information, in tandem with the major themes of the 360 data, indicated there was more work to be done on *how* Walt was leading his finance team. I referred to this as the "3R's," that is, his ensuring that he had the *right* people in *right* roles and that he influenced the *right* conditions for them to be successful. Walt would, in fact, make great progress on this.

## CONSOLIDATION PHASE

### *Coaching Wrap-Up Meeting*

Fourteen months after Walt's coaching commenced, the CEO, Walt, Ian, and I met to review progress made and to discuss next steps. In preparation for this meeting, Walt had completed a "coaching consolidation" exercise that revealed gains in each of his development areas—grading all three an "A" on his coaching report card. In addition, he felt that he had moved into frame 3 of his Visual Leadership Metaphor®—now acting more as the coach/manager instead of resident expert.

Walt was rewarded by this conversation. The CEO noted his continued progress and also made an interesting observation, "There's about to be some board turnover so you have a chance to 'start fresh' in their minds; your staying focused on how the entire board prefers to get its information from you will be key going forward. The old board saw you as too process-driven; the new board recognizes your progress away from that."

In terms of future steps, we agreed that I would extend the consolidation phase and meet with Walt once quarterly over the next year to ensure he leveraged gains made. Ian emphasized the need for Walt to stay equally focused on the technical and people competencies of his role. Ian's point was echoed in the CEO's closing comment, "There are two types of leaders—the ones who work through information and the ones who work through people. What Remington needs in a CEO is a hybrid of these two."

Before the first quarterly meeting with Walt, I spoke with the CEO who reported that a number of the board members were continuing to "see a change in Walt." Of note were comments that he was more engaged at a strategic level and more attuned in his interactions with them. The CEO emphasized that Walt would continue to impress board members as he displayed his ability to "consider business issues in a broader context (beyond finance)."

I encouraged the CEO to increase his constructive mentoring of Walt, which I referred to as his *conveyance of wisdom*.

During this phase, many of Walt's comments indicated the consolidation of lessons learned and of insights being applied. At one point he laughed, "I remember what you said about insight being cheap unless you use it, and I'm trying to do this!" His change effort was especially apparent when he said, "One of my bad habits has been my rushing to closure. I really see this now, and I understand that I've done this because I haven't been comfortable with ambiguity. I need to make progress on this." I made an interpretation stating how his intertwined fear of failure and need to control fostered this behavior—behavior that would continue to undercut the view of him as a confident and nondefensive leader.

Walt also noted improvement on another front, "I'm getting better in my large group communications—trying to be looser and less tied to the technical content. I know he (the CEO) wants me to think more like a board member, and I'm focused on this now." And perhaps of particular significance in terms of breaking a lifelong habit was his comment, "I'm also relieving myself of the burden of having to know everything." This relief was apparent in his body language—body language that now looked more relaxed than I had ever seen it. Further, Walt shared his pleasure regarding a recent "EQ moment" at a finance offsite meeting where his team—for the first time—engaged in candid and heartfelt discussions.

Toward the end of the consolidation phase, the CEO indicated that he was thinking of testing Walt's ability to deal with ambiguity by giving him responsibility for another part of the business. When Walt appeared uncertain about how much impact he could have in this area, I reinforced that this was a common step in CEO succession processes and that he should grab it with enthusiasm.[8] I also emphasized that in leading another team in the company, it would be an ideal opportunity for him to reveal his version of total brain leadership (TBL). To reinforce this, I shared a quote from a CEO whose development journey paralleled Walt's: "Leadership is about connecting two points in the longest distance in the world—the one between the head and the heart."[9]

### *Sudden Turn of Events*

When a series of business issues of significant magnitude became evident, the CEO advised, "The CEO role is now viewed by the board as far more complex and demanding. They've asked me to extend my retirement date which has obvious implications for the succession." He went on to emphasize how the company's landscape was changing quickly and placing enormous demands on their strategic planning and priorities. While Walt was still the leading internal candidate to succeed him, it was also clear that a few other internal candidates were under consideration as well.

In the wake of this development, I urged Walt to schedule even more frequent meetings with the CEO. I emphasized, and he understood, that the change in the CEO's expected retirement date was not a reflection on him as much as it was the board's perception of the sitting CEO being "the right leader at the right time." I also helped Walt frame a new set of interrelated leadership development criteria—criteria that reflected conversations both he and I had had with the CEO.

Using these criteria, Walt would now grade himself on a new report card focused on his: (1) greater comfort with ambiguity, (2) delivering his own analytic insights on key issues without being prompted by the CEO, and (3) forging a greater iterative dialogue with the CEO. We used this report card the rest of that year and into the last year (coalescence phase) of our work.

During this consolidation year of quarterly meetings with Walt, I continued communicating with the CEO and Ian. The CEO said he was comfortable with his internal slate of three succession candidates and was optimistic that one of them would be ready to succeed him probably within the next couple of years. He was consistent on the importance of Walt's demonstrating his capacity on the macro themes related to strategic thinking, broader leadership (beyond finance), and building relationships. While I shared this input with Walt, I also urged the CEO to provide it directly as part of his ongoing mentoring of Walt.

### Coach Gets Tough

With Walt, I stressed that this year was the necessary "lab time" for him to solidify progress made especially in terms of moving away from the habits that diminished his executive presence. Walt stated that he knew he had to step up his efforts to be "more aggressive" in projecting his capabilities both to the CEO and to the board. I agreed, and I also pushed back with an admonition, "Walt, we have dug a trench around us on the topic of your executive presence and how you need to project yourself more aggressively. Given all your talent, the insights you've gained, and the progress you've made, what's still getting in the way of your doing this?"

That took us right back to the beginning in terms of Walt's reflexively reserved nature—and confirmed (as indicated earlier) a concern I'd been harboring about the quality of his interactions with the CEO. Walt said he felt strongly about his need to be respectful whenever the CEO was in the room and that this reverence for authority prevented him from expressing his own thoughts—especially if they differed from those of the CEO. I interpreted Walt's black-and-white thinking—the flawed thinking that was not only keeping his "light" out of the room but would scuttle his candidacy as a CEO successor if he didn't alter this behavior.

As a tool, I urged him to practice any number of "qualifying phrases" that could, for example, precede his presenting an alternative view in a senior leadership team meeting. These included, "I know I may be coming at this from left field but..." or "What if we looked at this very differently..." or even "Maybe I'm missing something here, but what if we considered..." I continued to question how comfortable Walt was in making this behavior change. I worried that he wouldn't change enough. I kept searching for a way I could pierce his reserve, delete his reticence, and keep him focused on being his bolder self. I started to think about using metaphor as a tool for change.

### The Power of Metaphor as a Tool for Change

Knowing that Walt was an excellent and avid golfer, I used a golf term metaphorically to illustrate how he was still not applying the fullness of his capabilities and the consequence of that behavior (see chapter 6). Toward the end of the consolidation phase I said, "The more I listen to the CEO, and now as I listen to your explanation of why you're still reserved and reticent with him, you know what I hear? I hear that you're *under-clubbing* big time, and the more you under-club this, the less likely you're going to win." The look on Walt's face was worth the proverbial one thousand words. I'd delivered a core message that really hit the target. As he left my office that day, I wondered if I'd finally found a way to penetrate deeply enough to ignite the forceful and sustained manifestation of his capabilities.

### The CEO/CFO Interpersonal Dynamic

In an updating conversation with Ian, I explained that Walt felt like the CEO was usually more focused on his B's than on his A's whenever he provided feedback to Walt. This didn't surprise Ian. He went on to explain how he'd used the transactional analysis model of communication[10] with the CEO to illustrate how he was often in "critical parent" mode with Walt. He believed this exacerbated Walt's inclination to hang back in a deferential position. Ian shared this with Walt as well. In short, Ian and I were joined in our respective efforts to break through Walt's habit of "under-clubbing."

## COALESCENCE PHASE

As we entered the coalescence phase, Walt was giving himself all A's on his report card; the CEO noted that he continued to grow; and Ian described him as having "improved dramatically." Walt requested and received approval for one more year with me in the role of his trusted advisor (see chapter 10). We viewed this as the *final coalescence* of his learning and behavior change. Based on my year-end conversation with his boss, I knew we would have to continue to bear down on stubborn habits. The CEO reiterated, "Walt is a key contributor here. I look to him to demonstrate even more of a leadership presence in addition to his management skills. His continued growth in EQ areas, relationship-building, strategic thinking, and communications will all be key."

## DISCUSSION

Walt's many and impressive strengths made him an ideal CEO succession candidate especially as he used coaching to change work-related habits that were sabotaging his continued success. The open communication loop I was able to establish and maintain with the CEO and another external consultant was a critical factor in the progress Walt made. It ensured necessary alignment on the frequent and candid feedback we each provided to Walt in the service of his becoming more than a superb finance executive.

While specific development areas were identified initially and refined a few years later, from a broader perspective, as indicated earlier, the coaching fundamentally centered on Walt replacing old habits with more assertive, strategic, and relationship-oriented leadership. The enormity of this coaching agenda was understood in the context of his early familial dynamics, education, and career experiences. Walt was "wired" to strive for perfection, to form mostly transactional relationships at work, and to be deferential with his superiors. This pattern of behavior had been rewarded and reinforced earlier in his career but it had become a barrier in his pursuit of the CEO role at Remington.

A coaching approach that was both pragmatic and insight-oriented helped Walt see the underlying basis of his persistent habits—and how he could change them. Most prominently, the exploration of his perfectionism revealed the defensive purpose it served in terms of alleviating performance anxiety (*having all the right answers*), ensuring a sense of control, and avoiding ambiguity. Many tools, notably the coaching relationship itself, were used to keep Walt riveted on the goal of breaking old habits and replacing them with behaviors that would reinforce his full effectiveness as a leader and strong CEO succession candidate.

Working in collaboration with the CEO and Ian, the external leadership development consultant, I strove to maintain an objective perspective and, at the same time, to convey the progress Walt was making. I also acknowledged the challenge of maintaining gains in a changing and stressful business atmosphere—an atmosphere that could easily influence Walt's reverting to old, familiar leadership habits. In this sense, I increased my emphasis on the need for him to forsake his reserved style, step up to lead assertively, form strong relationships throughout the company, and to provide more input on pressing strategic issues. I also encouraged Ian to help the CEO recognize his part in triggering Walt's deferential behavior.

During the final coalescence phase of this engagement, Walt continued to make progress on breaking old habits and stretching into the broader leadership demands at Remington. Of note was a significant strategic planning effort led by Walt, which required a high level of collaboration and strong engagement with key constituents (including the board). At this juncture, he also benefitted from an in-depth development plan created by Ian and the CEO. Similar plans were put in place for the two other internal succession candidates as well, as the CEO succession process continued to gain momentum.

As the coalescence phase ended, my most persistent question was this: had I done all I could to ensure that Walt truly internalized his lessons learned? To what extent would he have the courage to use the insights acquired in coaching to abandon the force of old habits, to beat down the psychological barriers to change, and to sustain necessary leadership behavior? The answers would have to wait.

## CONCLUSION

At this writing, the next CEO of Remington had not been named; however, certain points were clear. If Walt was not appointed to the role, no member of the leadership team would want him to leave the company, he would likely choose to stay, and he would be welcomed by the new CEO as the superb CFO he had always been. Further, given the highly civil and mature nature of the company culture, as well as how well the CEO and Ian had orchestrated the succession process, the dynamics within the new leadership team would settle quickly and influence an atmosphere of healthy team-based leadership.

Finally, when this CEO succession decision is made, it will be driven as much by the candidate's preparedness to address specific business imperatives at the time as it will be by his leadership capabilities. This was stressed in the work with Walt especially as it related to the board's comfort with him and the projection of his combined strategic and operational capabilities. However it goes, Walt's evolution as a leader should influence his positive adjustment into the new normal at Remington buoyed by his commitment to the company, and his being equipped with whatever golf club he'll need to be swinging.

# Executive's Reflection

## INTRODUCTION

*Life is a journey*—I don't remember who said this originally, but it continues to be a constant truth.

Along the way, everyone makes decisions—sometimes for the better, sometimes not—that can have a meaningful impact on the path taken. As I look back, the opportunity to work with Karol was certainly one of those significant decisions.

Working with an executive coach may not be for everyone. You have to be in the right state of mind—open to feedback, willing to change, and with an appreciation that what you get out of the process is directly related to what you put in. It is also important to recognize that a successful coaching experience is a true partnership and heavily influenced by a strong match between the coach and the client.

## THE ENGAGEMENT

My initial investment in the coaching process involved a concerted effort to interview a number of prospective coaches and determine the best selection. The interviews focused on three key dimensions—the structure of the coaching process (what sort of approach is used), a discussion of proposed objectives (what do we want to achieve), and a sense of interpersonal fit (can we work well together).

From a process perspective, Karol's overall approach was based on a plan that focused on psychometric analysis, direct 360-degree assessments, and an identification of specific leadership development areas. The sequence and integration of these elements proved to be a very effective platform.

One of my primary objectives as part of the coaching process was to achieve a better balance between IQ and EQ. In this regard, Karol's experience in emphasizing Total Brain Leadership was very consistent with what I hoped to accomplish. This was an important differentiator in the engagement decision.

Finally, on the interpersonal side, I was fortunate to quickly confirm a high level of comfort with Karol from both a style and a communication perspective. This was a key consideration given the close working relationship that is essential to a successful coach/client interaction.

## THE EXPERIENCE

As I reflect on the overall coaching experience, I have little doubt in my mind that the benefits have exceeded expectations. The insights that I have gained are of lasting value, from both a personal and professional perspective. I am a firm believer that effective leadership can be attained by leveraging a combination of innate capabilities and learned competencies. Every leader is different but the key is to work through the process of better understanding yourself, your impact on others, and how best to leverage your available talents.

The best way I can describe the experience with Karol is focused yet flexible. Each session had its own intended goals that were part of the overall coaching plan, with the earlier ones being more structured and focused in their content. But that same plan, and in particular the later sessions, also allowed for a great deal of flexibility in terms of the discussion topics and the issues that were in play at a particular point in time. After each session, I left with an enhanced self-awareness and a better sense of what I needed to focus on to become more effective in my roles—both current and future.

In my case, much of the discussion about becoming more effective was centered on maturing as a leader. Specific areas of focus included deeper engagement with the organization (balancing people and process), sharing more strategic perspectives (painting with a broader brush), and communicating more thoughtfully (meeting the audience where it needs to be met). Karol's ability to offer her own unique perspectives and to help distill the feedback that I had received was instrumental in helping me internalize the desired changes. Quite frequently, the discussions boiled down to the quality of my relationships with people and how best to help the *true me* emerge—an idea that was as powerful as it was simple.

Another important part of the process involved interaction with key constituents. Our company puts great value on ongoing leadership development at all levels of the organization. This starts at the top with the CEO, but also has heavy involvement from our senior management team, midlevel managers, and the board of directors. At the very outset of the coaching experience, we had a joint meeting to discuss objectives and process. The meeting included Karol, my CEO, an outside advisor, and myself. It was very constructive in establishing a baseline of expectations and defining clear lines of communication. These lines of communication continued throughout the process as a very constructive way to maintain alignment and to allow everyone to remain comfortable with the progress being made.

One of the invaluable aspects of my relationship with Karol was the knowledge that my individual conversations with her were held in confidence. This is not to say that candid updates and progress reports were not provided to my CEO; they certainly were, on a regular basis. Rather, the confidentiality allowed me to explore certain issues in a one-on-one setting before sharing with a wider audience. In the end, there was very little that I did not choose to share more broadly, but the opportunity to work through things in advance was extremely helpful.

## THE EPILOGUE

One of the intended benefits of the coaching experience with Karol was to better prepare for potential additional executive responsibilities. At the time of this case study summary, the CEO succession question at our company is an active topic of discussion with the board of directors. Regardless of the outcome of those deliberations, however, I continue to feel very fortunate to have had the opportunity to work with Karol. I can't say enough about what this has meant to me personally.

As the saying goes, people don't really care how much you know until they know how much you care. In a way, this is the essence of my learning and I owe much of that to the experience I had during this process. To Karol, I value our relationship and the enhanced self-awareness that has come with this understanding. To my CEO, I continue to appreciate your support and counsel and the opportunities for ongoing development that our company willingly provides.

# CHAPTER 8

# The Reluctant President*

## INTRODUCTION

This engagement began as the grooming of a CEO successor candidate whose ambivalence about his new President role was at least matched by the ambivalence of the CEO/owner about the need to have a successor at all. It unfolded successfully with the President taking full command of his leadership challenges, and the CEO/owner becoming more resolved about his retirement transition as well as more trusting of his eventual successor. There was also secondary gain for the senior management team as it endorsed and embarked upon key organization development initiatives. What happened in between was a roller coaster ride during which my clinical training was as helpful as extensive experience I had had in business and coaching. Further, based on my experience with other *superkeepers* like Frank, a term coined by Berger (see Berger & Berger, 2003), this good outcome was influenced by three coaching process or meta principles—*traction, trust, and truth-telling*—as well as by four methodology factors—*a holistic approach, deep behavioral insight, the active involvement of top corporate executives*, and *sustained relationships*. These process and methodology considerations will be discussed in this chapter after presentation of the case.

## THE FACTS: CLIENT, CULTURE, BOSS

### *The Client*

Frank M. had been with Banyun, a privately held employee benefits consulting firm with annual revenue of approximately $50 million, for nine years when at age 40 he was made President. This unexpected appointment was widely perceived as a major step toward his eventually becoming CEO. In our first meeting Frank summarized his situation:

> I would have been content to just keep selling; but we were growing fast, things inside were getting more and more chaotic, the CEO had started to worry about perpetuation of the company, and before I knew it, I was President. This ticked off a couple of the other guys—one in particular who really wanted it—but for me, it's a pain. It's next to impossible for me to produce more business, manage my current accounts, and deal with all the infrastructure and people issues crucial for our continued success. John (the CEO) just doesn't want to spend the necessary time on this; I don't think he sees how complex things have gotten on the management side. All he wants to do is produce business, and he keeps raising the bar. Somebody's got to get a hold of this thing. It looks like that somebody is me, and I'm taking a financial hit to do it.

Frank had been recruited to Banyun based on his outstanding sales success at IBM. The combination of his potential for ownership, interest in learning Banyun's business, and a move to the East Coast was enticing enough for him to accept the offer and relocate his wife and three children. Within a few years of his hiring, he had become one of the top two business producers at Banyun—along with the CEO. In the midst of a health scare and based on counsel from his legal advisor, the CEO made the impetuous decision to appoint a President. Since he valued sales success above all else and had a relatively good relationship with Frank, he saw Frank as his best choice. While it was the right timing for appointing a President, John had little appreciation of what it would take to stabilize the firm through its rapid growth and to position it securely for the future. John's answer to any question about strategy was always the same: topline growth.

## *The Culture*

In this competitive, sales-driven culture, the business producers rapidly fell in and out of favor with the CEO based on their monthly results. This pattern of intermittent reinforcement had begun to create retention risks, another problem with which Frank would have to grapple. But good, bad, or ugly the culture was *strong*, and there was a lot about it that held appeal. Founded by the CEO's father, the company had long enjoyed a portfolio of prestigious corporate clients and had double-digit growth for several years running. It had a stellar reputation for quality service, customer focus, and integrity. Its employees were well-paid, loyal, and enjoyed the comfort of elegant surroundings. Appearances were paramount to the CEO, and the gestalt at Banyun was *Brooks Brothers crisp*. The company's success rested solidly on a foundation of excellent people, comprehensive technical training, an adherence to orthodoxy, and strong standards of accountability. For the most part employees were thriving in this atmosphere of innovation, competition, and an admixture of commitment to work-family integration and reward for beyond-the-beyond heroics.

There was also a darker side to Banyun's culture, manifested by an atmosphere of anxiety among the administrative staff and overt expressions of exasperation from professional and management employees. This was due primarily to the CEO's relentless micromanagement, crude attacks on people, impulsive firings, and obstinacy. For years he had waited to succeed his father; and when he did, his recrudescent narcissism (Levinson, 2003) washed over the company in undulating waves of need, self-aggrandizement, and inappropriate displays of power and dominance.

At the same time the firm's folklore abounded in stories about the CEO's incredible generosity and empathy for employees especially during times of family illness or death. In summary, a moat of eggshells lay between the splendor of his office and the staff beyond. As one senior manager described it, "As good as this place is to work, you can feel really whip-lashed, too." From the mail room to the board room, the firm's atmosphere tilted on the axis of the CEO's labile mood.

### The Boss

Beneath the surface of this seemingly impeccable gentleman was the wounded heart of an abused and emotionally impoverished child born to privilege but denied the psychological sustenance to thrive as a secure adult. Maintaining control was his leit motif; and since his locus of control was completely external, those around him were conditioned to provide frequent ego feedings and to avoid hitting the hot buttons of his massive insecurity.

The CEO frequently told employees about childhood traumas he suffered at the hands of his sadistic father. These stories were perceived as manipulative attempts to rationalize his bad behavior; horrifying as they were, they had long ago lost their potential to heal the wounds he inflicted. As Frank put it, "At some point, you have to get over it and move on."

Clearly, the CEO was a formidable challenge in this coaching engagement, a challenge that had to be met lest progress with Frank be sabotaged by John's narcissistic rage, especially as Frank became increasingly effective in his Presidential role. I would have to orchestrate a sequence of steps that produced an alliance with John, helped soothe his replacement fears, and reinforced his sense of trust with Frank.

### The Prelude

The prospect of executive coaching for Frank was the Human Resource Director's idea; he had grown weary of the CEO's tendency to complain about Frank and question—in earshot of others—whether he had done the right thing in appointing Frank President. While the HR Director knew the job was a stretch for Frank, he believed Frank was well-equipped to meet the demands of the job; and he knew how well-respected he was throughout the firm. The HR Director was also psychologically sophisticated enough to recognize that John's baseless complaints were a defense against his retirement fears.

With the CEO's agreement, the HR Director went on a round of initial screening interviews with prospective coaches. Toward the end of my meeting with him, the urgency and poignancy of the situation tumbled out when he said,

> I'm concerned that if Frank and John don't get their relationship right, Frank will leave; and that will be a major blow to the company. And as far as working with a coach, Frank's a tough street fighter kind of a guy. He's pragmatic and wants to stay focused on results. He's not into a lot of psychology, and I don't know how he'll do with a female coach.

To which I replied, "Let's see what he decides."

The initial meeting with Frank was memorable. Fit, polished, and direct, he got right down to business. He had already met with two other coaches, and I discerned quickly that he wasn't impressed with what he'd heard so far. In his words, "There are some things I need to learn about doing this job, but I don't think I'm going to learn much from people who haven't led anything or who don't understand the world I operate in. How do people like you do what you do?" In those opening minutes, I gave him a quick summary of my own business background, leadership experiences, companies I had consulted to, and an overview of my coaching model. Then I sat back and listened as he answered my question about what he needed to learn. Frank focused most on staffing, operational issues, and the challenge of managing the CEO. At the end of this two-hour meeting, he asked me for references. Having anticipated his request, I gave him names of both coached clients and company contacts. A few days later, Frank called to say he was ready to start the coaching. Of note in the phone call was his comment, "I don't want to contemplate my navel, but I think there's probably a connection between things that have happened in my life and what's going on for me at Banyun; so I'm assuming you'll take a good look at everything, right?" Right. In the midst of what adult development theorist Levinson (1978, p. 60) described as the BOOM effect, that is, "becoming one's own man," Frank was ripe for learning...and change.

## The Start-Up

After the introductory conversation with Frank, I facilitated an agenda-setting meeting in the CEO's office. Frank and I joined John and the HR Director for a discussion of the coaching methodology, our respective roles, the time frame, the boundaries of confidentiality, objectives of the coaching, and how we'd assess progress. We concluded with the selection of a representative group of people—14 in all—for Frank's 360 data-gathering.

My initial observations of the CEO tracked with what I had heard from Frank and the HR Director. He was a man of enormous energy and passion for his business; accomplished and flawed; commanding and insecure. A tinderbox for whom shame could easily produce an amygdala hijack (Goleman, 1995). A tormented person of dualities that could scuttle an orderly succession, endanger Banyun's future, and continue to erode the morale in the company. I also sensed his impatience with process so I was succinct:

- Methodology—I would use a four-phase model customized to the needs of this engagement: (1) data-gathering including a development history, a battery of psychometrics,[1] and face-to-face 360 data-gathering; (2) feedback when all the data would be synthesized and used to specify coaching areas; (3) coaching during which an array of learning resources would be used; and (4) consolidation of coaching gains.
- Roles—The CEO and HR Director would be active *collaborators* with Frank and me, that is, coaching would not be done in a vacuum. Both Frank and I would benefit from collateral information provided by them, and we wanted to make sure they felt in-the-loop.
- Time frame—Approximately 12–15 months for the four phases. During the coaching phase, there would be two-hour monthly meetings plus email and phone consultation as needed.
- Confidentiality—I emphasized that most data would be kept in complete confidence and explained the importance of this for my establishing and maintaining a strong working alliance with Frank. At the same time, it would be critical for us to maintain open lines of communication. I would have at least monthly conversations with them (John and Frank) in which we'd gauge progress, momentum, share new observations, and so on.

- Objectives of coaching—Two areas emerged in this meeting: (1) Frank's forging a stronger, more trusting relationship with the CEO; and (2) his building relationships with others throughout the firm (not just his sales peers and the CEO).
- Assessing progress—I would have a private meeting with the CEO at the 6-month point, a 12-month joint meeting with the CEO and Frank, and quarterly conversations with the HR Director. In addition, as indicated earlier, I would be available to the CEO and HR Director on an ad hoc basis.
- Selection of 360 sample participants—This concrete task initiated our four-way collaboration. It also provided some surprises/clues for Frank in terms of whom the CEO viewed as key stakeholders.
- Communication strategy—Since this was the first time Banyun had used an executive coach, and since there was a residue of envy and resentment surrounding Frank's appointment as President, I scripted the CEO and HR Director. They needed to speak of the coaching as a business resource, an investment in both Banyun's future and in Frank's development as *an even more effective leader*. We also agreed that I would interview everyone on site, beginning each conversation with a question exploring what he/she understood about my work with Frank. This would give me the opportunity to clarify any misconceptions and amplify the developmental intent of the engagement.

## THE WORK

Having grounded the coaching with the agenda-setting meeting, we moved on to complete the data-gathering phase. I took Frank's history in a three-hour face-to-face meeting and gave him the packet of psychometrics to complete on his own. Frank's early years were a Brothers Grimm tale of meager surroundings and emotional deprivation given his self-absorbed mother, a distant father, and later, an equally distant stepfather. Frank's one emotional anchor during his formative years was his maternal grandmother who remained a constant source of nurturance and affirmation until she died when he was in college. An outstanding athlete from grade school through college, Frank embarked upon an NBA basketball career, but a serious injury ended that pursuit. Through a serendipitous series of events, he wound up in sales eventually joining IBM where he surpassed quota after quota and was well-regarded by all who knew him. In his own words, "Sales was great for me from the beginning. You learn your products, know your goals, work harder than most, and you can measure your success. I'm a pragmatist who doesn't need a lot of love or stroking. I can take a lot, too."

True to the early signal Frank sent about a probable "connection" between his past and the present at Banyun, the synthesis of his history and the psychometric data was pivotal. It revealed a psychological insight that had important implications for both his personal life and leadership of Banyun. This insight was about his sadomasochistic pattern in significant relationships—including his spouse and the CEO. We moved quickly from history to immediate applicability of the insight: his tolerance for others' dysfunctional behavior kept him trapped in draining, toxic relationships that afforded him minimal appreciation, love, or acknowledgment of his accomplishments. Yes, he could "take a lot" but that also meant he had little psychic energy left to invest in his own personal growth and well-being. Moreover, given the leadership demands of his role, he had no time for the larger strategic and operational issues. Knowing I was trained clinically, Frank joked about "getting two for the price of one." I responded by explaining the need to maintain the boundaries of our work and by also indicating my willingness to refer him to a therapist, if he was interested. At a later point in the coaching, Frank did ask for referral to a marital therapist, an intervention that proved helpful. With Frank's permission, I shared relevant information with that clinician.

Based on the feedback, we finalized the coaching agenda. This agenda targeted three strengths to leverage—*business development ability, leadership potential*, and *relationship with the CEO*. We also agreed on two areas for development—*internal relationship building* and *people management*. These areas fundamentally tracked with what was discussed in the agenda-setting meeting, and Frank saw how they were inextricably linked to each other. Progress in any one area would likely have a positive effect on other coaching objectives. Of note was the fact that most people believed Frank managed the CEO better than anyone else at Banyun.

To anchor the coaching phase, Frank and I collaborated on the creation of a preliminary action plan, that is, the specific action steps he would take to make headway in the areas identified. The CEO and HR Director received copies of Frank's plan, and I urged them to give Frank positive reinforcement whenever they saw him "working" the plan well and to take advantage of their observations to give him constructive criticism when he wasn't working it well. During the initial months I interacted most with the HR Director, who proved to be a remarkably effective collaborator and who forged a strategic partnership with Frank. Regarding the CEO, once he realized the benefits of Frank's coaching for *himself*, he became more involved. He acknowledged Frank's progress (to Frank and others), and of greater significance was the fact that he was better able to express his annoyance and/or concerns directly to Frank—a behavior that had a positive effect on their relationship. The presence of the CEO's sadistic father and the healing effect of the shift in the John-Frank dynamic enveloped the CEO's comment, "I realize I don't have to worry about Frank blowing up at me when I'm not happy with something he's done."

The coaching was also anchored by the use of a technique I created some years ago—the *visual metaphor* (see figure 8.1). This pictorial representation of Frank's current, transitional, and future leadership states—as described by him—was a handy way for us to assess where we were in the coaching. We often referred to it at the outset of a coaching meeting. Frank's metaphor amplified the overarching importance of his managing the relationship with the CEO. In frame 1 (current state), Frank was in the midst of a major storm. Frame 2 (transitional state) indicated progress. And in frame 3 (future state), Frank saw himself working collaboratively with the CEO, staying focused on issues critical to the

**Figure 8.1**   Frank's Visual Leadership Metaphor® (VLM) #1.

company's future. After a year of coaching, Frank had moved into frame 2, and by the end of the second year, he was in frame 3 and working on solidifying that progress. Since he enjoyed movies, I used them as a resource especially during the consolidation phase (e.g., "Gladiator," "Hoosiers," "Mr. Holland's Opus," "The Big Kahuna," and "Elizabeth").

### Areas for Development

Regarding *internal relationship building*, Frank learned, primarily from the 360 data, that his results-oriented, no-nonsense approach was fundamentally a strength, though a double-edged one. People wanted more from him as President of the company. He came to appreciate that employees at all levels needed more access to him and to feel they could interact on a broader array of issues, that is, not just client-related problems or opportunities. Using emotional intelligence as a major learning vehicle (Goleman 1995 and 1998), Frank made enormous gains in this area. The coaching helped him generalize his emotional self, a self he had mostly suppressed defensively, across a broader array of situations. Frank's major actions included his: (1) displaying greater empathy regarding personnel issues; (2) conveying appreciation for the good work of sales support functions; (3) increasing casual interactions and being more visible throughout the firm; and (4) being more attuned to employees' personal events and acknowledging them with voice or emails.

To make headway on the *people management* development area, we used a Results/Attitude Grid (see figure 8.2). This helped Frank see where his direct reports stood and more importantly, what he needed to do developmentally with each of them. This led to key people decisions about which the CEO was especially pleased, for he was harboring unspoken resentment about "bad hires" Frank had made.

### Leveraging Strengths

In some ways, Frank's capitalizing on his strengths proved to be the more demanding part of his coaching agenda. Regarding *business*

**Figure 8.2**   Results/Attitude Grid.

| RESULTS/ATTITUDE GRID | |
|---|---|
| 1<br><br>    + R<br>    + A | 2<br><br>    – R<br>    + A |
| 3<br><br>    + R<br>    – A | 4<br><br>    – R<br>    – A |
| **Key:**<br>**Quadrant 1**: High potentials—what needs to be done to keep them?<br>**Quadrant 2**: Results lacking—what needs to be done to get results on track?<br>**Quadrant 3**: Attitude problem—is attitude adjustment possible? If yes, what's the plan? If no, is this person more trouble than he/she is worth? Answer to last question determines course of action.<br>**Quadrant 4**: Results and attitude problem—is person in wrong job? If so, and there is a better job fit in company, such people can move swiftly to quadrant 1. If not, separation from company is probably best. | |

*development*, he persisted in a difficult dialogue with the CEO about the growing demands of the Presidential role, that is, how it siphoned time away from his developing new business and how there needed to be a change in his compensation so that he was not so penalized financially for assuming the President role. The time spent on this issue in coaching meetings, as well as the coach's private conversations with the CEO, eventually produced a resolution that was satisfactory to Frank financially and had a positive effect on his overall enthusiasm for the job. He also became more intentional about coaching others' sales success.

It was gratifying for Frank to see *leadership potential* emerge as a strength from the 360 data-gathering. There were a number of coordinated action steps that produced rapid gains in this area. These included his (1) assuming a more forceful role at company-wide events when business results and plans for the future were communicated, (2) creating other opportunities to convey strategic plans, and (3) being more involved in the recruitment and assimilation of key people into Banyun. To support Frank's leadership impact further, I introduced him to respected resources in the areas of recruitment, organization development, and leadership development.

Of note, coaching meetings were influenced by my frequent challenge to Frank that "insight is cheap unless you use it." This resulted in his taking a number of courageous steps over the next couple of years. These included productive confrontations with chronic cynics at Banyun, the firing of nonperformers, persistence regarding strategic discipline, and censoring people's reflexive tendencies to trash the CEO.

While Frank made enormous headway on his *relationship with the CEO*, this coaching area would require continued vigilance into the future. We identified three action steps that served him well immediately: (1) increased *daily* communication with the CEO, (2) having monthly dinner meetings with John, and (3) ensuring that they displayed a "united front" to employees on all key business matters.

On a deeper level, Frank learned about the pros and cons of working for a narcissistic boss. His reading and our subsequent discussions of Maccoby's *Harvard Business Review* article (2000) was especially helpful. He realized that through it all, there was much he respected in terms of John's risk-taking, public visibility, and uncanny "nose for the business" that had propelled the company's growth. Frank also came to better understand—and even anticipate—the CEO's (1) swings between grandiosity and despair, (2) irrational distrust of others, and (3) maddening preoccupation with himself. Moreover, he became attuned to the subtleties and nuances of both his private and public interactions with the CEO. In his words, "I'm a lot clearer about what I'm dealing with, what I need to do to avoid setting him off, and how to influence a positive atmosphere." Frank's deepened attunement lead to actions he would intensify and sustain over time. These included his (1) creating opportunities for the CEO to be more visible both inside and outside the company, (2) working thorny business issues behind-the-scenes more thereby avoiding open dissent in the management committee, (3) reinforcing the CEO's better ideas and distracting him from bad ones, and (4) finding ways to give John frank feedback but without threatening the CEO's inflated self-image.

In tandem with Frank's efforts to manage the CEO, I continued to pursue my own agenda with John. Trust was built primarily through my empathy for his concerns. I also made considerable progress on his ability to see Frank as someone who deserved his trust, who was completely committed to the company, and who would be a superb successor *when John chose to retire*. As time unfolded, I made the most of opportunities to minimize the CEO's worst fears about retirement. I introduced him to the concept of *legacy* and facilitated his ability to verbalize what this would be for Banyun by the time he retired ("$100 million in revenue"). Further, I heightened his interest in exploring the arts, serving altruistic causes, and the possibility of using his wealth to fund "naming" opportunities at academic and other organizations. This effort ignited his awareness of the *glittering image* he could sustain, even after his time at Banyun.

## DISCUSSION

Many coaching tools were used to help Frank meet the challenges of the president's job. There were obvious tools such as a clear coaching agenda, the developmental history, a battery of psychometrics, the customized 360 data-gathering, selected readings, the frequency of coaching meetings, a cascade of valuable action steps, and the coaching relationship. There were more creative tools too like the visual metaphor, the Results/Attitude grid for assessing direct reports, and the use of movie scenes to reinforce learning about leadership. But in the end, the success of this work was influenced most by its grounding in the three coaching process (meta principles) and four methodology factors to which I referred in the introduction of this chapter. This approach reflects the integration of my experience in business, clinical training, research, consulting, and assuredly by what hundreds of executive clients have said about what helped them most. This is an approach that can lead to *sustained* results—with clients who want to learn, have the courage to change, and who perceive the need for change as one of life's continuous gifts.

Here's how these process and methodology considerations played out in the coaching of Frank, who in the end was no longer the "reluctant president."

### Three Meta Principles

*#1 Traction*

What I mean by traction in coaching is akin to the interaction between car tires and roads—a gripping of the surface while moving, but without slipping. This need to keep moving without slipping is fundamental to effective coaching. The work will falter, drift, or even fail without it.

There were many factors involved in attaining and maintaining traction in Frank's coaching beginning with my assessment of the "rightness" of the coaching referral. Had this been a certain derailment and/or no-win scenario, I would have passed or referred it to a colleague with appropriate warnings because I don't think companies should waste money on such coaching agendas (Wasylyshyn, 2003). While I had some reservations about Frank's trust in the value of coaching, and the climate of the coaching referral, I was swayed by his appetite to learn, willingness to invest sufficient time, and the potential for us to form a strong working alliance. In retrospect, his involvement in the choice of his coach was a key factor in our forming a rapid and strong working alliance.

Finally, due to the size of Frank's 360 sample—14 including the CEO and HR Director—his feedback was given in two sessions to help sustain traction. History and psychometric data were discussed in one three-hour meeting, and the 360 feedback was given in a second three-hour session that concluded with our final agreement on targeted areas for coaching. Both meetings were held in my office and were audiotaped for his future reference.

*#2 Trust*

This meta principle connotes a *reciprocal trusting* not just between the coach and coachee but with the two internal collaborators as well—in this case the CEO/boss and the human resources partner. As I got to know the CEO, his trust in me and the value of the coaching grew through the consistency of our conversations and, curiously, through my refusal to take on additional engagements at Banyun. Both Frank and he had invited my participation in other initiatives (e.g., company survey and leadership development program), and they were eager for me to coach other members of the management committee. My instinct to hold a strong boundary and not extend service beyond the initial coaching engagement paid off. Midway through the coaching, the HR Director said, "John respects your not getting enmeshed with us like other consultants have. This has helped your trust with him because he doesn't see you as more interested in getting business than in helping Banyun."

Overall, the HR Director served as an objective "translator" of events in the company and as such he was an invaluable source of collateral information. The CEO got increasingly better at expressing his true opinions, venting frustrations, and revealing his concerns about the future, so much so that I had to manage the boundary of our relationship carefully and in a way that was not narcissistically wounding to him.

In addition to my fostering these collaborative working relationships, there were two other key factors that influenced the building of trust: *confidentiality* and *emotional competence*. Always central to the issue of confidentiality is the question: "Who's the client?" While coaches vary in their perspectives on this question, I've not wavered from mine: the coachee is always the client, and the bill-paying corporate sponsor is just that, the sponsor. Wasylyshyn (2003) wrote:

> In terms of forming strong connections with clients, coaches who work from a perspective of the *executive as client* (versus the organization as client) are likely to form faster and more trusting coaching relationships. Seasoned coaches discover how to work from this perspective—satisfying both the coached executive and the sponsoring organization.

Having discussed the boundaries of confidentiality openly in the agenda-setting meeting, I was not compromised later by inappropriate questions regarding information that was off-limits such as history, psychometric or 360 feedback data, and specific content of coaching meetings. However, to foster the CEO's and HR partner's functioning fully in their roles as collaborators, I remained in frequent contact with them, capitalized on my private time with the CEO, and conveyed thematic material from the 360 data-gathering—particularly as it related to Banyun's culture. I also provided my general assessment of how the coaching was progressing and what each of them could do to gain most mileage from this investment.

Managing the meta principle of *trust* in coaching relationships also requires the coach to possess a high degree of *emotional competence*, which is defined as the awareness of and ability to manage one's emotions. I had to censor strong negative feelings about the CEO, as well as strong positive feelings about Frank. Obviously, maintaining objectivity was critical. Throughout the coaching I wanted what I taught and modeled in terms of key dimensions of emotional competence—self-awareness, discipline, empathy, and attunement to others—to help accelerate Frank's evolution as a leader.

Finally, as I had anticipated, coach gender was not an issue. It proved to be an asset manifested in numerous ways including Frank's (1) willingness to be vulnerable, (2) shedding of defenses, (3) exploration of emotions as a leadership asset, and (4) discussion of marital issues as they adversely affected his work-related relationships.

### #3 Truth-Telling

I think of the meta principle of *truth-telling* as a *double mirror*, that is, helping both client and company to see essential truths in the looking glass. Surely I helped Frank see what he needed to see. Through my relationship with the HR Director, I helped Banyun see systemic issues that had implications for effective leadership. These findings, based on 360 data, signaled concerns about micromanagement, insufficient strategic planning, lack of managerial bench strength, and the need to develop the next generation of effective leaders. This information influenced two constructive organization development initiatives: a company culture survey and a leadership development program for mid- and senior-level managers.

### Four Methodological Factors

### #1 Holistic Approach

Coaching executives from a holistic perspective means the coach has the inclination to get to know his/her client fully—not just through the myopic lens of work. It means the coach has the skill to weave a fuller, more luminous tapestry of the client's life making the connections that will matter most in the coaching. Working holistically means the coach will have the courage to address critical intersections between work and personal priorities. I refer to this as *work-family integration*—NOT *work-family balance*, the more common term—but a flawed semantic in that it raises an expectation on which it is virtually impossible for most senior executives to deliver.

While I maintained an appropriate boundary between the coaching agenda and issues of significant concern in Frank's private life, my willingness to serve in a triage capacity was helpful and much appreciated by him. Having led him to a competent marital therapist, for example, had a palliative effect and minimized his distraction at work.

Finally, coaches working holistically with executives has implications for executive retention. True to the Human Resources Director's worst fear, Frank's exasperation—given the dual tensions of managing the CEO and Frank's personal issues—produced thoughts about leaving Banyun. In the safety of the coaching relationship, Frank had a place to vent and to receive guidance that eased his frustration, helped him maintain perspective, and prevented a precipitous decision to resign.

*#2 Deep Behavioral Insight*

The rapid engagement of senior executives is often the initial challenge in coaching them. Bringing deep insight about behavior to the surface, especially as it relates to leadership, can be especially effective in meeting this challenge. Psychologist coaches, in particular, can tap into a broad armamentarium of tools for this purpose. My "good look at everything" for Frank was accomplished with the taking of a developmental history and a battery of psychometrics. I used the 360 data-gathering to surface relevant information about Frank's leadership and to learn more about Banyun's culture (see figure 8.3, Customized Interview Protocol). And I accelerated rapid engagement by setting two feedback meetings and getting to the first one quickly, so we could mine the history and psychometric data for deeper insights.

**Figure 8.3**  Customized Interview Protocol for 360 Feedback.

| | |
|---|---|
| 1 | Describe his strengths. |
| 2 | Give an example of when he used these strengths particularly well. |
| 3 | What could he improve so he would be even more effective? |
| 4 | Give an example of when these limitations were especially apparent. |
| 5 | Describe his management style. |
| 6 | How does he develop people? |
| 7 | How effective is he in getting the right people in the right jobs? |
| 8 | How does he relate to others specifically: Direct reports? Peers? His boss? Clients? |
| 9 | How would you describe Banyon's culture? What works? What doesn't? |
| 10 | Compare Frank's leadership style to John's. |
| 11 | How does Frank manage his work-family priorities? |
| 12 | If you were to offer him one piece of advice—advice that would help make him even more effective than he already is, what would you say? |

Frank's recognition of his pattern of sadomasochistic relationships had a lasting impact on him, as well as influencing much of what he learned and did throughout the coaching. Finally, his coaching was a carefully sequenced and nuanced process of delivering insight, supporting his courageous efforts to apply the insight(s), and then consolidating his behavioral gains.

#3 *Involvement of Top Executives*

Regardless of how secure they may or may not be, senior executives want to know where they stand with top management. And effective executive coaches will find ways to bring this information to their work—without it becoming the raison d'etre of the engagement.

In the work with Frank, this methodology consideration was both easy and difficult. It was easy in the sense that the engagement was riveted on his relationship with the CEO. The spigot of information was wide open, and, if anything, I was constantly making choices about the intensity of the water pressure. It was difficult in the sense that coaching meetings could have easily been overwhelmed by the Frank-John relationship agenda—at the expense of Frank's learning and attention to other dimensions of his leadership.

In this sense, the delineation of a full coaching agenda of strengths to leverage and development areas was most helpful. Further, the concrete preliminary action plan helped maintain focus on the broader agenda. As I said to Frank in one coaching meeting, "We don't want our work together to be a microcosm of what goes on at Banyun: total preoccupation with the CEO."

*#4 Sustained Relationships*

In my view, the coaching of senior executives is a boundary-less process—not a contained program. The coach does whatever needs to be done and is not trapped in a lock-step, company-endorsed model with a ceiling on engagement length. The coaching of super-keepers like Frank is more *relational* than *transactional*. This means that the coaching relationship is likely to be sustained, that is, it can hold value for the executive for a number of years. Specifically, after an initial body of work is completed, and progress on goals is achieved, the executive may choose to retain the coach further. This is not a scenario of dependency. Rather, it's the natural evolution of a valued business relationship to one in which the coach becomes a *trusted advisor*.

This is what occurred after 15 months of coaching Frank. We had accomplished our primary coaching objectives; and I would now, as trusted advisor, be an objective sounding board providing him a safe place to express concerns, test ideas, plan, and discuss people challenges—including the CEO. This relationship would also serve as an antidote to the isolation that often occurs for business people in senior leadership roles. Saporito (1996, p. 96) writes: "The fact of the matter is, the higher an individual moves in an organization, the less feedback he or she is likely to receive. Senior executives tend to get isolated from real-time, unvarnished feedback about the impact of their individual leadership."

Regarding other sustained interaction, we settled into a productive pattern of my having a June luncheon with the CEO, and the three of us sharing a Christmas luncheon at year-end. As enjoyable as these occasions were, they required careful planning in terms of the issues I needed to initiate, punctuate, or illuminate with John. In the relaxed atmosphere of these settings, I made the most headway with the CEO regarding both his retirement fears and his relationship with Frank. In one hyperbolic burst he said, "I would trust Frank with my life."

This shift from *coach* to *trusted advisor* warrants our attention because it holds enormous promise, especially for coaches working with top corporate executives. Sheth and Sobel (2002) wrote:

> When you've reached the final and most rewarding stage (of a client relationship), you'll become a trusted advisor who consistently develops collaborative relationships with your clients and provides insight rather than just information. At this stage you will have *breakthrough* relationships. Because of the broad, influential role you play and the unusual degree of trust that you develop, these relationships will be of a significantly higher order than the run-of-the-mill associations that so many professionals have with their clients. (p. 14)

## CONCLUSION

This case study illustrates how a timely executive coaching engagement helped accelerate the effectiveness and influence the retention of a company's top CEO successor candidate. Using a data-driven and insight-oriented approach, the executive and his coach identified specific coaching objectives with implications for the company's success, as well as for the executive's development. The case also represents how coaching at the top can influence *organizational* development—even in a culture dominated by the needs and whims of a partially dysfunctional CEO.

Finally, this case exemplifies the value of a long-term coaching model, a model that influenced the coach's role shift from coach to *trusted advisor*. But there are many coaching models for working effectively with senior executives. Rather than exploring or debating the differences among them, there are more compelling questions to consider: What's next for this strong application area within psychology? How will psychologists capitalize on trusted advisor relationships with powerful business leaders? How will we intensify the strategic use of psychology to not only aid business results—but increase the *nourishing*, and decrease the *agonizing* effects of the workplace?

## REFERENCES

Berger, L. A., & Berger, D. R. (Eds.). (2003). *The Talent Management Handbook: Creating Organizational Excellence through Identifying Developing and Positioning Your Best People*. New York: McGraw-Hill.

Goleman, D. (1995). *Emotional Intelligence*. New York: Bantam Books.

———. (1998, November–December). "What makes a leader?" *Harvard Business Review*, 93–102.

Levinson, D. J. (1978). *The Seasons of a Man's Life*. New York: Ballantine Books.

Levinson, H. (2003). From a paper presented at the APA Division 13, Phoenix, AZ, January 2003.

Maccoby, M. (2000, January–February). "Narcissistic leaders: The incredible pros, the inevitable cons." *Harvard Business Review*, 69–77.

Saporito, T. J. (1996). Business-linked execututive development: Coaching senior executives. *Consulting Psychology Journal: Practice and Research, 48*, 96–103.

Sheth, J., & Sobel, A. (2002). *Clients for Life: Evolving from an Expert for Hire to an Extraordinary Advisor*. New York: Simon & Schuster.

Wasylyshyn, K. M. (2003). "Executive coaching: An outcome study," *Consulting Psychology Journal: Practice and Research, 55*, 94–106.

# CHAPTER 9

# The Reluctant President Revisited

To date, there is little in the executive coaching literature that provides a longitudinal look at coaching engagements after their completion. This coaching update encompasses a continuous ten-year period (2004–2014) after the initial coaching (2002–2004, see chapter 8). In this client relationship, the coach's role had transitioned from executive coach to *trusted advisor* on issues related to the executive's ongoing effectiveness as a C-level leader. There are three primary segments in this coaching update that capture how the client, Frank, used the guidance of his executive coach/trusted advisor to: (1) make the decision to leave a company, (2) navigate a successful assimilation into a new firm, and (3) leverage the lessons he had learned in the initial coaching engagement.

A fuller title of this case study update could easily have been *The Reluctant President Revisited: Paradoxical Effects of a Successful Coaching Engagement.* Despite Frank's progress in the initial coaching, it became clear that his boss at this privately held entity had paid only lip service to Frank's growth as President of the firm. He cared for little else than new business development. On a deeper level, Frank's emergence as leader of the day-to-day operations (versus just one of the firm's biggest producers) fanned the flames of his boss's underlying insecurities, hostilities, and pernicious envy.[1]

## The Decision to Leave

Frank's having become a highly respected leader of the firm stood in stark contrast to the CEO/owner's reputation as a volatile cad and vindictive aggressor. Increasingly, John resented Frank's operations effectiveness and openly derided it as a *problem* that siphoned time away from Frank producing new business.

Clearly, Frank's growth as a leader was experienced as a narcissistic injury by John, and this wounded narcissist relished opportunities to attack and/or undermine his younger partner. It was no secret that Frank's youth, vigor, and physical appeal all grated on John, an infamous rake who was not aging well. Further, John rejected the author's attempts to convey the upside of Frank's growth, that is, how his focus on operations and processes actually freed time for John to leverage his major strengths of client management and new business development.

She also failed in her efforts to neutralize John's regressive and paranoid resentment revealed in comments such as, "Frank's gotten too big for himself and just wants to run everything now." In the words of Banyun's Human Resources Director, "It's like the better Frank gets as a President, especially in managing the people issues here, the more suspicious and critical John gets, and he has to look for ways to tear him down."

And tear him down he did in public rants when he blamed Frank for the lack of topline business growth, the firm's inability to recruit talented producers, and its spending on a leadership development initiative for the firm's high potential employees. John ultimately scuttled this program describing both it and its lead consultant as a "waste." One of Frank's colleagues told the author, "The truth about the leadership program is that John got a hate on for the consultant. He was infuriated by the negative stuff that came out about his bad leadership and the terrible effects he has on the culture. If we didn't make such a good living here, half of us would be out the door tomorrow." While trying to maintain objectivity, the author could not deny the toxicity of John's leadership. This was blatant in her own interactions with him, and actually influenced her writing of an executive vignette entitled "Cracked."[2]

In a meeting where an outside technical consultant was present, John went on a one-hour tirade about the firm's poor sales performance and accused Frank of "screwing up the entire company." In a subsequent private meeting, this consultant told Frank about the depth of John's resentments and how he wanted to punish Frank because he held an "inordinate amount" of the firm's stock, and he (John) regretted that he had ever made Frank President of the firm. While Frank could tolerate John's attacks on his Presidency, the possibility of John reneging on their agreement regarding firm ownership potential was intolerable. This signaled the eventual dissolution of their relationship for in Frank's words, "Am I really willing to do this whole job for less money and with half the stock I was promised?"

Despite the author's efforts of urging frequency and transparency of communication, the relationship between John and Frank continued to break down. In June of 2005 Frank told her, "I agree that our not communicating regularly is a problem, but I don't want to be babysitting him every two weeks. I want to have a 'partner' but the truth is John is not capable of being a partner."

Shortly thereafter, in the author's penultimate face-to-face meeting with John, she could not engage him in an objective assessment of how Frank had helped stabilize managerial aspects of the firm while continuing to develop significant business as well. Nor could she persuade him to discuss how Frank and he could get their relationship back on track. Clearly, he had "split" on Frank.[3] While she escaped his legendary impulses to insult and fire consultants, their mostly cordial meeting ended with his parting shot, "I doubt that I'll ever pay for someone like you again."

### Broken Contracts

In a comprehensive, last ditch effort to place things in perspective, Frank sent John a an extensive summary of the contributions he had made in his 15-year employment with the firm. It was direct, fact-based, and without emotion. However, it had no effect as John was mired in what appeared to be an increasingly irrational and venomous version of reality when it came to Frank.

When John gave Frank a new employment agreement, Frank had it reviewed by a lawyer who said, "This is not something that would be written for someone who's been a partner for 15 years. It really doesn't look like he wants you around." At that point, both Frank's psychological contract with the firm and business contract with John were broken, and he began to think seriously about leaving Banyun. While he would need to fight his resistance to change, the potential of a new start elsewhere was surely appealing.

An ideal opportunity in the same business and in a publicly owned company soon emerged for Frank. However, given his pragmatic and conservative nature, he was both cautious and thorough in his assessment of it. In one meeting with the author he said, "They are interested in me for all the right reasons, and I realize that I've become a lot more than a sales guy. There is something for me to build there, and I'm ready to do that." In the same meeting, he described his last dinner with John in which he expressed his disappointment given how unfair John had been, how unappreciative he was of all Frank had done for the firm, and most of all how John had gone back on his word in terms of Frank's ownership potential. The author noted the cathartic effect this conversation had had on Frank and agreed that it was time for him to move on.

### A Dignified Departure

Upon leaving Banyun, Frank sent a warm and diplomatic resignation message to all employees that evoked a strong emotional reaction. This news was experienced as a true loss for many, and for others it raised a serious concern about the pace of future business production. John said little publicly in the wake of Frank's departure, however, he persisted in his irrational belief that Frank had hurt the firm and that his leaving "had to happen."

## ASSIMILATION INTO NEW COMPANY

Within a month, Frank began his new role as CEO of the company mentioned earlier, a direct competitor of Banyun. Frank's holiday card to the author that year read on the front, "All is calm." Inside he wrote, 'I thought this was appropriate." The author and he agreed to continue their relationship with her serving as *trusted advisor* on issues related to his leadership, as well as his successful assimilation into the new company. In his words,

"My technical learning curve here is moderate; it's mostly going to be about reading the landscape and people leadership." They contracted for quarterly meetings, and during Frank's first year there, their conversations focused on his building a strong relationship with his new boss, the staffing ramifications of location consolidations, and his ensuring that he had the right people in key roles. With his trusted advisor, he created a new Visual Leadership Metaphor® (VLM) (see figure 9.1) to track progress in this role.

Near the end of that year Frank said, "This transition has been great; and my fears about change were unwarranted." Strategic priorities had been set, progress was being made on organization structure issues, and a number of good hires were made. While some of these people came voluntarily from Banyun, sword-rattling from John about employee piracy did not materialize into litigation. Most of all, Frank was experiencing the benefits of working for a mature and empowering boss whom he could trust and whose passion and entrepreneurial instincts fueled prospects of significant financial success and personal contentment.

Given Frank's open, candid, and frequent communication with his new boss, he readily conveyed his high standards, tenacity,

**Figure 9.1**   Frank's Visual Leadership Metaphor® (VLM) #2.

*Drawing by Joe Williams*

| FRAME 1 | FRAME 2 | FRAME 3 |
| --- | --- | --- |
| It's like I'm on one of those game shows and you just don't know what's behind the door. Every time you open one, there are more problems— things that need to be fixed. | Now it's like I'm juggling 15 balls simultaneously. | It's like I'm with a chessboard now: I have myself and everything else settled down and organized so I can go about things systematically. |

accountability, and ability to handle the managerial aspects of the company. Unlike John, Frank's current boss appreciated this but it was neither his interest nor strength, and when not developing business, he spent his time with local and state political figures, as well as on his significant philanthropic activities. He was happy to leave the day-to-day management of the company completely in Frank's capable hands, and he gave him the resources he needed.

Instead of second-guessing Frank, he challenged him. In Frank's words, "He's having a real stretch effect on me. I feel myself reaching for bigger goals faster, and I'm putting myself out there in a very different way now." Having been contained, scrutinized, and belittled for so many years, the effects of this new boss relationship were liberating and released in Frank heightened levels of confidence, commitment, and certainty about his career path forward.

In this time frame, Frank sent the author a thank you card in which he wrote, "I read the 'Reluctant President' (see chapter 8) again. I must have breezed through it before because now I see how hard we had tried to make it work for me at Banyun. I really appreciate all you've done." The author remembered thinking that leadership progress like Frank's didn't happen without the intention of a talented and fully engaged client. She believed her efforts were less about building Frank's leadership competency than they were about his discovering and releasing dormant capabilities.

### Unexpected/Fortuitous Business Event

Within a few years, their business was spun out of the parent and Frank commenced the next chapter of his evolution as a leader. He relished their full independence and appeared as confident as his boss about the growth prospects of their company. Over the next four years, it would establish a national presence. Frank continued to produce new business and manage the firm with a focus on creating a team-based leadership culture. In his words, "A lot of people were worried about what this would mean for them, but the truth is we'll have all the benefits of a small company environment with all the resources of a major corporation."

When asked where he was in his new Visual Leadership Metaphor® (see figure 9.1), Frank's continued progress was evident when he said,

I'm clearly in frame 2, and I think prioritization is my major challenge now. It's about the business and the people, and increasingly, I see the importance of communication. The employees need to hear enough from senior management, so we're having mini town hall meetings and creating a new website and a general brochure, too so everyone is clear about what we are—and their place in it.

### Complementarity with Boss

As they predicted, business boomed with Frank and his boss building on their special brand of complementarity. Not one to boast or otherwise tilt toward self-aggrandizement, Frank described his boss as the "inspirational rainmaker" and himself as the "pragmatic captain of the ship." His boss described Frank as "the best hire I ever made." Together they continued to focus on two major strategic issues: (1) managing their rapid growth—largely a function of several acquisitions, and (2) assessing the pros and cons of their selling the company.

### Maintaining Focus on Top Priorities

Aside from major strategic issues (cited earlier), the interrelated themes in discussions with Frank over the next couple of years were: (1) the relentless tension between developing new business and managing people; (2) need to break the firm's dependency on Frank and his boss as the "perpetual rainmakers," that is, to create and sustain a strong sales force; (3) the need to better mentor key talent; and (4) his desire for more personal time (Frank was now in his fifties).

Frank and his trusted advisor discussed the chronic nature of themes one and two as inevitable. In other words, that this was the bane of any sales-driven culture where business development rested on the shoulders of a certain few who possessed a distinctive and rare array of skills and behavioral assets. This is not to say that

Frank gave up on searching for such talent. At the author's prodding, he spent time thinking about what comprised the "magic sauce" of talented business producers so as to better inform their outside recruiters and company interviewers.

Frank also made headway on theme three (mentoring others). He recognized that he needed to get more granular in his discussions with key sales producers particularly on issues such as how to qualify a meaningful client prospect. While this was something he could gauge quickly (*I can pretty much tell immediately if something is worth chasing*), it was not as reflexive a talent for others. He also became more demanding with top managers regarding their discernment of what warranted their time versus necessary hand-offs to others (*You need to be clear about when you really need to be in a client meeting, for example, and when it's better for you to give that shot to someone else*).

By 2012, Frank felt that he had moved into frame 3 of his Visual Leadership Metaphor®, and there were signs of progress on theme four (more personal time) as well. He had built his dream house at the beach and was intentional about spending more time there. Surely information technology tools supported an effective "virtual" working model. Further, his leisure time now included international travel, as well as more quality time with his sons. One was still in college while the other had graduated and seemed to be embarking upon a career in sales. Whether or not he would join Frank's company remained to be seen but in the meantime, Frank had rightly encouraged him to first earn his stripes elsewhere.

## Leveraging Lessons Learned in Initial Coaching

Perhaps the most compelling question aroused by this case study update is the extent to which Frank had internalized lessons learned from the initial coaching engagement. In brief, he deserved high marks for continuing to apply what were originally identified as his "strengths to leverage"—business development, leadership potential, and relationship with boss. He had also made gains in his two "development areas"—relationship-building and people management. These areas would warrant his continued attention. What follows is a more granular look at his progress in each of these areas.

### Strength to Leverage—Business Development

Developing new business would always be Frank's "power alley." He relished the chase, and while he was constrained by a three-year noncompete agreement with Banyun, when that lifted, he was able to resume relationships with former customers, as well as develop new business with them. The ongoing challenges for Frank in this area would be recruitment of great business producers and mentoring.

If Frank had his preference, he would focus all his time "hunting" new business unencumbered by his company leadership responsibilities. However, by now he had learned that the perpetuation of a business was not just about topline growth. This required intentional leadership as well, and he had modified his behavior to capitalize on his leadership potential.

### Strength to Leverage—Leadership Potential

There were numerous instances of Frank's having evolved his leadership potential but one of the biggest indicators of progress was when he said of his prospective new employer, "They are interested in me for the right reasons, and I realize that I've become a lot more than a sales guy. There is something for me to build there, and I'm ready to do that."

Other indications of Frank's leveraging this strength were his: (1) maturity when he left Banyun, that is, the time he took to compose a resignation letter that hit the right notes; (2) recognition that the demands of his new role would largely be about his leadership and ensuring he put the right people in place; (3) personal sense of "stretch" in his new role and the leadership implications of that; (4) emphasis on ensuring clarity of strategy, structure, objectives, and rewards; and (5) recognition of the importance of prioritization as a leader.

In many conversations with Frank, his strong preference for the production side of the business emerged like a shooting star in all its power and speed. However, through his coaching one of the strongest leadership insights—an insight with lasting implications for his behavioral change—was the utility of his *slowing down to go fast*. Specifically, when Frank slowed down and made the time to mentor and/or coach others, he was rewarded by their progress in producing new business and their contributing to the strong reputation and rapid growth of the company.

### Strength to Leverage—Relationship with His Boss

Given what Frank had learned through his experience at Banyun, he was acutely focused on what the relationship dynamics might be with his new boss. This wasn't just any boss; this was the chairman of the company, and as has already been indicated, he was a significant player in local and state politics, and a heavy hitter in community philanthropic circles, too. While Frank was drawn to his new career opportunity, the initial prospect of this boss was tinged with equal elements of intrigue and wariness.

What became apparent almost immediately was that his new boss, like Frank himself, was a pragmatist who valued competence, commitment, competition, and stellar results. Therefore, Frank formed an immediate and strong bond with him. To a large degree this was due to their mutual respect, drive, tenacity, and excitement about building something neither could have built alone. On a deeper level, the platinum quality of their relationship was a function of their reciprocal engagement, that is, it produced something significant for both of them (Baldoni, 2010).[4] Further, having learned from his dysfunctional relationship with John, Frank ensured frequent communication with his new boss abetted by the fact that their offices were right next to each other. Given his boss's significant time away from the office, Frank remained opportunistic about when he could "catch him" for the issues they needed to discuss together.

### Development Area—Relationship-Building

Frank would be the first to emphasize that he was never going to be a "warm and fuzzy" guy. However, he had learned that he could influence stronger performance from people if he made an effort to connect. This realization influenced behavior change that found him more willing to discuss people's anxieties, fears, and elations about the work and even to do a better job of celebrating their accomplishments. Such relationship-building remained an ongoing focus in discussions with the author who used emotional intelligence as a development tool, as well as what she modeled about caring connection in their relationship.

Regarding emotional intelligence, over a decade Frank became more self-aware especially in terms of his impact on others. He was also better able to channel his emotions—both positive and negative—as a resource for achieving objectives. Further, he became more attuned to others' concerns, and as has already been mentioned, he was more mindful about making a personal connection with others versus being so transactional.

### Development Area—People Management

Frank's holding the "people side" of the business as a top priority influenced a sustained behavior change in his leadership. He learned that he could drive more change and business growth by staying focused on talent management. Specifically, he maintained a commitment to the strong recruitment, employee assimilation, technical training, management development, and performance management efforts necessary to build a vibrant and thriving business organization.

Ongoing conversations with his trusted advisor focused on how one leadership approach could not fit all. The ultimate pragmatist, Frank wished that this could be the case, but nothing would replace his clearing time for quality face-to-face interactions with his direct reports—and key others as needed. Frank's reflection on the *conveyance of wisdom* appeared to have had positive effects on his mentoring others on both business production and leadership issues. However, clearing time for these interactions would be an ongoing challenge. His hiring of a seasoned and gifted HR leader gave him the inside partner he needed.

## Discussion

The author's long-term *trusted advisor* relationship with Frank is at the center of this case study update.[5] For context, the original case study (see chapter 8) helps ground an understanding of how the author transitioned from executive coach to trusted advisor.[6] In short, the more successful her efforts were to deliver on the coaching remit of helping her client, Frank, become an effective leader, the more agitated his CEO seemed to become. Her attempts to influence a productive peace between John and Frank resulted in only fleeting days of détente. Further, as time went on, it became clear that Frank's vigor, vitality, and now increased admiration of his multifaceted leadership efforts within the firm were experienced by John as a huge narcissistic injury.

As John's public criticisms of Frank mounted, and Frank's tolerance level of this behavior declined, the author conveyed her concern to John regarding Frank's becoming a potential retention risk. In the profane tirade that followed, John expressed his wish that Frank would indeed leave the company because, in John's view, Frank was the source of "all the firm's problems." While recognizing the magnitude of John's defensive projection, the author phoned him anyway to verify his position vis-á-vis Frank. Her inquiry was met with his loud and stinging adamancy couched in the crudest of terms.

Now free to participate in Frank's consideration of leaving Banyun, the author could aid in his objective appraisal of other opportunities. For example, she created a Stay-Go Exercise (see figure 9.2) for him to use as he zeroed in on his final decision. By the end of the initial coaching engagement, Frank had achieved his leadership objectives, as well as a fundamental insight. This insight involved his underlying masochism, and it explained why he was able to tolerate John's sadistic behavior for so many years. Their pattern of masochism and sadism actually worked well for them—until Frank's coaching, and then he grew out of it.

The coach's unsavory experiences with John may have contributed to the bond she shared with Frank. However, in the end it was the learning and growth Frank had experienced in the coaching, and his recognition of the ongoing value of input from a leadership

**Figure 9.2** Stay-Go Exercise.

**Exercise instruction:**

1 To make this exercise as relevant as possible to your current situation:
   o Read all the factors
   o IGNORE factors that do not apply
   o Add new factors under the "Other" section—factors that match your current situation
   o Make a copy of this exercise *before* you fill it out. You may want to have someone who knows you well fill it out independent of you. Comparing your respective ratings should prove useful.

2 Rate each factor on a 1–5 scale, with 5 as the highest rating. For each relevant factor, place a rating in *both* the **Stay** and **Go** columns.
   For example, if you think the *Relationship with Boss* factor is very negative, you would put a 1 or 2 under **STAY** and a 4 or 5 under **GO**.

   Conversely, if you think the *Opportunity to Learn* factor is quite positive, as compared to another company, you would put a 4 or 5 under **STAY** and a 1 or 2 under **GO**.

3 Add the scores you've placed in both columns. A big difference (more than 10 points) in the **STAY-GO** ratings is a clear signal in favor of the **STAY** or **GO** option, i.e., the column with the highest score.

4 If there is not a big difference in the **STAY-GO** ratings, this indicates a caution for you to reflect carefully and make sure you do not make an impetuous decision.

Rate factors on a 1–5 scale, 5 being highest

| Factors | Stay | Go |
|---|---|---|
| Autonomy—level of empowerment | | |
| Creative latitude—freedom to pursue/apply one's own ideas | | |
| Daily level of stress | | |
| Desire to pursue something different altogether (e.g., MBA, law school, another career objective) | | |
| Intellectual stimulation | | |
| Job security | | |
| Money (current) | | |
| Money (future potential) | | |
| Pace of work—fast, medium, or slow | | |
| Peerage—relationships with peers foster real collaboration | | |
| Potential for bigger role in the organization | | |

*Continued*

**Figure 9.2** Continued

| | | |
|---|---|---|
| Power—ability to influence boss and others | | |
| Professional legacy—work provides opportunity to mentor, teach, influence others | | |
| Recognition—stature, respect for work done | | |
| Relationship with boss—effects of this in terms of mood, morale, motivation | | |
| Relationships (colleagues, staff) | | |
| Resources—staff and other resources needed to meet job objectives | | |
| Self-actualization—becoming all one can be | | |
| Span of impact | | |
| Travel—enough opportunity to travel; travel is not excessive | | |
| Visibility to senior management and the board | | |
| Work environment/location—comfort, positive aesthetics, reasonable commute | | |
| Work-personal integration; negative effects of role on personal life | | |
| *Other factor (if any)* | | |
| *Other factor (if any)* | | |
| *Other factor (if any)* | | |
| **TOTALS** | | |

expert with both a business background and training in clinical psychology that most influenced her becoming his trusted advisor. This was the springboard into a productive and enduring next phase of their relationship.

### *Trusted Advisor Aids Client's Continued Success*

Working with Frank as his trusted advisor flourished on the foundation of all he had already learned. He had the emotional attunement to navigate effectively in a new situation, the confidence to stretch to the limits of his capabilities, the clarity about how to apply his leadership capabilities, the wisdom to capitalize on a mature relationship with his new boss, and the courage to build something of significance. His role in *building* this company would likely be the capstone to Frank's career.

Metaphorically, the author's role as *trusted advisor* involved a combination of dimensions that she has described as echo, anchor, mirror, and spark (for a fuller discussion, see chapter 10). As echo, she knew when to holler into the canyon reminding Frank of the lessons he had already learned—lessons that had applicability in his new role. As anchor, she exhorted him to stay steady in the practice of his best leadership habits such as mentoring other business producers. As mirror, she reflected candid observations of his leadership whenever he needed them. And as spark, she brought him the examples of other good leaders, the optimism, and the encouragement that would inspire his most effective leadership.

## CONCLUSION

This case study update provides a rare inside look at how a superb senior executive worked with an executive coach/trusted advisor in a long-term partnership. Spanning over a decade, this extraordinary partnership rewarded both participants and the organizations they served. For the executive, there was heightened self-awareness, the discovery of the full range of his capabilities, and his sustained use of them. For the executive coach/trusted advisor, there was the initial walk through a fire that seared at the edges but mostly fanned her resolve about how to deal with "stars"—and the monsters who try to devour them. And then later, there was the deep—and shared—satisfaction of watching a client's hard lessons learned influence the building and steady growth of one of the most respected and envied entities in its field.

The pragmatic captain of the ship had ridden a turbulent sea, and arrived at his destiny.

# Executive's Reflection

The suggestion of my involvement in "coaching" was initially received very cynically by me. The suggestion came from the company's patriarch who while very successful was also troubled and had been seeing a psychologist regularly for years. My reluctance was a function of my not having the time, and not being able to conceive of an "academic" having much valuable insight. The fact that my boss embraced the idea was not surprising to me because of his state of mind.

I reluctantly gave our HR head the "go-ahead" to seek out some "qualified candidates." While I did undertake the process with an open mind, I had serious doubts that I would meet someone who gave me the necessary confidence to commit myself to an initiative of this magnitude. I did meet more than a couple of "duds" before meeting Karol. One openly admitted that he had no experience with business people, but was anxious to transition into this line of work as it would be more "lucrative." Karol had excellent references, years of experience, and she had what sounded like a sound process. In addition, I sensed a good chemistry.

Our initial work (i.e., testing, 360 interviews, etc.) took the better part of six months. Anything short of this thorough process would have been inadequate for me to "wake up and smell the coffee." In my case, the transition from sales leader to President created mixed emotions in the organization, which I had underestimated. I couldn't imagine that the entire organization wouldn't welcome the change with a sigh of relief. The reality was I needed a real lesson in emotional intelligence and had to come to grips with the fact that "perception was reality" and in order to be effective, I needed to develop a plan to deal with the resultant issues. My work with Karol for some time afterwards focused on not changing who I was, but being more thoughtful about changing some of those perceptions.

We collectively succeeded in much of what we set out to do in our game plan. A very smooth transition was accomplished, and the coaching related to emotional intelligence was successful. Unfortunately, while progress was being made on this front, the psyche of my partner (and the majority shareholder) went in the opposite direction. It became obvious very quickly that he had buyer's remorse from the start. While intellectually he knew it was wise to turn over the reins, his ego couldn't deal with it. While we achieved great success from an objective standpoint, we remained a dysfunctional organization.

As a result of this dynamic, my work continued with Karol for another couple of years before my departure. We met quarterly and unfortunately our time was frequently consumed revisiting the appropriate strategy to continue driving results and coexist with a dysfunctional partner. Karol's efforts were key to our continuing to operate effectively as a company, and for me to maintain my sanity. While our work together should be credited with extending my tenure at the company, it was inevitable that I would eventually leave.

Ironically, I stepped into another situation where I had my hands full, albeit a much different scenario. My success heading up company A put me in a position to approach the same business, which was twice its size and one of the largest in the country. The mission at company B was to create a brand for an operation, which was the by-product of 17 acquisitions in seven years. In addition, a sales culture needed to be developed and professionals needed to be recruited in order to position the company to take advantage of the large opportunities they were failing to capitalize on.

I felt that this transition would have been more difficult than it already was if I had not had Karol, my trusted advisor, available. She knew me well, and through her work with me had come to know our industry. She encouraged me to take this challenge and was there to help me as this was a much bigger engagement, with four more moving parts. Her best advice was delivered with a prop. A small Lucite box filled with different sized rocks. The message was dealing with the big rocks (issues) first. If I tried to deal with all of the multitude of issues at once, nothing would get done.

Over the last seven years in my current position, Karol and I have continued to meet quarterly. Invariably there are issues at hand that I am happy to have her available to discuss as an informed outside party. In the first 15 months the parent company (a bank) was put on the blocks and eventually sold. Simultaneously, we purchased the insurance business and immediately thereafter sold off businesses that the bank looked at favorably but we did not. We changed the company name, moved out of the bank's facilities, transitioned to a new computer system, and so on. The end result is that we now have one of the largest privately held firms of its kind in the country, it is the region's leader, and it's the envy of our competition. I have made many decisions over the last ten years in which Karol was an influence. I would say the return on investment has been exceptional.

# CHAPTER 10

# From Executive Coach to Trusted Advisor

## INTRODUCTION

Each of the eight case studies in this book is distinguished by its own objectives, contextual factors, interpersonal dynamics, and outcomes. However, seven of them have one thing in common: my role shifted from executive coach to *trusted advisor*, and the relationships with these business leaders ensued for many years thereafter.[1] While the term "trusted advisor" is familiar in business,[2] it has been used less frequently in the field of consulting psychology.[3] Freedman and Perry used it when they described how the emergence of trust with a senior executive was the central factor in his (Freedman) ultimately becoming a trusted advisor to that organization.[4] My use of this term is applied to the consultant who has coached a senior executive, and upon the completion of that engagement, the executive coach is invited by the client to provide consultation on issues related to this leader's ongoing effectiveness.

My trusted advisor relationships have involved either continuous connections over many years, or they have been episodic, that is, preexisting relationships were reignited as a function of an executive's new leadership responsibilities. While some may argue that long-term relationships of this nature foster dependency, my experiences underscore something quite different. Specifically, the enduring trust, mutual respect, and committed presence of an objective outsider who, in my case, has a dual background in business and clinical training in psychology provides the executive with an additional and distinctive resource for leading effectively. This includes the trusted advisor providing unfiltered feedback[5] as well as ensuring that the executive leverages relevant insights and lessons learned during the coaching.

Surely there are differences in how coaches form trusted advisor relationships with their executive clients. At the core of my approach is a hybrid stance between my primary identity as a business person and my sensibilities as a clinically trained psychologist and consultant. However, I offer my conceptualization of this role as potentially useful to anyone who wants to discover his or her way of making the coach to trusted advisor transition. Further, this conceptualization may also be of interest to seasoned consultants who have already established this level of client *intimacy* with senior business leaders. More later on *intimacy* and the sense of *relatedness* that trusted advisors can establish with their clients.

## Prelude to Becoming a Trusted Advisor

The shift from executive coach to trusted advisor is typically preceded by a number of factors. First, the coaching engagement was significantly successful, that is, the objectives were achieved, and the executive is buoyed by the fact that he or she is more effective than was the case before the coaching commenced. Second, the chemistry between the executive and the coach is not just good— it's superb, having grown on a strong foundation of mutual trust, respect, and personal resonance with the other. Third, there are continuing issues related to leadership effectiveness that can be readily addressed by the trusted advisor given his or her knowledge of both the executive and the company as gained through the coaching engagement. These issues include executive recruitment, the development of high potential employees, and succession planning for top roles. And finally, the organization values and is willing to financially support the work of the trusted advisor.[6]

Certain professional and personal background factors are also germane to becoming a trusted advisor—as they are in establishing credibility at the outset of a coaching engagement. In my case these included: (1) a decade of employment in a Fortune company; (2) doctoral training in applied clinical psychology; (3) an internship in a management assessment firm where I learned how to give psychological feedback to business people; (4) several years as a partner in a sales-driven career management firm where I learned how to "sell" psychological consulting services; (4) my commitment to forming strong collaborative partnerships with the human resources (HR) professionals in the organizations that engage me; (5) a business model that emphasizes long-term relationships with both global entities and well-established privately held companies; and (6) having done my own psychological "work." This last factor is, perhaps, my greatest insurance against abusing or otherwise contaminating the necessary boundaries of mature and valuable trusted advisor relationships with my clients—relationships that are maintained over many years.

### Intimacy *and* Relatedness *in the Executive Coach to Trusted Advisor Shift*

Based on my experience and observations, senior consultants who move fluidly from executive coach to trusted advisor possess a strong capacity for intimacy, that is, they readily establish a close working alliance with a client that deepens over time and is characterized by mutual authenticity and absence of ego.[7] By this time, any concerns the executive may have had about vulnerability[8] have been replaced by the freedom to "just be" with no thoughts about weakness or over-dependence given the special *relatedness* to the trusted advisor. Josselson wrote, "Relatedness and individuality are not dichotomous. Action takes place only within a relational matrix; the self is realized through others; development concerns both maintaining our ties to others *and* differentiating from them."[9] This relatedness is welcomed by the executive, and thrives on the trusted advisor's fundamental commitment and intimate orientation to the client:

> You have let me in, and I "see" you. I see what others see, and I see what they don't see. I am aware of your distinctive talents and of your lesser talents, too. I am aware of the relentless pressures you endure, of the restless nights, and the cold sweats, too. I know that the rhythm of your life is more staccato than smooth, and often more lonely than not. I know that there is less glory and more angst in your role than others realize. I know that you can be battle-weary, and you can be battle tough—but whatever stance you're in, we have created a safe and steady sanctuary

in which you can trust, be vulnerable, reflect, and contemplate issues in a manner that ensures you're leading with the full force of all your capabilities.

In the vocabulary of this relationship—this intimate *relatedness* with the trusted advisor—the executive can count on getting what he or she is pressed to give others but receives little of in return: affirmation, optimism, hope, and empathic responsiveness, as well as constructive guidance and feedback. At times, the responsiveness of the trusted advisor can/should be tough and pointed, however, it always seeks to release the positive emotion of the leader for both its individual and organizational effects.

There are significant implications of this for business leaders. Fredrickson wrote, "Because an individual's experiences of positive emotions can reverberate through other organizational members and across interpersonal transactions with customers, positive emotions may also fuel optimal organizational functioning."[10] Further, both neuroscientists and psychologists to include Seligman[11] and Hanson[12] maintain that we can take advantage of the plasticity of the brain to cultivate and sustain positive emotions. (What an honorable objective for the trusted advisor!)

Finally, I believe compassion is embedded in the trusted advisor's focus on positive emotion—especially self-compassion as a tool for mitigating the negative effects of the harsh self-criticism so common among senior business leaders.[13] Perhaps there is also an individual corollary of the systems change discipline of appreciative inquiry.[14] Specifically, as an orientation in the trusted advisor relationship, consultants can help clients discover the positive and anticipatory images of the future for both themselves and the organizations they're leading.

## The Trusted Advisor: Four Dimensions

There are four dimensions in this conceptualization of the trusted advisor: *echo, anchor, mirror,* and *spark* (see figure 10.1). As a trusted advisor, I have given guidance from all of these dimensions trusting my intuitive weaving of a client's inner and outer realities as to which dimension would be most useful, and when. The difference

**Figure 10.1** Trusted Advisor—Four Dimensions.

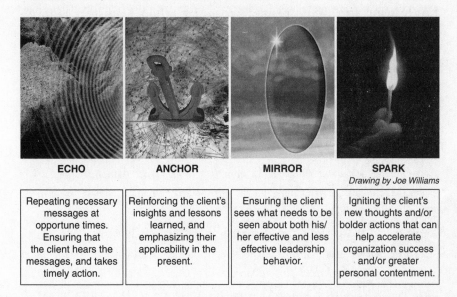

| ECHO | ANCHOR | MIRROR | SPARK |
|---|---|---|---|
| | | | *Drawing by Joe Williams* |
| Repeating necessary messages at opportune times. Ensuring that the client hears the messages, and takes timely action. | Reinforcing the client's insights and lessons learned, and emphasizing their applicability in the present. | Ensuring the client sees what needs to be seen about both his/ her effective and less effective leadership behavior. | Igniting the client's new thoughts and/or bolder actions that can help accelerate organization success and/or greater personal contentment. |

between my stance as a trusted advisor (more directive) versus that of coach (less directive) involves a fundamental difference between consulting and coaching. As trusted advisor I am consulting to—or directly advising—the leader based on what I have already learned and discovered about him/her (through insight) in the previous coaching phase.

Given business circumstances—or at times the confluence of business and personal events—I have advised a leader primarily from one dimension or from one or more of these dimensions even in the same meeting. Often, a client and I were moving in and out of each dimension as fast-moving events necessitated. In short, the role of the trusted advisor is never static—it is as dynamic as the business conditions with which our clients are confronted. The value of the role—as presented here—is to be able to read what circumstances require of you as the trusted advisor, and to be accurate and nimble enough to meet your client wherever he or she needs to be met.

### Echo *Dimension*

The *echo* dimension of this conceptualization of the trusted advisor involves the focused listening skill and steel trap memory of the advisor. Based on a deepened understanding of the client and what I'm hearing in the moment, I recognize when I must metaphorically, of course, yell a certain message into the canyon. This is a right message at the right time—a message that will reverberate in a relentless echo loud and clear enough for my client to hear its significance. The message may be a warning: (*Your team is not aligned on the strategy—not aligned! Not aligned! Not aligned!*). The message may be a strong suggestion: (*Take another look at that candidate before she's hired, she may not be a good "fit" with the team—take another look! Take another look! Take another look!*). Or it could be an exhortation: (*Be bold—take action, trust your gut! Trust your gut! Trust your gut!*).

Advising from the echo dimension, I frequently reminded Frank (chapter 9) of his former boss's emotional instability: (*You were expecting rational decision-making but he is not rational! Not rational! Not rational!*). I urged Max (chapter 6) to be courageous in the exploration of his "next self" (*Pursue your desired path, face yourself! Face yourself! Face yourself!*). And for Walt (chapter 7), my echo into the canyon emphasized the need for him to be less constrained by his content in large group presentations and doing more to connect to his audience: (*Step away from your content, show them more of you—loosen up! Loosen up! Loosen up!*).

### Anchor *Dimension*

The *anchor* dimension of this trusted advisor conceptualization is based on the reinforcement—or anchoring in the learner—of past lessons learned in the coaching phase. My intention is to ensure that the executive can leverage these lessons and insights in ways that support—and even accelerate—the pursuit of current business objectives. By relating from the *anchor* dimension, the trusted advisor also helps ensure the executive's behavioral consistency and his or her ability to be a source of sturdy and steady leadership for others.

Advising from the anchor dimension for Rachel (chapter 4) found me reinforcing lessons about the clash between her company's culture and her preferred way of leading: (*Be mindful of the culture but, at the same time, do not be unduly apologetic about how you're leading. When your boss is critical of your leadership, don't let that erode your power. Emphasize how you've motivated your team to achieve good results).*

One of the most powerful lessons emphasized (anchored) for Kathryn (chapter 2) was that her boss's enigmatic ways had more to do with him than her: (*We've seen this behavior before. Remember there is something in his dynamic with others that can spill over into his interactions with you. So question yourself less, and attune to him more*). And for Ted (chapter 1), one lesson he needed to remember was not to overidentify with the aggressor: (*When a business decision is not going your way, challenge yourself to put forth another argument versus strafing the landscape and grinding your opponent into the ground*).

### Mirror *Dimension*

The *mirror* is perhaps the most straightforward of the four trusted advisor dimensions. Advising from this dimension necessitates vigilant and constructive efforts to ensure that clients see what they need to see about themselves as leaders. Using astute powers of observation and courage, the trusted advisor performs at least two invaluable tasks by holding up a mirror: (1) as a candid truth-teller; and (2) as an enthusiastic affirmer of work well done. There are also myriad other ways that advising from the mirror dimension can add value. These include the trusted advisor signaling the need to celebrate in the wake of achieving key milestones; using humorous observations to cut through tension; challenging assumptions; and helping executives forgive themselves for mistakes, that is, keeping these in proper perspective, and (as indicated earlier) having sufficient self-compassion too.

Using the mirror dimension, I reminded Walt (chapter 7) that his habit of rubbing his hands together detracted from his projecting a strong executive persona: (*I notice that you rub your hands like that a lot when you're speaking. This makes you look anxious or uncertain so try to do less of that*). For Ravid (chapter 5), my holding up the mirror was intended to ease his mind about the sale of his company: (*There are times when you look and sound dejected as if you should have been able to avert the sale of the company—but you did all you could. This was about majority shareholders wanting the money*). And for Max (chapter 6), I held up the mirror often to help bolster his confidence in a contemplated career change: (*Try to keep balancing your concerns about this change with a focus on your proven talent and natural affinity for this new pursuit*).

### Spark *Dimension*

The spark dimension of the executive-trusted advisor relationship is about igniting leaders' continued success and/or personal contentment. The most immediate and obvious benefit of advice given from this dimension is its influence on the executive's ability to deliver on his or her strongest aspirations for the company. The trusted advisor influences the executive's actions in a manner that helps ensure his or her collaboration with a leadership team so together they achieve and even surpass objectives set for the enterprise.

Sometimes an emotionally charged personal event, as in the case of the death of Jean Paul's father (chapter 3), finds the trusted advisor striving to ignite a greater sense of emotional resolution: (*I'm going to introduce you to a bilingual bereavement counselor who can help you grieve so you will be less distracted by this huge loss*). Or, in the case of Max, advising from the spark dimension required referral to another resource: (*I'm going to recommend someone who can help you actually map out your new career*). And with Ravid, a clearer picture of the future began to emerge as he considered his life through the lens of my Five-P model for retirement planning: (*For many CEOs, the Purpose factor in the model may be the most difficult. You will be invited to do many things, and while you will feel the inexorable pull to keep busy, this is the time when you can be selective about what you really want to do—the activities that will give you the most satisfaction and meaning now*).

When a senior executive approaches retirement during the relationship with his or her trusted advisor, guidance given from the spark dimension can help ignite comprehensive planning for entrance into this life stage. For many senior executives, retirement

**Figure 10.2**  A Five-P Model for Retirement Planning*

| |
|---|
| **Purpose**—What do I want to do and/or get involved with that will provide a real sense of meaning in my life now? |
| **Place**—Where do I really want to live now? What locations(s) will be most compatible with my desired lifestyle? |
| **People**—Who are the people with whom I want to spend the most time? |
| **Physical**—What do I need to do to ensure my physical well-being? |
| **Prosperity**—What more might I need to do to ensure my long-term financial stability? |
| * For some executives, i.e., those who are craving a greater spiritual component in their lives, there is a sixth factor that can be spelled "phaith" thus making it a "Six P Model." This involves a different type of introspection that may lead one back to a religious practice—or not. It matters not what "it" is; rather, the importance is the identification of this need and then a targeted response to it. |

can initiate a hail storm of doubt, anger, and loss. It is the emotional equivalent of the midlife identity crisis. The trusted advisor can provide a methodical approach that replaces mental evasion or denial with a careful consideration of essential factors. This "Five-P Model" for retirement planning can be a helpful spark for both piercing unspoken anxieties at this life stage, and for initiating proactive planning. See figure 10.2 for this model and the interrelated questions that can inform postcareer planning.

Helping an executive ignite holistic and reflective planning for the after career life stage can be an especially rewarding endeavor for the trusted advisor. It is an opportunity to intervene in a manner that can promote ego integrity and avert the potential despair of the life stage between age 55 and death.[15] Wasylyshyn wrote, "When dissatisfaction, hostility, and/or restlessness predominate (in this life stage), individuals can fall into a deep sense of despair looking back on their lives with gnawing feelings of unrequitedness, anger, and frustration."[16]

## CONCLUDING THOUGHTS

While the four dimensions of *echo, anchor, mirror,* and *spark* are offered as a practice framework for building trusted advisor relationships, some words of caution about this role are also warranted. Given the intimacy of this bond between executive and consultant, the latter must guard against losing objectivity about the client. We must also protect the professional boundary of this relationship. While sharing dinners, for example, can be scheduled as a time for important conversations, trusted advisors are encouraged to balance these occasions with meetings that occur during business hours. It is often wiser to resist other business-social invitations as well—unless doing so would constitute a major faux pas in the relationship.[17]

Further, despite the intimacy of these relationships and the confidential nature of the conversations that transpire within them, trusted advisors must keep their own egos in check. While they have a special access to power, trusted advisors must remember that they are not—and never will be—true "insiders." They are "outside insiders" and as such it is incumbent upon them to not only keep this in perspective but to also make a concerted effort to foster relationships with other key stakeholders in the system (e.g., the corporate head of Human Resources). To not do so the trusted advisor runs the risk of being isolated from an ongoing flow of collateral and objective information that can, in fact, enrich consultation to the executives whom they serve.

Finally, while this may be obvious, the relationship between an executive and his or her trusted advisor—the type of advisor depicted in these case studies—is as unique and fragile as any close relationship. It is a privilege to have it. It requires special attention to maintain it. And maintaining it involves something more visceral than the advisor's obvious credibility (business knowledge and expertise in human behavior). It is his or her steadfast *presence* rooted in trust and commitment to the executive's success. It is magnified by the advisor's capacity to form an intimate and compassionate connection with the leader whilst still maintaining sufficient objectivity to be an effective truth-teller. Invariably, it can be counted on as a catalytic container in which leaders' fears are eased, anxieties are neutralized, eye-to-eye validation is provided,[18] and courage is amplified—all in the service of the organizations the executives are leading.

It is in the committed *presence* of the trusted advisor—in this quiet away from the cacophony of quarterly pressures, in this safety apart from the feasting critics or gutless pessimists, and in this encouragement—that leaders can clear any psychological debris and rise into themselves. In this relationship, they are helped to see and hear themselves differently. In Josselson's words, "Who we are in others' eyes affects our sense of our reality—who we are in our own eyes...we need others to validate our experience of ourselves and, beyond that, to offer us sometimes a better version of ourselves than we know ourselves to be."[19]

In the intimacy of relationships with their trusted advisors, business leaders hear necessary messages reverberating in the canyons around them. They practice lessons of lasting wisdom. They see their glittering images in balance with humility and authenticity. Their best efforts are ignited by sparks of clarity and conceptual depth. In all these many ways, and others, too, they are helped to realize their destinies to lead.

# CHAPTER 11

# Client and Coach Views Compared

These eight clients' perspectives on their coaching as provided in candid *executive reflections* make a timely contribution to the field of executive coaching. In the brief summaries that follow, the author compares their comments to her view of the key points in each case—with an eye toward contributing to research and practice considerations. As Stevens wrote, "Hearing the clients' voices about what happened behind closed doors in coaching meetings is a way to strengthen our theoretical and practice foundations."[1]

*Three Suprises*

There were three surprises for the author that related to both what these clients did—and did not—mention as key in their coaching. First, despite what other coaches may perceive as fostering dependency, these senior executives were emphatic about the value of their long-term relationships with the coach who eventually became their *trusted advisor* (as defined in chapter 10). Second, while significant psychological insights were at the core of most of these coaching outcomes, they were not always acknowledged by the clients. And third, while the author found her collaborative partnerships with company sources (boss and HR professional) to be critical to positive and sustained coaching outcomes, only a few clients cited this factor.

*Four Expectations Realized*

Four points mentioned frequently by these clients were not surprising to the author but bear emphasis as they reinforce sound practice in the coaching of senior executives. First, these clients did not have coaching or a particular coach imposed upon them. In other words, they valued the opportunity to gauge the potential utility of coaching for them, as well as to assess "chemistry" with a prospective coach. Second, the clarity of both coaching goals and ways to track progress on them was key. Third, they valued a focus on leveraging their strengths, as well as on addressing limitations. And fourth, their comfort in the coaching was increased by the coach/trusted advisor maintaining appropriate boundaries of confidentiality.

## TED—*THE RELENTLESS CHAMPION*

The points of agreement between the perspectives of Ted and his coach included: (1) the tough scrutiny upfront about the strength of his intention to participate in the coaching (*I wanted to prove her initial assessment of me wrong and impress her with the changes that I was capable of making in a successful coaching endeavor*); (2) the proactive role of a Human Resources (HR) professional (*I trusted and respected [him] immensely*); (3) the importance of two particular coaching tools (Gestalt technique of imagining his coach sitting next to him in meetings, and the notion of his career *legacy*) that helped him achieve his leadership *statesman* aspiration (*I wanted to be more successful so this was the time to be thinking about legacy*); and (4) the coach's stance of honoring his strengths and conveying her steady belief in his potential as a leader (…*her belief in my potential…contributed significantly to the crowning achievements of my career*).

What was not mentioned by the client but proved to be essential in the outcome of this case was the coach's integration of the "psychological residue" from his traumatic childhood with the implications of this material for his leadership behavior. This behavior included his difficulties in trusting others, insatiable needs for affirmation and recognition, and inability to tolerate others disagreeing with his positions. Further, this integration had to be accomplished in a manner that was consistent with the objective of the coaching engagement, that is, not drift into psychotherapy.

## KATHRYN—*DESTINED TO LEAD*

By her own description, Kathryn had *always been a very independent person*. Therefore, it was not easy for her to accept a coach but their agreement about key points in the coaching is clear. These included: (1) her recognition that, at this stage in her career, she could benefit from having a sounding board (*She was a rock in a very rocky period*); (2) her valuing the insights the coach provided about what motivated Kathryn and others (*I had found a partner who focused me on the underlying drivers*); (3) the coach's combined business and psychology background (*This enabled a fuller discussion of the issues*); (4) the continuity of their relationship and steadfast presence of the coach/trusted advisor (*This was someone who counseled me through highs and lows*); and (5) the help Kathryn received in managing her enigmatic CEO.

There were only a few key points that Kathryn did not mention in her *executive reflection* that the coach saw as significant in the coaching. First, the coach's interpretation of Kathryn's primarily left brain leadership style (highly analytical engineer's approach). This influenced her impatience and missing clues about the need to build key stakeholder relationships especially with board members. And second, how trust in the relationship with her coach was increased by the coach's firm position as a development versus evaluative resource. In other words, the coach would not be "voting" on Kathryn's candidacy as the CEO successor.

## JEAN PAUL—*THE RECOVERING PERFECTIONIST*

There appeared to be complete agreement between Jean Paul and the author on the major points of his coaching—and subsequent relationship with her as his trusted advisor. These points were: (1) the recognition of the initial coaching as a collaborative partnership for his benefit (*I understood that this process was for me*); (2) how the coach's manner and commitment to confidentiality eased his initial sense of vulnerability (*Her caring behavior and thoughtful approach to the process made being vulnerable a natural stage. A trusting and lasting relationship was born, and my fears were gone*); and (3) the focus on leveraging strengths (*concentrating on what differentiates you from other players*).

While the author expected it would be difficult to engage a leader who was already so effective, they also agreed on his key learning breakthroughs: (1) minimizing the dark side of his perfectionism; (2) an insight about "ambiversion" as a strength (*I learned that I had behavioral elasticity that enabled me to adapt to different situations very quickly…this is especially valuable to me as I travel through different regions of the world intent upon connecting well to local employees*); and (3) the value of the concepts of total brain leadership (TBL) and emotional intelligence (EQ) (*It is strange to look back at all these years. TBL and EQ are now part of my everyday language and what I look for in the people around me*).

### RACHEL—*THE DUALITY WITHIN*

Client/coach perspectives on this engagement were highly aligned. While the coaching began with the explicit goal of improving the relationship with her boss, an underlying disconnect between Rachel's values (*leading my way*) and the company culture (*hierarchical…discussions in meetings very much geared toward the highest ranking person in the room*) was identified. This would likely influence an eventual decision for her to work in another global company—or to pursue something entrepreneurial.

Both coach and client considered the major breakthrough in the work to be an insight they named her *duality within*. This referred to the conflict between Rachel's aspiration to lead in *her way* and her concern about financial security—a concern that prevented her from being more proactive in her career.

The client and coach perspectives differed in that Rachel did not mention an issue that the coach saw as potentially sabotaging the success of the coaching. This was the boss's failure to become an active partner in the engagement. This did not surprise the HR partner (*He'll only give the coaching time if he sees an advantage in it for him*) who feared that Rachel had reached a career plateau. This was due primarily to her boss's failure to advocate for her, and the company culture in which "her way" of leading was not valued despite its positive impact on her business.

### RAVID—*THE DEMON SLAYER*

The perspectives of both client and coach compared well as related to three distinct phases of a relationship that spanned over 20 years.

They each highlighted his: (1) discovery and bolder use of all his capabilities (*I started to see myself differently*); (2) resolution of underlying issues (*It was humility to a fault; I was overcoming my own demons*); and (3) achieving his CEO aspiration and maintaining interaction with the coach who had become one of his trusted advisors (*I maintained contact with Karol for over 20 years*).

A very private man, perhaps it was no surprise that he did not mention how he and his wife had participated in an *executive couple module* with the coach. Nor did he mention the help his trusted advisor provided in the early stage of his career retirement transition. This was also not surprising in that it was unlikely that Ravid would ever retire completely.

## Max—*A Midlife Reinvention*

Where the perspectives of Max and his coach differed most was in the recognition of the inherent tension between his expectations of the coaching (assimilation into a new role, plus the exploration of another career aspiration) versus those of his boss—which were focused exclusively on Max's effectiveness in his new role. It was necessary for the coach to pace two phases of work with Max and collaborate with the boss in a manner that resulted in his actually anointing the second career exploration phase that Max desired.

Their alignment on what transpired in the coaching was greatest in three significant areas: (1) the emergence of a significant insight that explained his lifelong tendency to "hold back" (*My lifelong pattern has been about me under-clubbing! I'm really old enough now to stop and think more about what club I need to be using!*); (2) how he used the *structured and safe sanctuary* of coaching to make development progress in areas that included prioritization, reflection, and enriched self-awareness; and (3) the importance of other relevant insights that would ultimately influence his decision to leave his corporate role (e.g., feeling like the *rejected outsider*, and his strong need for affiliation).

There was also an unexpected surprise in Max's *executive reflection*: that as he transitioned into his own consulting practice, in a realm somewhat similar to that of the coach, he perceived his former coach as his *mentor*. While she had some pause regarding his possible overidealization of her, she was pleased to support the development of his practice.

## WALT—*FIGHTING THE FORCE OF OLD HABITS*

In comparing Walt's comments on what mattered to him in the coaching, the difference between his language and that of his coach is notable. While Walt described the focus of his coaching as his *maturing as a leader*, his coach conceptualized it as his "fighting the force of old habits" that could sabotage his becoming CEO of his company. For Walt, his maturation as a leader involved: (1) *deeper engagement with the organization*—balancing his focus on people and on processes; and (2) strategy in terms of his *painting with a broader brush*. His coach's language was at a higher decibel: (1) his needing to be less transactional in his relationships; and (2) formulating and conveying to the CEO his best strategic thoughts about the business. On a third area of leader maturation, communication effectiveness, Walt and his coach were in agreement regarding the importance of his *meeting the audience where it needed to be met* (especially board members). He was focused on evolving a presentation style that was less stiff and bound by his technical (financial) content.

The major points of client/coach agreement were: (1) the value of the open communication loop among the CEO, Walt, another external consultant, and the author (*maintaining comfort with the coaching process*); (2) insights about his reserved style (*helping the true me emerge*); and (3) how his learning in the interrelated areas of total brain leadership (TBL) and emotional intelligence (EQ) were helpful (*a better balance between IQ and EQ*).

## FRANK—*THE RELUCTANT PRESIDENT REVISITED*

In this comparison, there were several points of convergence between client and coach perspectives that can be considered in two groups: (1) the initial coaching when he was at Banyun, and (2) his assimilation into another company.

Regarding Frank's coaching when he was at Banyun, the key points upon which he and his coach concurred were: (1) how his boss's psychopathology was exacerbated in the presence of Frank's coaching progress (*He had buyer's remorse about the coaching*); (2) that it became untenable for Frank to remain at Banyun (*Karol's efforts were key to our continuing to operate effectively as a company, and for me to maintain my sanity… (but) it was inevitable that I would eventually leave*); and (3) how the coaching had helped increase his self-awareness and appreciation for his impact on others; this greatly aided his effectiveness as a leader, that is, he had *become more than just a new business producer.*

As Frank joined his new company, the coach transitioned to the role of trusted advisor and abetted his assimilation (*Her best advice was delivered with a prop—a small Lucite box filled with different sized rocks. The message was to deal with the big rocks/issues first*). Their respective perspectives tracked well in terms of: (1) his feeling ready to meet the new leadership challenges with the full force of his abilities; and (2) this being his opportunity to truly build something (*We now have one of the largest privately held firms of its kind in the country*).

The one major point of divergence between the perspectives of Frank and his coach/trusted advisor was on what she considered to be the most significant insight in her work with him. Specifically, Frank had failed to mention his lifelong pattern of masochistic behavior, and how this was a factor in why he had tolerated the toxic behavior of his previous boss for so long. Further, she had underscored the importance of his guarding against this dynamic in both his business and personal relationships.

## Conclusion

With this first collection of executive coaching case studies, my intentions were to stimulate an open conversation about coaching at the top, and to share practices that have been refined through hundreds of my engagements. Both the aforementioned surprises and the expectations realized as conveyed by these leaders in their *executive reflections* serve to inform the intertwined areas of research and practice. If we listen to these clients' voices, a number of topics emerge as warranting further investigation. These topics include: (1) the value proposition of the coach to trusted advisor transition, (2) how to achieve sustained impact in the coaching of senior executives (insight-oriented and other coaching models), and (3) the utility of forming and maintaining collaborative partnerships with organization sources (boss and HR professional) whilst coaching top business leaders.

In terms of what really matters to the coached client, these particular clients remind us of specific practice considerations. These practice considerations include: (1) the importance of executives themselves electing to be coached and choosing with whom they'll work, (2) the setting of clear coaching objectives and concrete ways to assess progress, (3) the value of focusing on both identified weaknesses and leveraging strengths, and (4) the need to ensure an inviolate boundary of confidentiality; coaches must be explicit in the contracting phase of a new coaching engagement regarding what will and will not be shared with the client's organization.

These comprehensive case studies and the specific input from the coached executives themselves enrich our understanding of the privilege and challenge of working with such senior business leaders. Hearing their voices here, and looking behind the closed doors of their coaching meetings, we are reminded that as evolved and brilliant and resilient as they may be, they can continue to learn and will be rewarded by the sanctuary of a steady and safe relationship with a coach or trusted advisor. So, what of the future of the field of executive coaching?

# Coda: As to the Future...

The future of executive coaching appears to be at a challenging inflection point. After roughly 30 years of explosive growth—there are approximately forty thousand coaches worldwide[1]—marketplace dynamics have shifted and demand a nimble response if the field is to capitalize on its robust beginning. The coached executives in *Destined to Lead* have, with their input, indicated one such response. Specifically, their emphatic endorsement of the long-term nature of their coaching/trusted advisor relationships suggests that *more may be more* when it comes to the length of these engagements.[2] Further, the potential value of these relationships is amplified as we consider the steady stream of senior executive flame-outs in recent years—often brilliant executives but who nevertheless failed given problems with *how* they lead.[3] I therefore suggest that a next evolution for the field of executive coaching would involve more practitioners making the coach to trusted advisor transition (see chapter 10). But I am getting ahead of myself—some context is warranted.

## Marketplace Dynamics

As decision-makers in business organizations have become more savvy about executive coaching, inevitable questions about cost and quality have been raised and these decision- makers are driving notable changes. These changes include companies developing their own coaching models to which external coaches are expected to conform; creating lists of "approved" coaches; enforcing fee structures that influence commoditization; forming internal networks of coaches; and in a significant move that may be indicative of a future trend, pharmaceutical giant GlaxoSmithKline has established an actual "center of coaching excellence" staffed and run by its own managers. Obviously, these changes have implications for the future of executive coaching and will, in my view, be best met with timely and collaborative responses from executive coaching practitioners.

It may take several years for there to be an objective assessment of the value of the aforementioned marketplace changes but in the meantime, sound reactions to them from the coaching community must include a steady flow of case literature and empirical research that demonstrate the continued ROI of executive coaching. As the first executive coaching casebook, *Destined to Lead* joins the most impressive compendium on coaching practice and theoretical considerations.[4] Further, it is hoped that this book's indicators for both coaching practice and research (see chapter 11) will influence continued investigation and thought leadership especially in the context of senior executive development.

Given the urgency of the current inflection point for executive coaching, ongoing discussions and debates in the field[5] should continue but they must do so in tandem with proactive responses to marketplace developments. These responses may include executive coaches forming collaborative (mentoring) relationships with internal coaches, and providing them information on applicable advances in the field. However, one thing is clear: senior business leaders will continue to resist working with internal coaches primarily for reasons related to conflict of interest, confidentiality, and trust.[6] Therefore, the potential of such engagements continues as a singular opportunity for external coaches who, through their stellar work, will help perpetuate and advance the field to its next plane.

## The Next Plane: A Third Wave of Executive Coaching Practice

If we accept what the senior executives in *Destined to Lead* have revealed in terms of their strong preference for—and valuing of— long-term relationships with a coach/trusted advisor, we can consider this as an evolution in the field. I refer to this as the *third wave* of executive coaching practice. The first wave, occurring in the 1970s and through the 1980s, focused mostly on *remedial* engagements. These individuals were often de-railing and were described as needing to be "fixed." In the second wave of coaching, unfolding between the 1990s and today, the assignments have become more *developmental*. While these coaching clients are usually competent leaders, there is often that certain leadership competency and/or behavioral limitation that needs to be "changed" if they are to receive greater responsibility and/or be fully effective in the roles they occupy.

And now, well into the twenty-first century, a third wave of practice includes what I term *essential* executive coaching that is focused on already outstanding and established leaders. These leaders are clearly gifted. Most have no limiting soft sides or blind spots. There are no questions about their performance. They are usually among the most senior business or functional executives in their organizations. They may even be at the pinnacle of their careers. Notably, they express a desire to evolve beyond their current levels of effectiveness.[7]

This third wave of executive coaching practice is distinguished from *developmental* engagements by the fact that seasoned practitioners have earned an opportunity to make the transition from executive coach to trusted advisor (see chapter 10).[8] In these longer-term relationships, business leaders are "stretched" in ways that help ensure they leverage the full force of their capabilities, and that they remain steady in turbulent socioeconomic and geopolitical conditions. In the author's experience, significant "stretch" gains are made through her clients' increased application of emotional intelligence (EQ) and their stronger integration of analytical thinking and interpersonal capabilities.[9]

Senior practitioners' continued efforts to establish these relationships—and to provide distinctive service in them—should advance *essential* coaching/trusted advisor practice, and solidify its use as a primary executive development resource. Further, the broader field of executive coaching should benefit as the recipients of high quality *essential* coaching are often in positions through which they can approve coaching resources for individuals at lower organization levels.[10] A final consideration of *why* and *how* these *essential* coaching/advising relationships happen (see later) may influence more practitioners to pursue them or to set this work as an aspirational goal—a goal that can be informed by the case studies in this book, as well as by other case literature and empirical research on coaching senior leaders.

### Why *Trusted Advisor Relationships Happen*

Based on my experience and collegial conversations with other trusted advisors, I believe that these relationships happen because coaching engagements at this level readily deepen and unfold on a more personal level once the initial coaching objectives are met. After all, these people are typically among the best and brightest in their fields. They don't need to get any smarter nor any wiser in their technical realms. What they do need—and what many are hungry for—is a *safe place to be* with someone who "gets" their world and can resonate with both the darkness and light of it. They may be unduly weighed down by the free-floating anxiety attendant to domestic political and economic issues, as well as unsettling investors at home and abroad. They may be tempted to respond to the head hunters who are luring them elsewhere. They may be weary of the pounding tension between delivering quarter-by-quarter results and the need to drive growth. They may have health and/or personal issues interfering with the focused attention and clear decision-making their roles require. The most senior among them may be conflicted about their succession or, they may be more ready to retire than others are willing to accept. More often than not, they are feeling under siege or isolated or uncertain given the complexity and unpredictability of the business issues before them. And surely they do not want to fail.

For all these reasons and myriad others too the coach to trusted advisor relationship happens because it is one of the few places senior leaders can go to express their fears, to quell their concerns, and to receive the steady and candid input they need. As one CEO told the author, "Most of my peers now have someone like you—we need the trusted outside sounding board and recognize that if we don't have it, we really don't have all the resources we should!"

## How *Trusted Advisor Relationships Happen*

While the semantic of "trusted advisor" may change, this role bears the potential to assume greater prominence among the resources made available to top business leaders. As indicated earlier, trusted advisors can become an *essential* resource for these executives. *How* this happens involves a number of interrelated factors (see chapter 10) including the quality of the initial coaching and the chemistry between the coach and the executive. Once coaches become trusted advisors, they are capable of providing imminently more value given their deep understanding of their clients, their company cultures, and their business dynamics, too. Reflecting on his long-term relationship with a trusted leadership advisor, a retired CEO of a global company commented to the author, "This relationship was definitely a part of my taking care of business."

*How* this happens also involves trusted advisors' interpersonal and other behavioral assets. Yes, they are intellectually strong, possess an armamentarium of coaching tools, can make piercing interpretations, and have the courage to speak truth to power. Their egos are in check. But in the end, I believe what differentiates them in these uncommon relationships are all of these factors *plus* their steadfast *presence*, compassion, and capacity to maintain a truly *authentic* and *intimate* connection with a client.

The conversations within this connection help ensure clients' successes in the present, and can influence actions that foster the steady growth of their enterprises into the future. Regardless of one's theoretical or practice orientation, it is this connection, this presence, this intimacy that trusted advisors foster in the relationships with senior business leaders that is the *red thread* I cited at the outset of *Destined to Lead*. When/if this thread is woven into the fabric of executive coaching—of trusted advising—relationships, the future of this field will likely reach another plane.

On this plane, in this third wave of executive coaching practice, the work of senior practitioners will have cascading effects for coaching as a leadership development resource of choice. Further, trusted advisors will not only leverage their past experiences, they will also seize the present and the future differently—especially in their work with the next generation of top business leaders. The Mark Zuckerbergs, the Marissa Mayers, the Sheryl Sandbergs—all these brilliant wunderkind are moving fast, they are bold, they are certain about where they're going, but they can also stumble badly because they have simply not had enough time on the planet nor sufficient mentoring to be fully effective leaders. In the *constancy of relationships with their trusted advisors*, they should flourish as they learn how to integrate their passion for innovation and value creation with the hard lessons of how to lead people well.

In closing, this metaphor of the *red thread* reminds me of an East Asian myth, referred to as the "red string of fate." According to this myth, the gods tie a red cord around the ankles of those who are to meet one another in a certain situation or help each other in a certain way. In this sense then, I believe the destinies of those of us who are so privileged to do this work are tied irrevocably to our clients' destinies to lead.

# NOTES

## INTRODUCTION

1. R. R. Kilburg, "Trudging towards Dodoville: Conceptual appro-aches and cases studies in executive coaching," *Consulting Psychology Journal: Practice and Research, 56*(4) (2004): 204.
2. R. L. Lowman, "Executive coaching: The road to Dodoville needs paving with more good assumptions," *Consulting Psychology Journal: Practice and Research, 57*(1) (2005): 90–96.
3. As throughout this book, "senior business leader" refers to exec-utives in top corporate level roles or to those who are carrying responsibilities of that magnitude.
4. S. Ennis, L. R. Stern, N. Yahanda, M. Vitti, J. Otto, and W. Hodgetts, *The Executive Coaching Handbook*. Wellesley, MA: The Executive Coaching Forum, 2003 (http://www.executive-coachingforum.com). This work offers a general definition of "executive coaching": "Executive coaching is an experiential, individualized, leadership development process that builds a leader's capability to achieve short- and long-term organizational goals. It is conducted through one-on-one interactions, driven by data from multiple perspectives, and based on mutual trust and respect. The organization, an executive, and the executive coach work in partnership to achieve maximum learning and impact."
5. T. Irwin, *Derailed: Five Lessons Learned from Catastrophic Failures of Leadership*. Nashville: Thomas Nelson, 2009.
6. K. M. Wasylyshyn, "Behind the door: Keeping business lead-ers focused on how they lead," *Consulting Psychology Journal: Practice and Research, 60* (Winter 2008): 314–330.
7. V. Hart, J. Blattner, and S. Leipsic, "Coaching versus therapy: A perspective," *Consulting Psychology Journal: Practice and Research, 53* (2001): 229–237.

8. I am indebted to my friend and colleague Paul Koprowski, who, based on his brilliant work with entrepreneurial business owners, helped me see what I was too close to see in my work with senior business leaders: the significance of the coach and/or trusted advisor's committed, astute, and humane *presence* in which all can be said, considered, understood, and even resolved absent concerns about reproach or weakness.

9. R. R. Kilburg, "When shadows fall: Using psychodynamic approaches in executive coaching," *Consulting Psychology Journal: Practice and Research, 56*(4) (2004): 246–268.

10. T. J. Saporito, "Business-linked executive development: Coaching senior executives," *Consulting Psychology Journal: Practice and Research, 48* (1996): 96–103.

11. K. M. Wasylyshyn, "Coaching the superkeepers," in L. A. Berger and D. R. Berger (eds.), *The Talent Management Handbook: Creating Organizational Excellence through Identifying Developing and Positioning Your Best People*, Chapter 29. New York: McGraw-Hill, 2003.

12. J. Quick and D. Nelson, "Leadership development: On the cutting edge," *Consulting Psychology Journal: Practice and Research, 60*(4) (2008): 296.

13. These leadership competencies include: (1) setting strategy, (2) business acumen, (3) people management, (4) innovation management, and (5) driving business results.

14. These emotional resources include: (1) self-awareness, (2) self-control, (3) psychological resilience, (4) attunement to others, (5) passion, and (6) grit.

15. A. L. Duckworth, C. Peterson, M. D. Matthews, and D. R. Kelly, "Grit: Perseverance and passion for long-term goals," *Journal of Personality and Social Psychology, 92* (2007): 1087–1101.

### 1 THE RELENTLESS CHAMPION

1. D. Coutu and C. Kauffman, "What can coaches do for you?" *Harvard Business Review Research Report*, 2009, p. 93.

2. E. H. Erikson, *Childhood and Society*. New York: W.W. Norton & Company, 1950.

3. A written report was given to Ted. This report represented the major themes identified through "live" or telephonic interviews with the 17 people in his 360 data-gathering sample.

4. Given my coaching model, I would "touch base" with both Ted's boss and his HR partner before every meeting with Ted so that I was as current as possible on his progress or lack of same. The HR partner was particularly communicative and became a remarkably strong collaborator providing an ongoing flow of valuable collateral information. At my suggestion, she also reinforced action steps that Ted could take to support his coaching progress.

5. R. E. Kaplan and R. B. Kaiser, "Developing versatile leadership," *MIT Sloan Management Review, 44*(4) (Summer 2003): 19–26.

6. M. Mikulincer and P. R. Shaver, *Attachment in Adulthood: Structure, Dynamics, and Change.* New York: Guilford Press, 2007.

7. L. Horowitz, S. Rosenberg, and K. Bartholomew, "Interpersonal problems, attachment styles, and outcome in brief dynamic psychotherapy," *Journal of Consulting and Clinical Psychology, 61*(4) (1993): 549–560.

8. M. Maccoby, "Narcissistic leaders: The incredible pros, the inevitable cons," *Harvard Business Review* (2000, January–February): 69–77.

9. See chapter 10 for a discussion of the conceptualization of "trusted advisor."

10. R. R. Kilburg, "When shadows fall: Using psychodynamic approaches in executive coaching," in R. R. Kilburg and R. C. Diedrich (eds.), *The Wisdom of Coaching: Essential Papers in Consulting Psychology for a World of Change* (p. 187). Washington, DC: American Psychological Association, 2004.

11. F. S. Perls, *The Gestalt Approach and Eyewitness to Therapy.* Palo Alto, California Science and Behavior Books, 1973; New York: Bantam Books, 1976.

12. C. K. Germer, *The Mindful Path to Self-Compassion: Freeing Yourself from Destructive Thoughts and Emotions.* New York: Guilford Press, 2009.

13. K. M. Wasylyshyn, *Behind the Executive Door: Unexpected Lessons for Managing Your Boss and Career.* New York: Springer, 2011.

2 Destined to Lead

1. T. Saporito and P. Winum, RHR Executive Insight newsletter, *28*(1) (2012): 2.

2. The corporate Head of Human Resources (HR) at the time was a business person rotating through that role. He proved to be a helpful source of collateral information throughout the coaching as was another member of the CEO's staff who was also a longtime employee of the company.

3. The author uses the more apt term "work-family integration" instead of the popular "work-family balance" terminology. For top talent individuals, work-family balance—if considered literally as a balance between the two domains of work and family—is an impossible objective to achieve. On the other hand, everyone should strive to find her/his version of work-family integration.

4. The data-gathering for this case, as well as for the seven others in this book, was based on a multitrait-multimethod (MTMM) approach. A. H. Church and C. T. Rotolo, "How are top companies assessing their high-potentials and senior executives? A talent management benchmark study," *Consulting Psychology Journal: Practice and Research*, 65(3) (2013): 199–223.

5. Kathryn sent this email separately to the people in her 360 sample: "I am writing to invite you to meet with my executive coach, Dr. Karol M. Wasylyshyn. We are focusing on ways I can be even more effective as a leader and this organization-based feedback will be helpful. This confidential one-hour conversation with Karol will occur either 'live' or by phone, and I thank you in advance for your candid participation."

6. Erik H. Erikson, *Childhood and Society*. New York, NY: W. W. Norton & Company, 1950.

7. K. M. Wasylyshyn, H. Shorey, and J. Chaffin, "Patterns of leadership behaviour: Implications for successful executive coaching outcomes," *The Coaching Psychologist*, 8(2) (2012): 78–85.

8. M. Maccoby, "Narcissistic leaders: *The incredible pros, the inevitable cons*," *Harvard Business Review* (2000, January–February): 69–77.

9. The psychometric battery consisted of; the Myers-Briggs Type Indicator, Watson-Glaser Critical Thinking Appraisal, Life Styles Inventory 1, Revised NEO Personality Inventory (NEO PI-R), and the BarOn Emotional Quotient Inventory (EQi).

10. Whenever I gather 360 data, the interview protocol is customized so as to elicit the most targeted input possible, that is, maximum "grist for the coaching mill." Further, these interviews typically last one hour and are conducted face-to-face whenever possible.

11. R. R. Kilburg, "When shadows fall: Using psychodynamic approaches in executive coaching," *Consulting Psychology Journal: Practice and Research,* 56(4) (2004): 249.

12. D. Goleman, R. Boyatzis, and A. McKee, *Primal Leadership: Realizing the Power of Emotional Intelligence.* Boston: Harvard Business School Press, 2002.

13. D. Goleman, "What makes a leader?" *Harvard Business Review* (1998): 93–102.

14. J. Kabat-Zinn, *Wherever You Go, There You Are: Mindfulness Meditation in Everyday Life.* New York: Hyperion, 1994.

15. K. M. Wasylyshyn, *Behind the Executive Door: Unexpected Lessons for Managing Your Boss* (p. 4). New York: Springer, 2011.

16. R. E. Kaplan and R. B. Kaiser, "Developing versatile leadership," *MIT Sloan Management Review,* 44(4) (Summer 2003): 19.

17. M. W. McCall, M. Lombardo, and A. Morrison, *The Lessons of Experience: How Successful Executives Develop on the Job.* Lexington, MA: Lexington Books, 1988.

18. J. A. Sonnenfeld, *The Hero's Farewell: What Happens When CEOs Retire* (p. 3). New York: Oxford University Press, 1988.

19. From RHR Executive Insight newsletter, (2012), *Volume 23, Number 2.*

20. While circumspection is one of my inherent traits, this had been reinforced strongly by the psychoanalytic theoretical orientation of my graduate training in clinical psychology.

21. Kaplan and Kaiser, "Developing versatile leadership," 19–26.

22. Wasylyshyn, *Behind the Executive Door.*

23. H. Ibarra, R. Ely, and D. Kolb, "Women rising: The unseen barriers," *Harvard Business Review* (2013, September): 59–64.

24. Saporito and Winum, RHR Executive Insight newsletter, 1–2.

### 3   The Recovering Perfectionist

1. Originally named Leadership 2000 when it was implemented in the late 1980s, it was renamed Leadership 3000 at the outset of 2000.

2. K. M. Wasylyshyn, "Chapter 20: Developing top talent: Guiding principles, methodology and practice considerations," in L. A. Berger and D. R. Berger (eds.), *The Talent Management Handbook*, second edition. New York: McGraw-Hill, 2011.

3. This was in contrast to most other business organizations. According to this company's HR leader, "Too many companies are caught in a pattern of leadership development du jour and this constant change in competencies and models does more to confuse that to truly engage people in their ongoing development. It's not about the models: it's about the quality of the relationships among the people charged with developing high potential talent."

4. Participants in these phases were considered to be members of the participant's ongoing development "brain trust." The members were the CEO, a participant's boss, the HR leader, and the consulting psychologist.

5. The psychometric battery consisted of the Myers-Briggs Type Indicator, Watson-Glaser Critical Thinking Appraisal, Revised NEO Personality Inventory (NEO PI-R), Rorschanch Ink Blots, Guilford-Zimmerman Temperament Survey, Personality Research Form-E, the Herrmann Brain Dominance Instrument and the Operationalizing EQ Inventory (author-created).

6. D. J. Levinson, *The Seasons of a Man's Life*. New York: Ballantine Books, 1978.

7. D. Stoop, *Hope for the Perfectionist*. Nashville: Thomas Nelson Publishing, 1987.

8. A. M. Grant, "Rethinking the extraverted sales ideal: The ambivert advantage," *Psychological Science*. Published online April 8, 2013, http://pss.sagepub.com/content/early/2013/04/08/09 56797612463706, 1–7. DOI: 10.1177/0956797612463706.

9. This comment was consistent with information I had read about the American/French difference. Specifically, when it comes to the concept of a business partnership, Americans tend to be objective-oriented, see process and rules as binding the partnership, and it is not equated with friendship. The French business person is relationship-oriented, believes trust and engagement bind a partnership, and tend to equate partnership and friendship.

10. D. Whyte, *The Heart Aroused: Poetry and the Preservation of the Soul in Corporate America* (p. 207). New York: Doubleday, 1994.

11. The Visual Leadership Metaphor® (VLM) is a technique created specifically to assess the progress of a coaching engagement. The executive's language is given to an artist who draws the imagery. This sequence of three images (current, transitional, and future leadership states) is then laminated on a sheet

of paper with the imagery on one side and the language on the back. One copy is given to the executive and the other is kept in his or her file. It is referred to frequently throughout the coaching with the coach's question, "Which frame are you in now?" The goal is for the executive to feel he or she has reached frame 3 by the end of the coaching. Executives are encouraged to keep their VLMs in a visible place as a reminder of their coaching goals.

12. K. M. Wasylyshyn, *Behind the Executive Door: Unexpected Lessons for Managing Your Boss and Career.* New York: Springer, 2011.

## 4 The Duality Within

1. In my executive coaching model, I strive to establish and maintain a close working partnership with the boss and HR professional. I believe the quality of the coaching work will be enriched by the steady flow of collateral information from the boss and HR partner. Often there is also "secondary gain" for them and their development through the discussions of how to help the coached executive evolve as a leader.

2. This warranted careful attention in that senior executives here, unfamiliar with current leadership development tools, could have a reflexive cynical response.

3. A. Olson, "The theory of self-actualization: Mental illness, creativity and art," *Psychology Today* blog series Theory and Psychopathology, August 13, 2013. Retrieved from http://www.psychologytoday.com/blog/theory-and-psychopathology/201308/the-theory-self-actualization.

4. Not every initial client meeting concludes this way. Often executives indicate—and I encourage—time to reflect on the discussion before making a decision to commence coaching.

5. D. B. Peterson, "Coaching and mentoring programs," in K. Kraiger (ed.), *Creating, Implementing, and Managing Effective Training and Development.* San Francisco: Jossey-Bass, 2002.

6. In addition to this half day, my Office Manager worked closely with Rachael's Administrative Assistant to set all the monthly coaching appointments. While there are the inevitable changes that need to be made, we have found this is the best way to ensure coaching traction (frequency of meetings).

7. The Visual Leadership Metaphor® (VLM): The VLM language is given to an artist who draws the visual tool—pictures on the front, client's words on the back. A laminated copy of the VLM

is given to the client as a reminder of the coaching journey to be made. I keep one in his or her file and often begin a coaching meeting with the question, *Where are you in your effort to get to frame 3 in this coaching?* Of note is the fact that many clients who complete coaching and retain me thereafter as a *trusted advisor* create a new VLM in which frame 1 is frame 3 from their first VLM.

8. I would have preferred more time, but this was what I could negotiate. It is not unusual for a coaching engagement to be extended—especially when progress is noted, and the coach presents a strong rationale for further work to be accomplished.

9. Typically the data-gathering phase includes (1) an agenda-setting meeting in which my client and I meet with the boss and HR partner, and (2) my gathering 360 feedback from the organization. However, given the contextual factors described earlier, the initial data-gathering was limited to conversations with human resources, the psychological measures, and the life history.

10. The psychometric battery consisted of: the Myers-Briggs Type Indicator, Watson-Glaser Critical Thinking Appraisal, Life Styles Inventory 1, Revised NEO Personality Inventory (NEO PI-R), and the BarOn Emotional Quotient Inventory (EQi).

11. This life history taking was based on Erik Erikson's eight life stages and the psycho/social tasks to be accomplished in each stage.

12. K. M. Wasylyshyn, H. Shorey, and J. Chaffin, "Patterns of leadership behaviour: Implications for successful executive coaching outcomes," *The Coaching Psychologist*, 8(2) (2012): 77.

13. Amy Chua, *Battle Hymn of the Tiger Mother*. New York: The Penguin Press, 2010.

14. K. M. Wasylyshyn, *Behind the Executive Door: Unexpected Lessons for Managing Your Boss and Career*. New York: Springer, 2011.

15. D. Goleman, R. Boyatzis, and A. McKee, *Primal Leadership: Realizing the Power of Emotional Intelligence*. Boston: Harvard Business School Press, 2002.

16. D. Goleman, "What makes a leader?" *Harvard Business Review*, 76 (1998, November–December): 93–102.

17. M. Maccoby, "Narcissistic leaders: The incredible pros, the inevitable cons," *Harvard Business Review* (2000, January–February): 69–77.

18. B. Peltier, *The Psychology of Executive Coaching: Theory and Application*, second edition. New York: Routledge Taylor & Francis Group, 2010.

19. Unfortunately, due to an illness for which he was hospitalized, this conversation never occurred. The author's follow-up efforts to communicate with him by email went unanswered. My HR contact said Rachael's coaching was "probably not a priority for him."

20. We did not yet know if the deal would be completed. Her boss was aware of the potential deal but few others were—so in this I maintained confidentiality—until the time was right for a debriefing with HR.

### 5  THE DEMON SLAYER: CONQUERING A DARK SIDE OF DEFERENCE

1. K. M. Wasylyshyn, "Developing top talent: Guiding principles, methodology and practice considerations," in L. A. Berger and D. R. Berger (eds.), *The Talent Management Handbook,* second edition. New York: McGraw-Hill, 2011, Chapter 20.

2. My conceptualization of "trusted advisor" can be found in chapter 10 of this book.

3. This work became well-established in the company and when year 2000 arrived, it was renamed *Leadership 3000.*

4. K. M. Wasylyshyn, "Coaching the superkeepers," in L. A. Berger and D. R. Berger (eds.), *The Talent Management Handbook: Creating Organizational Excellence through Identifying Developing and Positioning Your Best People* (p. 322). New York: McGraw-Hill, 2003, Chapter 29.

5. Having read the 2010 work of Peter Cappelli, Harbir Singh, Jitendra Singh, and Michael Useem (2010), "Leadership lessons from India," *Harvard Business Review,* 90–97. I realized the prescient nature of my HR colleague's guidance. In reflecting on Ravid's career years later, I recognized that his commitment to community service (social mission), investing in employee learning and development, discovering innovations through a company's value chains, and driving company growth through identifying and meeting the needs of long-term customers were similar to that of other Indian business executives.

6. The psychometric battery consisted of the Myers-Briggs Type Indicator, Watson-Glaser Critical Thinking Appraisal, Revised NEO Personality Inventory (NEO PI-R), Rorschanch Ink Blots, Guilford-Zimmerman Temperament Survey, Personality Research Form-E, the Herrmann Brain Dominance Instrument and the Operationalizing EQ Inventory (author-created).

7. These interviews were conducted by the author either face-to-face or telephonically. Through the duration of Leadership

3000, she interviewed over one thousand employees of the company.

8. A. M. Grant, "Rethinking the extraverted sales ideal: The ambivert advantage," *Psychological Science*. Published online April 8, 2013, p. 1, http://pss.sagepub.com/content/early/2013/04/08/095 6797612463706, 1–7. DOI: 10.1177/0956797612463706.

9. The active participation of the CEO in these action-planning meetings is notable and indicative of the company's commitment to the "conveyance of wisdom" principle—a principle that contributed significantly to the value proposition of Leadership 3000.

10. D. Goleman, *Emotional Intelligence*. New York: Bantam Books, 1996; *Working with Emotional Intelligence*. New York: Bantam Books, 1998; "What Makes a Leader?" *Harvard Business Review* (1998, November–December), 93–102.

11. The rationale for the company-sponsored and optional Spousal Module was that there could be value in an executive couple exploring the work-family integration issue. Its major potential was in helping the couple manage the relentless tension between career and personal priorities thus minimizing the executive's being distracted by these inevitable concerns. Thus far, the author has been able to influence only this company and one other about the contribution of the Spousal Module to an executive's development. This may well be a fruitful research topic.

12. M. Kerr and M. Bowen, *Family Evaluation: An Approach Based on Bowen Theory*. New York: W.W. Norton & Company, 1988.

13. T. J. Saporito, "Business-linked executive development: Coaching senior executives," *Consulting Psychology Journal: Practice and Research, 48* (1996): 96–103.

14. D. Keltner, J. Marsh, and J. A. Smith, *The Compassionate Instinct: The Science of Human Goodness*. New York: W.W. Norton & Co., 2010.

## 6   A MIDLIFE REINVENTION

1. The psychometric battery consisted of the Myers-Briggs Type Indicator, Watson-Glaser Critical Thinking Appraisal, Life Styles Inventory 1, Revised NEO Personality Inventory (NEO PI-R), and the BarOn Emotional Quotient Inventory (EQi).

2. Given my coaching model, Max would own whatever data got generated in the coaching, and he was free to choose how he

might share this material with others. What I would share with the company included the areas we agreed to focus on in the coaching, updates on Max's progress, and my thoughts on how the boss and HR partner could help accelerate Max's ongoing progress in the coaching.

3. This case illustrates the advantage of a long-term relationship with a business organization. Specifically, each new coaching or other consulting engagement builds on the work that has preceded it. Armed with deep knowledge of a company's culture and of its senior executives, the consultant can get rapid traction, and the work is inevitably enriched by previous experiences there. A caution, of course, is to manage the credibility that comes with an established track record in one organization whilst also maintaining necessary confidentiality about all work that has occurred before a new engagement.

4. In my coaching model, I refer to the coached executive as the "client" and the paying organization as the "sponsor." All of my engagements are "sponsored" by a business organization.

5. H. Littman-Ovadia and D. Nir, "Looking forward to tomorrow: The buffering effect of a daily optimism intervention," *The Journal of Positive Psychology*, published online October 2013.

6. In the Driving Force exercise, the client is asked to draw a circle and write in the middle of it whatever is the most pressing need he or she has at that time. In Max's case, it was staying focused on his top business objectives for the year. Whenever one is asked to become involved in something, he or she must challenge the self with this question: "Does this support or detract from my staying with my current driving force?" If the request is a distraction, the individual must say "no" and perhaps offer an idea about whom else might be helpful with the rejected request.

7. K. M. Wasylyshyn, "Behind the door: Keeping business leaders focused on how they lead," *Consulting Psychology Journal: Practice and Research, 60* (Winter 2008): 314–330.

8. Years later, I asked Max if we had missed an important path in our work by not pursuing the race factor. He replied, "Absolutely not. If I had been on the couch, then we could have gone there, but I was in the chair and by this time in my life, I had learned to deal with it." While I wasn't convinced, his response reminded me of the fact that consultants who are trained clinically must stay alert about the boundaries of their consulting contracts and not veer into directions for which there is no contract.

9. The Coaching Report Card is another tool used to gauge progress in coaching. At each meeting, the client grades him or herself in each of the areas being worked on in the coaching. The coach also invites the HR partner to grade the executive as a way of assessing her client's objectivity regarding progress.

## 7  FIGHTING THE FORCE OF OLD HABITS

1. K. M. Wasylyshyn, "Behind the door: Keeping business leaders focused on how they lead," *Consulting Psychology Journal: Practice and Research, 60* (Winter 2008): 314–330.
2. K. M. Wasylyshyn, *Behind the Executive Door: Unexpected Lessons for Managing Your Boss and Career.* New York: Springer, 2011.
3. The psychometric battery consisted of the Myers-Briggs Type Indicator, Watson-Glaser Critical Thinking Appraisal, Life Styles Inventory 1, Revised NEO Personality Inventory (NEO PI-R), and the BarOn Emotional Quotient Inventory (EQi).
4. The Visual Leadership Metaphor® (VLM) is a technique created specifically to assess the progress of a coaching engagement. The executive's language is given to an artist who draws the imagery. This sequence of three images (current, transitional, and future leadership states) is then laminated on a sheet of paper with the imagery on one side and the language on the back. One copy is given to the executive and the other is kept in his or her file. It is referred to frequently throughout the coaching with the coach's question, "Which frame are you in now?" The goal is for the executive to reach frame 3 by the end of the coaching. The coached executive is encouraged to keep his or her VLM in a visible place as a reminder of the desired progress to be made in the coaching.
5. D. Goleman, R. Boyatzis, and A. McKee, *Primal Leadership: Realizing the Power of Emotional Intelligence* (p. ix). Boston: Harvard Business School Press, 2002.
6. Whenever I gather 360 data, I work with my client to customize an interview protocol that will draw data that relate specifically to the issues we are working on in the coaching. I also review the sample of participants with the boss and/or my HR partner to ensure it is representative versus just members of my client's "fan club."
7. Wasylyshyn, "Behind the door," 314–330.
8. M. W. McCall, M. M. Lombardo, and A. M. Morrison, *The Lessons of Experience: How Successful Executives Develop on the Job.* New York, NY: The Free Press, 1988.

9. B. Concannon, Personal communication with CEO candidate, July 25, 2007, Haemonetics, Braintree, MA.

10. E. Berne, *Games People Play: The Basic Handbook of Transactional Analysis*. New York: Ballantine Books, 1996.

## 8 THE RELUCTANT PRESIDENT

* Reprinted with permission—Copyright 2005 by the Educational Publishing Foundation and the Society of Consulting Psychology— DOI: 10.1037/1065–9293.57.1.57. *Consulting Psychology Journal: Practice and Research*, Vol. 57, No. 1, 57–70.

1. Psychometric battery consisted of Watson-Glaser Critical Thinking Appraisal, Myers-Briggs Type Indicator, the Life Styles Inventory, the NEO PI-R, and the BarOn Emotional Quotient Inventory.

## 9 THE RELUCTANT PRESIDENT REVISITED

1. Frank's initial coaching focused on three strengths to leverage: (1) business development ability, (2) leadership potential, and (3) relationship with the CEO. In addition the two development areas were: (1) internal (firm-wide) relationship-building, and (2) people management.

2. K. M. Wasylyshyn, *Standing on Marbles: Three Leader Types in Verse and Imagery* (pp. 84–85). Philadelphia: TrueNorth Press, 2011.

3. The psychological defense of splitting is used here as an indicator of the instability of John's relationships. As with Frank, he was capable of suddenly turning on people or of radically changing his view on them. To a significant degree this was based on the extent to which they gratified his needs—or not.

4. J. Baldoni, "Employee reciprocity," *Bloomberg Businessweek*, November 30, 2010. Retrieved December 2013, http://www.businessweek.com/managing/content/nov2010/ca20101122_272375.htm.

5. I believe in the value of long-term relationships between senior executives and their trusted advisors. As I have written (see chapter 10), "While some may argue that long-term relationships of this nature foster dependency, my experiences underscore something quite different. Specifically, the enduring trust, mutual respect, and committed presence of an objective outsider who, in my case, has a dual background in business

and clinical training in psychology, provides the executive with an additional resource for leading effectively."

6. In the initial engagement the author, a licensed psychologist, had to walk the ethical line between being paid by a company to aid in the development of a top executive, and then eventually be able to support this executive's decision to leave the company. Embedded in this ethical challenge and the steps she took to manage it were the fertile seeds of the deepened trust that fostered the long-standing trusted advisor relationship with Frank.

## 10   FROM EXECUTIVE COACH TO TRUSTED ADVISOR

1. Rachel's case (chapter 4) did not evolve into a long-term relationship. This was a first engagement in her company and a time-frame limitation had been negotiated at the outset of the work.

2. D. H. Maister, C. H. Green, and R. M. Galford, *The Trusted Advisor*. New York: Free Press, 2000.

3. J. Sheth, *Clients for Life: Becoming a Trusted Advisor*. Program presented at the Society of Consulting Psychologist, February 2003, Div. 13, Scottsdale, AZ.

4. A. Freedman and J. Perry, "Executive consulting under pressure: A case study," *Consulting Psychology Journal: Practice and Research*, 62(3) (2010, September): 189–202.

5. T. J. Saporito, "Business-linked executive development: Coaching senior executives," *Consulting Psychology Journal: Practice and Research*, 48 (1996): 96–103.

6. In my experience, compensation of the trusted advisor is always paid by the business organization.

7. This was the central point in an important conversation shared on February 12, 2013, with one of the most prolific researchers, writers, and practitioners in the field of executive coaching, my friend and colleague Dick Kilburg.

8. B. Brown, *TEDx talk The Power of Vulnerability*, June 2010. Retrieved from http://www.ted.com/talks/brene_brown_on_vulnerability.html.

9. R. Josselson, *The Space between Us: Exploring the Dimensions of Human Relationships* (p. 15). Thousand Oaks, CA: Sage Publications, 1996.

10. B. L. Fredrickson, "Positive emotions and upward spirals in organizations," in K. Cameron, J. Dutton, and R. Quinn (eds.), *Positive Organizational Scholarship*. San Francisco: Berrett-Koehler Publishers, Inc., 2003, p. 163.

11. M. E. P. Seligman, *Learned Optimism: How to Change Your Mind and Your Life*. New York: Vintage Books, 2006.

12. R. Hanson, *Hardwiring Happiness: The New Brain Science for Contentment, Calm and Confidence*. New York: Crown Publishing Group, 2013.

13. T. Brach, *Radical Acceptance: Embracing Your Life with the Heart of a Buddha*. New York: Bantam Books, 2003.

14. D. L. Cooperrider, D. K. Whitney, and J. M. Stavros, *Appreciative Inquiry Handbook: For Leaders of Change*. Brunswick, OH: Crown Custom Pub, 2008.

15. E. H. Erikson, *Childhood and Society*. New York: W.W. Norton & Company, 1950.

16. K. M. Wasylyshyn, *Behind the Executive Door: Unexpected Lessons for Managing Your Boss and Career* (p. 13). New York: Springer, 2011.

17. I have accepted invitations to weddings and other celebratory events. Observations made at such events have been another source of insight about my clients.

18. Josselson, *The Space between Us*.

19. Ibid., p. 111.

II    CLIENT AND COACH VIEWS COMPARED

1. J. H. Stevens, Jr., "Executive coaching from the executive perspective," in R. R. Killburg and R. C. Diedrich (eds.), *The WISDOM of coaching: Essential Papers in Consulting Psychology for a World of Change* (p. 414). Washington: American Psychological Association, 2007, Chapter 39.

CODA: AS TO THE FUTURE . . .

1. International Coach Federation, Global Coaching Study—Executive Summary, February 2012. http://www.coachfederation.org/coachingstudy2012.

2. These executives made numerous comments in their *executive reflections* on the long-term nature of the relationship with the author who had become their *trusted advisor*. These comments included: (1) Having a trusted advisor (for over seven years), someone who—no matter what the issue—is there to reflect, walk all the way around the issue with you, to challenge . . . this is invaluable; (2) the results of this development work (for a number of senior leaders), tabulated over 20 years, showed marked improvement in the ten areas (competencies)

and our business results showed we were in the top ranks when compared to industry peers; and (3) Karol's efforts (over three years) were key to our continuing to operate effectively as a company, and for me to maintain my sanity (working for a dysfunctional boss).

3. Talented executives who failed in recent years primarily for problematic leadership style issues include Jill Abramson (The New York Times), Dennis Kozlowski (Tyco Int'l. Ltd), Mark V. Hurd (Hewlett-Packard Company), Stephen P. MacMillan (Stryker Corp.), Edward C. Forst (Goldman Sachs), and Al Dunlap (Scott Paper and Sunbeam).

4. In R. R. Kilburg and R. C. Diedrich (eds.), *The Wisdom of Coaching: Essential Papers in consulting psychology for a World of Change.* Washington, DC: American Psychological Association, 2007, pp. 185–205.

5. As with any nascent field, collegial discussions and debates are necessary to inform sound practice principles and research. Ongoing topics of focus within the field of executive coaching include: its definition, how it differentiates itself from other popularized forms of coaching such as "life coaching," essential coaching competencies, coaching credentials or certifications, and the relevant merits of various coaching models.

6. K. M. Wasylyshyn, "Executive coaching: An outcome study," *Consulting Psychology Journal: Practice and Research, 55* (Spring 2003): 94–106.

7. As indicated at the outset of this chapter, inevitably there are gifted leaders who are vulnerable for failure given certain flaws in how they lead. They could well benefit from the objective, steady, and courageous input of an executive coach/trusted advisor. However, whether or not they would seek and/or accept such assistance is the challenge.

8. Even when working with the most senior business leaders, the author has maintained collaborative partnerships with their HR professionals and bosses. When her clients have been CEOs, rather than her having a boss partner, she has often had ongoing interactions with board members who proved to be valuable sources of collateral information.

9. I refer to this as total brain leadership (TBL).

10. In this third wave of *essential* coaching/advising, the delivery of *developmental* coaching continues with individuals at lower organizational levels, and successful work can be accomplished in shorter-term coaching models. However, the author advises

against companies investing in coaching that is primarily *remedial* in nature. These instances are fraught with peril that does not bode well for the cost-effective and credible use of executive coaching. For example, there may be managerial abdication, i.e., a boss is expecting that the coach will deliver negative feedback to an individual who has already lost major credibility in the company—these coaching referrals rarely work out well. Further, in *remedial* circumstances, the coaching is usually too-little-too-late given long-standing performance issues, damaged relationships, or the individual may just be in the wrong role with no other job option in the company. Finally, in these situations, prospective coaching clients typically lack the necessary intention to participate in a manner that would enable them to benefit from coaching.

# INDEX

*Page numbers in italics refer to information in tables and charts.*